REFLECTIVE PRACTICE
for Educators
Second Edition

*Professional Development
to Improve Student Learning*

Karen F. Osterman ▪ Robert B. Kottkamp

CORWIN PRESS
A Sage Publications Company
Thousand Oaks, California

For information:

Corwin Press
A Sage Publications Company
2455 Teller Road
Thousand Oaks, California 91320
www.corwinpress.com

Sage Publications Ltd.
1 Oliver's Yard
55 City Road
London EC1Y 1SP
United Kingdom

Sage Publications India Pvt. Ltd.
B-42, Panchsheel Enclave
Post Box 4109
New Delhi 110 017 India

Printed in the United States of America

Library of Congress Cataloging-in-Publication Data

Osterman, Karen Figler.
Reflective practice for educators: Professional development to
improve student learning / Karen F. Osterman, Robert B. Kottkamp.—2nd ed.
    p. cm.
Includes bibliographical references and index.
    ISBN 0-8039-6800-0 (Cloth) — ISBN 0-8039-6801-9 (Pbk.)
    1. Teachers—In-service training—United States. 2. School administrators—
In-service training—United States. 3. School improvement programs—United States.
4. Reflective teaching—United States. 5. Learning. I. Kottkamp, Robert B. II. Title.
LB1731.O78 2004
370'.71'5—dc22   2003026987

This book is printed on acid-free paper.

04   05   06   07   10   9   8   7   6   5   4   3   2   1

Acquisitions Editor:	Robert D. Clouse
Editorial Assistant:	Candice Ling
Production Editor:	Diane S. Foster
Copy Editor:	Cheryl Duksta
Typesetter:	C&M Digitals (P) Ltd.
Proofreader:	Andrea Martin
Indexer:	Teri Greenberg
Cover Designer:	Michael Dubowe
Production Artist:	Lisa Miller

Contents

Preface

Ten years have passed since the first edition of this book. In that time, we have learned a great deal, deepened our appreciation of the importance of reflective practice, and strengthened our conviction that it holds powerful, empowering, and healthy possibilities for change and betterment in the educational community. We are optimistic, but we have also lived another ten years of educational history.

During these last ten years, we have seen wonderful things happen in education, particularly at the elementary school level. With the introduction of new approaches to literacy and an increasing emphasis on project-based learning intensified by many children's easy access to literally a world of people, information, and ideas, the learning experience in many schools is indeed a rich one, far distant from the experience of these students' parents and grandparents. On one hand, we seem to be coming to a renewed appreciation of the importance of engaging children in learning. At the same time, there are many schools where children are not learning; there are many "good" schools where some children's learning needs are still neglected; and many schools where the joy of learning has been suppressed by pressure to pass the test. Unfortunately, the approach to reform remains the same.

Ten years ago, we referred to a variety of solutions that were on the agenda at the time: new and higher standards, integrated curriculum, better teacher preparation. Now, ten years later, we still observe an educational system struggling to address what it defines as failure. The fix-it mentality and model of change still reigns supreme, but there is a new iteration, an almost maniacal pursuit of the Holy Grail of high-stakes testing. Establishing thoughtful, comprehensive standards is essential to reform. Similarly, gathering and collecting outcome data is invaluable for organizations to assess performance relative to those standards. With data in hand, the most effective organizations then engage their staffs in a critical analysis of their own performance. With evidence before them, they critique their work, develop and implement alternative strategies, and use data to assess their efforts. Unfortunately, in many instances, the test has become an end in itself, and accountability demands have had little positive effect on practice and have aggravated the very conditions they were designed to address. While standards and assessment are two integral and essential processes, the legislatively empowered evil twin of high-stakes testing, by promoting reliance on single—and faulty—indicators of educational performance, has suppressed and marginalized the critical voice of standards, its important counterpart (Thompson, 2001). For all practical purposes, the once vaunted authentic standards-based reform has joined many of its predecessors among the *desaparecidos.* For those concerned about the impact of high-stakes testing, however, history offers some comfort because today's solution soon becomes yesterday's initiative.

Unfortunately, that is the problem. In the history of school reform, one new program follows another, yet the more things change, the more they stay the same. Seeing this fix-it history repeat itself, we are firmer in our conviction that short-term behavior adjustment only maintains the status quo in the long run. It is simply not enough to develop a new program, however well designed, if the process of implementation does not provide an opportunity to explore the ways of thinking, seeing, and believing that affect what we do and how we do it. Without this conscious dialogue, even the best solution will not be sustained in the face of continual demand for newer and better solutions.

We remain convinced that the most enduring changes will take place in schools as teachers, administrators, and parents ponder how students learn and how the adults responsible for their learning can best support them. In fact, research is becoming increasingly clear that schools most successful in creating change are those functioning as learning organizations, schools where every person and the organization itself are consciously and continuously learning. We believe firmly that reflective practice is an important and effective change process that is integral to the learning organization. At the same time, we are not so naive as to believe that a practice that cannot be packaged, distributed, and imposed with a promise of immediate results will be readily embraced by schools, school districts, or policy makers who are looking for quick solutions to complex problems. Reflective practice lacks cache. Nonetheless, the term has become embedded in the language of education, and, more important, there are a growing number of schools and districts that have adopted the principles of reflective practice to create effective schools that are indeed meeting the diverse learning needs of their students.

OUR THEORETICAL PERSPECTIVE

There is a rich theoretical and critical literature on reflective practice. This book focuses on the application of reflective practice in school settings, yet it has a theoretical perspective that distinguishes it from similar books. Although the term is widely used, conceptions of reflective practice differ. Some authors emphasize the reflective aspect, equating reflective practice with silent introspection and retrospection; others emphasize practice, viewing this thoughtful process as a means of developing a better solution to a problem. Our conceptualization stays close to its roots in the work of Argyris and Schon (Argyris, 1982, 1993; Argyris & Schon, 1974, 1978): It emphasizes thought and action as integral processes but extends beyond to consider how context and culture shape both thought and action. Our description of reflective practice respects the autonomy of the learner but recognizes the value of incorporating lessons drawn from theory, research, and practice. For others, thought or cognition holds primacy; in our conceptualization, systematic observation of practice emphasizing thought, action, feelings, and consequences is the keystone of the process. As we explain in a later chapter, reflective practice depends on careful observation and data-based analysis of practice as well as experimentation with new ideas and new strategies.

Argyris has continued his work, describing a process that he calls action science (Argyris, Putnam, & Smith, 1985). This process, like action research, is another formulation of reflective practice. What these processes all share are systematic procedures for critically examining thought and action in an effort to improve our professional practice. While action research does not intentionally highlight the importance of examining assumptions and beliefs, the process often leads to this deep analysis.

We advocate reflective practice under a definition that always encourages the possibility of deep change in assumptions, thoughts, and actions. Our interest is in profound (double-loop) learning and change, in an educational paradigm shift that goes beyond thought to action and beyond action to thought. As we explain in Chapter 1, our goal is to transform existing educational organizations into true learning organizations. For this reason, our notion of reflective practice is grounded in the concept of community and communication. While organizational change or cultural change will not come about without individual change, organizational change will not come about until dialogue about change absorbs the whole community (Cambron-McCabe, 2003; Kottkamp & Silverberg, 2003).

Over the last ten years, our conception of reflective practice has not essentially changed; however, we have come to a deeper appreciation of the richness of reflective practice as we have explored its connections with other major schools of thought (Kottkamp, 2002; Kottkamp & Silverberg, 1999b; Osterman, 1999). As a process of learning, reflective practice builds on and draws from experiential learning, constructivism, situated cognition, and metacognition, and the critical literature on professional development frequently incorporates these important principles.

Reflective practice is also rooted in the notion of intentional action. This cognitive perspective that what we believe, what we value, and the way we view the world is indeed reflected in our action is evident in much research about teachers, administrators, and children. Within the organizational change literature, we see similar ideas and processes in Senge's (1990; Senge et al., 2000; Senge et al., 1999) discussion of system thinking as he encouraged practitioners to examine problems thoroughly, examine their mental models, articulate and share their vision, and work collaboratively to improve practice. In the research on leadership and school leadership, through the work of Leithwood and others (Leithwood, 1995; Leithwood, Begley, & Cousins, 1994; Leithwood, Jantzi, & Fernandez, 1994; Leithwood & Steinbach, 1995), we find increasing attention to cognition and intention and an emphasis on the clear articulation of goals or vision and also on the continuous assessment of performance relative to those standards of performance.

Fullan and Hargreaves (Fullan, 1997; Fullan & Hargreaves, 1996) wrote about the importance of deep dialogue, collaboration, and reflection and the often anxiety-producing nature of this endeavor. Elmore and colleagues (Elmore, 1992, 1995; Elmore, Peterson, & McCarthey, 1996) are among others who have come to appreciate that structural reform without change in the underlying beliefs about teaching and learning leads to naught. Conversely, we are beginning to see the power of collective energy as educators unite, often with the guidance and support of transformational leaders, to engage in an ongoing analysis of their practice. In these learning organizations, we see educators engaged in reflective practice and the potential for change realized in meaningful ways.

It is nice to be part of a broadening stream of thought and dialogue focused on improving our ability as professionals to learn and, as educators, to serve our very important clientele in an ever-improving manner. In some settings, reflective practice has become an integrated part of organizational life. At the same time, there is still a long way to go until the exception becomes the norm.

HOW THE BOOK HAS CHANGED

The format of this edition is similar to its predecessor. Topics are similar, but in most cases the ideas are far more developed. Because we feel that cognition is such an important determinant of action, we continue to pay a great deal of attention to developing a deep understanding of reflective practice. Kofman and Senge (1994) argued that simple formulas, "seven step methods to success" or "similar how-to's," are not very practical because "life is too complex and effective action too contextual" (p. 17). We agree and believe that a strong theoretical understanding provides educators with greater flexibility to integrate reflective practice, formally and informally. We also share Fullan's and Leithwood's appreciation for problems. In Fullan's (1997) words, "problems are our friends"; they're "inevitable and you can't learn without them" (p. 15). From our perspective, the problem, or the discrepancy between where we are now (the current situation) and where we want to be (the preferred situation), is an impetus for change. Accordingly, we develop that contrast throughout the book.

The original book was targeted to school administrators. At the time, there were many resources dealing with reflective practice for teachers and prospective teachers but very little information that would explain its value and application for school leaders and schools. In addition to defining and explaining the process, we included three case studies describing administrators engaged in reflective practice and facilitator strategies. One described prospective administrators' introduction to reflective practice in a graduate class and its effects. The second looked at a professional development program designed to facilitate leadership renewal among experienced school principals. The third depicted school district administrators involved in an ongoing effort to incorporate reflective practice in their own work. While these cases are not reprinted here, they remain valid and may still be of interest (Osterman & Kottkamp, 1993).

Since the first edition, our priorities have sharpened. This volume also includes three cases drawn from our own work, but they focus specifically on how reflective practice facilitates change in the classroom. While reflective practice has important applications and can benefit professionals at every organizational level, ultimately, the primary concern is student learning, and our deepest concern is for those children who are consistently failed by our schools. We believe that all children can learn; we also believe that achieving this goal requires a very different approach to teaching. To illustrate how reflective practice can facilitate this change, all of the cases in one way or another deal with marginal students: those children who stand out from the rest because of behavior or learning problems. In many cases, they are children who are poor and of color. In other cases, they are children from affluent homes in predominantly White districts. Regardless of their demographic status, most are perceived as troublesome. They are the children who, in teachers' words, drive them nuts, the ones who give them gray hair, the ones who make teaching difficult. For these children, there are no expectations of success and often attributions that they are responsible for their own failure because they lack ability or motivation. These cases show teachers confronting these assumptions and changing their beliefs and their practice, often in very dramatic ways and with dramatic results. In one situation, the teachers are prospective administrators and the stimulus is a class assignment. One involves teachers and administrators working with one another to address important issues of classroom practice. The third shows teachers and children engaging in reflective practice as they change their approaches to teaching and learning.

Our intention here is not to place all responsibility for children's learning in teachers' hands. To the contrary: Within the school, there is no question that teachers play the most critical and direct role in student learning. At the same time, it is very clear that organizational conditions, including the nature of leadership, directly influence the quality of teachers' work. As Fullan and Hargreaves (1996) noted, schools that have bad teachers usually deserve them. It is also clear that leaders can create environments that enhance teaching and learning. By creating trust; promoting inquiry, dialogue, and initiative; encouraging critical examination of current practices and continuous and collaborative learning; and providing resources that foster personal growth, leaders directly influence the quality of teachers' work (Murphy & Datnow, 2003a, 2003b; Silins, Mulford, & Zarins, 2002). Essentially these are the same conditions that facilitate reflective practice, and we hope this book supports leaders' efforts to create these positive learning environments. At the same time, we believe that this book is important for educators at all levels who want to become more effective through their work with their colleagues. Schools where everyone assumes responsibility for student learning are more effective schools. This book is also useful to educators who wish to engage in this process of continuous improvement and to educators in higher education who wish to develop reflective skills in preparation programs.

These cases illustrate another difference in our thinking over the years. It is possible to engage in reflective practice without using that label, and reflective practice, while it may lead to surprising and even astounding insights, does not necessarily lead to conflict or anxiety. In each of these situations, educators engaged in reflective practice, but no one called it that. The first case was intended to generate reflective practice but was focused on problem framing. The second was an action research project initiated in a school by an elementary principal concerned with bullying and victimization. In the third, children and their teachers engaged in reflective practice and critically examined their own learning without ever using the term. What these cases also illustrate is that reflective practice can be integrated into professional life, with minimal disruption but maximum effects. In fact, we would argue that reflective practice cannot be sustained as an add-on. We also downplay the conflict-generating potential of reflective practice. The cases we present show educators encountering very critical information about their own practice and sharing that information openly with colleagues without distress. We attribute this to professional commitment, a supportive environment, and the teachers seeing this information as a means to improvement.[1]

In the first edition, there was more attention to the facilitator role. In each of the cases, the facilitator played a direct role in structuring the reflective practice. In this book, the facilitator plays an important role in initiating, framing, and supporting the process but is less visibly directive. The most important responsibility of the facilitator is to promote problem identification and data gathering. Once educators become engaged in data gathering and analysis, the process takes on its own momentum, and the key role for the facilitator becomes one of active listening, as Chapter 4 explains.

The final chapter is essentially unchanged. We believe now, as we did then, that reflective practice is an empowering process that has far greater effects on people than most other learning experiences and produces visible outcomes, including changes in attitudes, beliefs, and assumptions, relationships with professional colleagues, and behavior. While recognizing the value of articulating core values and beliefs, we now give greater significance to the role of information as the stimulus for reflective practice and professional development. Knowing where you stand as an educator is one critical piece of information, but it is also essential to understand other elements of your practice: what you want to accomplish and your effectiveness, the strategies you use and more broadly how you experience and interpret your work, and most important the underlying ideas that shape your action. Equally important is sharing data openly in a collaborative and supportive setting. Communicating openly to improve professional practice enables educators to draw on and develop their expertise. It enables them to create knowledge; it helps to build professional community and learning organizations. Finally, reflective practice works because it respects the professionalism of educators and empowers them to assume personal responsibility for their own learning and professional growth. As we explain, it is an empowering process that enhances educators' self-efficacy.

We concluded earlier by seeking "colleagues who will join us in this quiet approach to change . . . " and opined that "If we have learned anything in our personal journeys with reflective practice, it is that only through changing ourselves do we have any hope of changing others" (Osterman & Kottkamp, 1993, pp. 188-189). We reaffirm these positions and feel gratified when we look around to see people actually doing it and often marveling at the outcomes.

HOW THE BOOK IS ORGANIZED

The book consists of two sections. The first, including Chapters 1 through 4, explain reflective practice, provide a conceptual framework or rationale, detail the stages of the process, and outline basic ideas and strategies that facilitate reflective practice. In Chapter 1, we explain our understanding of reflective practice as a professional development strategy and its potential for creating meaningful individual and organizational change in the context of our current reform efforts. Chapter 2 describes reflective practice as an experiential learning cycle, providing a detailed explanation of each phase. Reflecting our belief that valid information is one of the most important aspects of the reflective practice cycle, Chapter 3 outlines ways to gather data about the different dimensions of our practice as a means to facilitate reflection. In Chapter 4, we talk about introducing reflective practice in an organizational setting. Here we explore organizational obstacles to reflective practice and identify important assumptions and strategies to facilitate this new form of interaction.

As in the past edition, the second section describes and explains reflective practice in action. Reflective practice is a form of problem-based learning, and the next three chapters deal with important problems confronting educators. Chapter 5 considers the "problematic" student and shows educators confronting their unstated assumptions about these children. In Chapter 6, working with their principal, teachers engage in action research to break the cycle of bullying and victimization in the classroom. Chapter 7 describes how new data about their learning help children and teachers to join forces in a radically different response to concerns about test results. Chapter 8, as noted previously, offers final thoughts on the efficacy of reflective practice as a professional development strategy.

NOTE

1. McLaughlin (2001) made a similar point, noting how access to data and opportunities to analyze those data relative to their own performance actually help to create communities of practice.

Acknowledgments

While there are many people whose conversations and work have contributed to the development of our thinking about reflective practice and about this book, we would like to offer special thanks to a few whose contributions were very direct.

To the reviewers, who not only pointed out sins of omission and commission but also commended us and gave excellent suggestions to improve the final product, we deeply appreciate the time they spent carefully reading and reacting to our work.

To our graduate students and graduates, who have worked with us over the years, reading and reacting to our ideas and our work, engaged in reflective practice as students in the classroom and professionals in the workplace, and extended research on the topic in important ways, we would like to offer particular recognition to cohorts of administrative preparation and doctoral candidates who looked very closely at problematic students in their classrooms and schools, and particularly to Wafa Deeb-Westervelt, who permitted us to present her work in detail here in Chapter 5; to Karen Siris, whose excellent research is reported in Chapter 6; and to Ruth Powers Silverberg, who made valuable contributions to the work in Chapters 5 and 7 and whose conceptual analysis of the transformational experience of teachers helped us to articulate more clearly the important role of self-understanding as a stimulus to change. We would also like to recognize the important contribution of Maria Bonich, whose skill in computer graphics brought some of our presentations into the twenty-first century.

While we were not able to provide detailed descriptions of their work in this book, we would also like to mention two other excellent studies that used reflective practice effectively. Susan Fishbein (2000), whose work is referenced here, completed a study of the socialization process of administrative interns. Specifically, the research team, including the interns, focused on a particular problem—the gap between teachers and administrators. Throughout the research process, the interns gathered data through observation. Through their analysis, they were able to reconceptualize their own understanding of the problem and develop alternate strategies. Joyce Montalbano (2001) also completed an action research study that, similar to Siris's work, engaged teachers in reflective practice. Her study focused on teachers' working with at-risk elementary students during a summer program. Like the teachers in Siris's study, these teachers, too, through observation and analysis, developed a new understanding of themselves and their students. In this situation, the children's needs for belongingness and autonomy were dominant. Addressing these needs led to dramatic changes in students' sense of efficacy in the classroom and profoundly affected teachers' understanding of their roles and their practice.

To our colleagues: We are fortunate to work in a very collegial environment and recognize the intellectual and emotional support of our department colleagues. Two professionals from our extended professional family have also offered continuous support and stimulation. Christine Johnston, who as originator, theoretician, and ongoing creator of the Let Me Learn Process, the subject of Chapter 7, moved us from assuming reflective practice to be an adult domain to the realization that children as young as third grade may engage it in the fullest sense. She is friend, steady confidant, honest critic, and colleague in a vision of what really matters. We are privileged to have grown and learned from the generativity of her confluence.

Susan Sullivan is an amazing professional with an outstanding knowledge of the New York City schools, school leadership, and supervision. She has also been an advocate and an innovator in her work to understand, apply, and teach reflective practice. The supervisory texts that she and Glanz developed (Glanz & Sullivan, 2000; Sullivan & Glanz, 2000) not only espouse reflective practice by educational leaders but also adopt reflective practice strategies to introduce concepts and develop skills. Her editorial skills and her willingness to offer important critical feedback were also very helpful in motivating us to go back to the drawing board for even more revisions beyond the point where we thought we were done.

There are also many professionals working in teacher education and administrative preparation who have done remarkable work exploring reflective practice as a concept, demonstrating how to integrate reflective practice in professional education, and enabling professional educators to take reflective practice into the workplace. While the thoughts expressed in this book are our own, the development of our thinking reflects the ideas, effort, and accomplishments of our professional community. To all of them, far too many to mention here, we extend our deepest appreciation.

Corwin Press gratefully acknowledges the contributions of the following individuals:

Philip Bigler
Director/Professor
The James Madison Center
James Madison University
Harrisonburg, VA

Nelda Cambron-McCabe
Professor
Miami University
Oxford, OH

Tim Egnor
Principal
Spruce Creek High School
Port Orange, FL

Gail Ghere
Project Coordinator
University of Minnesota/St. Paul Public Schools
Minneapolis, MN

Timothy Reagan
Associate Professor
School of Education
University of Connecticut
Storrs, CT

William Sommers
Executive Director
Minneapolis Public Schools
Minneapolis, MN

About the Authors

 **Karen F. Osterman** is currently Professor and Chairperson in the Department of Foundations, Leadership, and Policy Studies at Hofstra University. She received her BA from Emmanuel College, an MPIA at the University of Pittsburgh Graduate School of Public and International Affairs, and a PhD from Washington University. Her teaching and research focus broadly on motivation in a social context with particular emphasis on organizational structures and processes that affect the workplace behavior of adults and students. Her work has appeared in the *Journal of Management Science, Journal of School Public Relations, Journal of School Leadership, Education and Urban Society, Newsday, Phi Delta Kappan, Review of Educational Research,* and *Urban Education.* Recent work explores the way that school and classroom policies and practices affect the quality of peer relationships, bullying, student violence, and disengagement from learning.

 **Robert B. Kottkamp** is Professor and Doctoral Director in the Department of Foundations, Leadership and Policy Studies, Hofstra University. He received his BA from DePauw University and an MAEd and PhD from Washington University. His teaching and research foci include problem framing, reflective practice, and change and pedagogy in leadership preparation programs. He has coauthored four books and has had works published in *Phi Delta Kappan, Journal of Research and Development in Education,* the *Alberta Journal of Educational Research, Educational Administration Quarterly, Teachers College Record,* and *Leadership and Policy in Schools.* Recent work includes development and research with the Let Me Learn

Process described in Chapter 7 and leadership in the Taskforce to Evaluate Educational Leadership Preparation and Effectiveness supported by the University Council for Educational Administration and the American Educational Research Association Special Interest Group on Teaching in Educational Administration.

Reflective Practice, School Reform, and Professional Development

This is a book about reflective practice. It is also a book about children. Reflective practice is a meaningful and effective professional development strategy. Even more, it is a way of thinking that fosters personal learning, behavioral change, and improved performance. Through systematic inquiry and analysis, it is a way for individuals to create meaningful and enduring change by changing themselves. It is a way to address problems rather than symptoms. As a basic learning strategy, reflective practice is relevant for any type of organization and in any walk of life. Here, however, we focus primarily on its value for educators—and for the children they serve.

In this chapter, we develop a conceptual understanding of reflective practice as a professional development strategy and explain its potential to create meaningful change in schools. In schools, reflective practice is ultimately a way for educators to search for ever-improved ways to facilitate student learning. Reflective practice is based on a belief that organizational change begins with individuals. Unless we as educators change the way we do things, there will be no meaningful educational change. Unless we identify new ways of acting, we will make little progress in achieving our goals. Reflective practice also incorporates the belief that much resistance to change is rooted in unexamined assumptions that shape habit. To create change, then, we must examine current practice carefully and develop a conscious awareness of these basic assumptions. We also consider the organizational conditions necessary to support reflective practice and the way reflective practice, in turn, can help develop a learning organization. To understand reflective practice as a change strategy and its significance for schools, we begin with a critical perspective on school reform.

UNDERSTANDING THE FAILURE OF SCHOOL REFORM

In this new century, critiques of public education remain pervasive, and, with the erosion of public confidence, increasing numbers of parents are seeking alternatives through charter schools, voucher systems, or home schooling. The common perception is that schools are failing, and our children are not being prepared well academically or socially to meet the challenges of life in a rapidly changing and complex world. While some argue that criticisms of public education are inaccurate and oversimplified (Berliner & Biddle, 1995), the societal response to these concerns has been aggressive.

Over the last 40 years, governmental agencies, business leaders, profit and nonprofit organizations, elected officials, universities, special interest groups, and professional organizations—through financial incentives and disincentives, legislation, research, product development, and political persuasion—have bombarded schools with innovations designed to reform education. While the thrust of these reforms has shifted, the intention has been constant—to fix problems through a constant and continually changing barrage of externally developed and often mandated initiatives intended to change how and what teachers teach, how school leaders lead, the organizational conditions under which learning takes place, and how schools establish accountability and assess learning. The list of so-called solutions is long. Organizationally, schools have introduced site-based management and shared decision making—involving teachers, parents, and community—while manipulating schedules, reorganizing teachers into interdisciplinary or grade-level teams, and shifting students from tracks to heterogeneous age and ability groupings. School leaders have been encouraged to develop effective schools by adopting new and improved leadership strategies. In the classroom, teachers encounter constantly changing directives: new math, old math, back to basics, balanced literacy, phonics, interdisciplinary and integrated learning versus subject specialization, computer-assisted instruction, drill and skill, push outs and pull ins, cooperative learning, and problem-based learning. These are only a few of the procedural, programmatic, and structural changes that have been prescribed and implemented—sequentially or simultaneously—in schools struggling to improve learning while addressing public concerns. What is omitted here is a list of perhaps thousands of individual programs developed for schools—packaged, marketed, and sold—complete with training and new materials. As one administration gives way to another, as one fad gives way to another, in response to carrots and sticks, schools adopt new, different, and costly programs—programs to improve instruction in reading, math, and science; in-class and afterschool programs to meet the needs of special children, such as gifted students, students with learning disabilities, non-English speakers, and children who simply fail; and programs to address special interests, such as school violence, bullying, character education, sex education, or multicultural education. Programs, programs, and more programs, all designed to solve one or more problems.

Implementing these constantly changing strategies requires substantial investment in professional development. In 1995, a Consortium for Policy Research in Education (CPRE) policy brief indicated that most states and districts had no idea what they were actually spending for professional development but estimated that state investments alone probably ranged from less than 1% to more than 3% of total state spending on public education (Corcoran, 1995). In 1993 alone, the federal government spent more than $615 million on teacher development programs in only one programmatic area: math, science, and technology. Information on total expenditures is not available, but it is clear that reform has attracted extensive resources. Cost aside, what benefits have we reaped? The answer to that question is obviously not a simple one, but costs seem to exceed benefits. In some cases, reform efforts have led to actual change. Recent research on comprehensive school reform, for example, shows that consistent, focused, research-based, and integrated schoolwide efforts that engage staff in collaborative efforts to examine and address educational problems have led to observable improvements in student achievement (Borman, Hewes, Overman, & Brown, 2003; Murphy & Datnow, 2003a, 2003b). With few exceptions, however, little has changed.

As Tyack and Cuban (1995) explained, "For over a century, ambitious reformers have promised to create sleek, efficient school machines 'light years' ahead of the fusty schools of their times. But in practice their reforms have often resembled shooting stars that spurted across the pedagogical heavens, leaving a meteoric trail in the media but burning up and disappearing in the everyday atmosphere of the schools" (p. 111). Despite devoting extensive fiscal and human resources to reform, and despite good intentions and sound ideas in general, the way that schools are organized and the way that teachers teach has not changed in important ways.

From a researcher's perspective, the more things change, the more they stay the same (Sarason 1971, 1990). From the perspective of an enlightened teacher commenting on the teaching practices in her own school, "you'd think it was 1950." Despite the intensive and continuous involvement in change, how schools are organized, how teachers teach, and how children learn in the majority of our schools is very similar to the way we did things in the 1950s or even in the 1920s. Students are organized in age-graded, daylong classes and presented with lockstep curricula (Berliner & Biddle, 1995; Tyack & Cuban, 1995). Many classrooms are still teacher directed rather than student centered; our emphasis is still on information transmission and recall rather than the development of critical analytic skills. In classrooms, students spend little time actually reading and writing, discussing what they read, thinking about issues with elusive answers, or working in independent activities or group projects (Cuban, 1984; Goodlad, 1984; Newmann, 1992). The advent of standards-based education and the emphasis on accountability through frequent mandated and publicly compared testing, in some cases, seems to have reinforced enduring practice and widened the gap between advantaged and disadvantaged students. Critiques of high-stakes testing, for example, note negative effects on teacher creativity and the richness of the curriculum, as teachers and students devote even more time to test preparation. Of even greater concern is the disproportionate rate of failure and dropout of students from low socioeconomic and minority backgrounds, and some argue that attention to the test distracts us from deep discussions of problems confronting children who live in poverty (Amrein & Berliner, 2002; Berliner & Biddle, 1995; Fullan, 1999; McNeil, 2000; Tyack & Cuban, 1995).

Little has changed in the classroom, and little has changed in the ways that schools are organized and operated. Despite decades of calls for restructuring, site-based management, shared decision making, and the development of professional communities, many schools retain traditional bureaucratic practice. For many teachers, working conditions are still characterized by overload, isolation, exclusion from decisions about their work, and a lack of meaningful professional development opportunities (Fullan & Hargreaves, 1996; Ingersoll, 2003). Efforts to reform education by changing the way that teachers relate to students and to each other through structural changes—in schedule, student groupings, and teacher groupings—have also encountered resistance. Changes are difficult to make and difficult if not impossible to sustain, particularly at the secondary level. More important, even when structural changes are introduced, the anticipated changes in teaching and learning do not materialize. While "standard ways of organizing schools may limit teaching practice and undermine good teaching," we "have so little evidence that changes in organization lead directly to changes in teaching and practice, and ultimately to changes in student learning" (Elmore, Peterson, & McCarthey, 1996, pp. 213-214).

Professional development, too, has had little effect on teaching practices (Little, 2001). While some reform strategies may be ineffective or counterproductive, many of the reform proposals introduced are based on sound research, often drawn from the experience of exceptionally successful schools and classrooms. Despite the quality of the program or proposal, despite the commitment to the goal or the enthusiasm for the particular strategy, efforts to enact even the best-conceived proposals are frequently unsuccessful. Changes are not implemented as designed and intended, or changes are implemented but, over time, cannot be sustained. As Hargreaves, Earl, and Ryan (1996) explained, while "the surface and style of schooling may have changed," the deep structures "have been reproduced from generation to generation" (p. 2).

Why have these reform efforts failed to achieve their objectives? There are a number of factors that affect the efficacy of change initiatives. Basically, this approach to change is symptomatic rather than systemic and externally imposed rather than internally designed. It's a piecemeal, patch-up approach that works around and essentially ignores basic structural flaws. While the problems are complex, the solutions are frequently quick fixes that are universally applied, regardless of the specific features of the organizational, social, or cultural context. Solutions are developed and imposed—on districts, administrators, and teachers—without the input or involvement of those who must implement them. Without commitment to change, new ideas—like new materials—will be shelved sooner or later as educators get back to business.

Even when professionals are involved and committed, translating new ideas into practice is a complex process and a goal that has largely eluded professional development efforts. From the perspective of critics, professional development efforts are frequently "limited and misguided" (Fullan & Hargreaves, 1996, p. 16) and ignore important principles of learning. Different staff development initiatives are often unrelated to one another or to teachers' problems or concerns. As educators are bombarded with one new "solution" after another, this fragmented approach actually mitigates against sustained change.

Further, and most important, professional development assumes a mechanistic approach to change—that simply presenting new ideas or strategies leads to changes in practice. Elmore et al. (1996) examined three schools deeply invested in reform, and all three "looked like models of enlightened practice" (p. 222). The schools provided a supportive collegial environment and actively involved teachers in change decisions. Teachers held high standards for children's learning and believed all children could learn. They were committed to student-centered learning and worked hard to introduce new practices into their work. When the researchers evaluated the process, however, they found that, despite enthusiasm and effort, the majority of the teachers were unsuccessful in implementing changes. There was a major discrepancy between what they said they wanted to do and what they accomplished. The researchers concluded that accomplishments were limited because teachers lacked a deep understanding of what they were doing and because professional development did not provide ample time for them to explore their assumptions and beliefs about their work. "The assumption was that if the teachers had access to good ideas, they would know how to put them into practice" (p. 231). While incorporating many valuable change principles, this effort, like many others, ignored the fact that behavior—and teaching—is a complex phenomenon, reflecting ideas, experience, and judgment within a social context.

> How teachers teach at any given time is a composite of how they taught in the past, how they think they ought to be teaching in the present, and how they reconcile the latter with the former. Teachers are not ciphers for their organizations; they do not simply and immediately translate the prevailing ideas about teaching practice in their schools into some new form of teaching. Teachers are active decision makers who are constrained in their capacities to act on new ideas by their past practice, by their judgments about what is worth doing, and by deeply rooted habits that are often at odds with their own espoused views of what they ought to do. (Elmore et al., 1996, pp. 238-239)

Further complicating reform is a sense of powerlessness among many educators. Paradoxically, educators are involved in an almost continuous process of change, yet are cynical about the value of new mandates and prospects of change. Organizations consist of people, ostensibly working together toward a common purpose. Yet individuals get lost in the shadow of the system. We understand organizations as highly rational, impersonal, and mechanistic systems (Weber, 1947). Rules and regulations rigidly determine behavior, and decisions are typically made by someone higher up. These bureaucratic procedures preclude individuals from becoming actively and wholeheartedly engaged in the search for truly effective change. In this impersonal context, individuals are submerged, invisible, and seemingly powerless, and the system takes on a life of its own.

Within the system, change consists mainly of mechanistic approaches—hiring outsiders to fix this and that or add a bit of something here or there. Educators are told how to implement somebody else's solution but are seldom involved in identifying the problem or developing the response. In fact, many of the solutions seem designed to fix the educators themselves. In the face of continuously changing and externally mandated changes that fail to change educational practice in important ways, many educators become passive, thinking, "You can't beat the system."

The most recent innovation soon gives way to the next, and educators comply, sometimes wholeheartedly, sometimes begrudgingly, knowing that the tide will soon turn—or return—to another miracle cure. They hunker down and reassure themselves that this, too, shall pass (Tyack & Cuban, 1995). As seasoned educators know, what goes around often comes around again. While whole language temporarily captivated the educational community, phonics is once again in vogue, with the assistance of federally supported research and new federal mandates (Taylor, 1998). Ditto sheets displaced by math manipulatives soon regained cache as part of the back to basics movement. Efforts to introduce authentic assessment are overshadowed by increasing accountability demands that require paper-and-pencil tests easily administered on a mass scale. Despite almost continuous change, little changes. "The more things change, the more they stay the same" is both an accurate descriptor and a self-defeating prophecy.

REFLECTIVE PRACTICE: A DIFFERENT APPROACH TO SCHOOL REFORM

Reflective practice offers a more optimistic perspective on school reform: Meaningful change is possible. It also offers a very different road map, one based on a very different set of assumptions about personal and organizational change.

For Schools to Change, Educators Have to Change

Whether schools are effective in facilitating student learning is the result of the efforts of all those involved in the learning effort: teachers, administrators, guidance personnel, custodians, secretaries, the students themselves, parents, and community groups. The actions they take, individually and collectively, determine whether children succeed. School improvement, then, requires a change in actions. Although organizations certainly exert powerful influences on the people who inhabit them, organizations are human creations guided by human intentions and decisions (Greenfield, 1986, 1991), and individuals have the potential to shape organizations to their purposes.

Change Requires More Than Good Intentions

Reflective practice takes an optimistic perspective: Real change is possible. At the same time, it recognizes the seemingly intractable nature of organizational and personal behavior. Despite what we know about "good" practice, these "behavioral regularities" (Sarason, 1971, 1990) are tenacious. Even though our conscious ideas—about teaching, about administration, about our relationships with parents and community—change, we continue to behave in the same old ways. Despite a stock of new knowledge and our best intentions, we tend to resist change and to behave in very predictable ways. Despite the substantial body of research demonstrating the superiority of heterogeneous over homogeneous grouping, schools still track students and assign children to different ability groups for instruction. Despite a growing body of research demonstrating the effectiveness of collaborative decision making, many administrators resist involving staff and parents in meaningful ways. Despite considerable evidence of the failure of fix-it model change efforts, we continue to prescribe one fix after another. It is the aggregation of these behavioral patterns that constitutes the organizational status quo. Organizations won't change until these patterns are interrupted. Yet, as we have seen, introducing new instructional or leadership patterns is difficult, even when we recognize the impotency of old approaches and accept the need for change. So how do we understand this we-believe-in-it-but-can't-seem-to-do-it phenomenon?

New Approaches Require New Ways of Thinking

Many of our previous reform efforts were based on an assumption that structures shape people's actions. To a certain extent they do. Nonetheless, research and experience on the effectiveness of structural reforms basically show that few of these efforts in school reorganization led to meaningful change in how teachers teach or how students learn (Elmore et al., 1996). The consensus is that real change depends on a change in ideas and beliefs. Unless educators examine and modify their mental models, there will be no important changes in behavior. Quoting Tyack and Cuban (1995), "better schooling will result in the future—as it has in the past and does now—chiefly from the steady, reflective efforts of the practitioners who work in schools" (p. 135).

Reflective practice, as a learning model, emphasizes the importance of cognition, maintaining that thought influences action. In essence, personal action theories, our ideas about the world, govern our behaviors—the decisions we make, the actions we take. Typically, *theory* connotes abstract ideas about issues detached from the world of practice. In reflective practice, however, theories are linked closely with daily experience. They are simply the assumptions and beliefs we hold about how things should and do work (Argyris & Schon, 1974). Everyone has action theories: Teachers have theories about discipline and instruction, administrators have theories about leadership and supervision, parents have theories about child rearing and discipline, and change agents have theories about facilitating change. Some action theories are stated in formal language; others appear in aphorisms: for example, "spare the rod and spoil the child" and "learning should be fun." In reflective practice, however, two distinct types of personal action theories are key to understanding behavioral stability and change: espoused theories and theories-in-use.

Espoused Theories

Of the two forms, espoused theories are easier to understand. They are simply what we are able to say we think and believe. Espoused theories have two distinct characteristics: They exist at a conscious level, and they change with relative ease in response to new information. Individuals often emerge from professional development and university courses able to articulate new ideas and goals. Their espoused theories have changed. And since espoused theories reflect conscious ideas, intentions, and beliefs, if we want to know what they are, we simply ask. Responses to questions likely indicate an individual's broad range of information and beliefs acquired through experience and formal education.

Traditional models of education generally presume that espoused theories guide our actions, but this is often not the case. To illustrate, consider professional development. While attending a course or workshop, we encounter exciting new ideas that we may be eager to try. Despite good intentions, however, we return to the office or classroom, find ourselves bombarded by the usual demands, and, lacking support or sufficient experience to introduce the new strategies with ease, our practice remains unchanged. The more things change . . .

While it is relatively easy to develop new ways of thinking, these new ideas often remain distanced from and independent of our practice. While our espoused theories may change, these changes will not necessarily lead to changes in behavior, and our behavior is not always consistent with our espoused theory. We do not always practice what we preach. While knowing the research on constructivist teaching, we put aside project-based activities to cover the material. While talking collaboration, we retain decision control and reward compliance.

Theories-in-Use

If espoused theories don't directly influence behavior, what does? As Figure 1.1 illustrates, it is theories-in-use that directly, persistently, and consistently influence behavior. In much the same way that genetic code influences our physiological development, these theories are the ideas that actually guide our behavior. Consisting of beliefs and assumptions, the theories-in-use are our mental models. Consisting of tacit knowledge, they account for the apparent resistance to change in professional and organizational behavior (Argyris & Schon, 1974; Senge, 1990; Senge et al., 2000; Sergiovanni, 1991, 1992).

Unlike espoused theories that develop through conscious and intentional thought, theories-in-use develop through acculturation. As we grow from infants to adults, society shapes our understanding of how the world works. Just as traditional societies pass on understandings about childbirth, family, natural forces, and the relationship of human beings to the cosmos, so too does our culture transmit, through the daily processes of living, interpretations of the world that shape our behavior. As adult members of that society, we no longer focus consciously on many of our behaviors or the assumptions behind them. In many aspects of our organizational behavior, we function by rote, doing what others have done before us. We may be unable to articulate the reasons for our actions; we may also lack full awareness of what we're doing and its effects.

Language acquisition illustrates the nature of theories-in-use. We learn a native tongue through immersion, that is, acculturation. Through listening, imitating, practicing, and receiving feedback from others, we acquire a very complex set of beliefs and knowledge, or a theory-in-use for language. The knowledge component includes grammar, syntax, and vocabulary. We also learn how to make meaning, not only from words and structure but also from vocal and facial nuance, tone, volume, and other factors. By age five years—no matter what our culture or language—we possess a very complex language theory-in-use that enables and governs verbal communication. But, while the five-year-old can use the language adeptly, he or she will be unable to explain the grammar and syntax. It is apparent that the child knows the rules governing the language but can't explain them. Being able to demonstrate but not describe is what Schon (1983) describes as knowing-in-action.

In the same way that we learn language, we also learn rules governing how things work and how we should behave in different situations and in different roles. A clear example of the force of cultural influence in creating habitual behavior is the schooling process itself. Educators are perhaps the most thoroughly socialized of all professional groups. Some

Figure 1.1   Reflective Practice: A Conceptual Framework

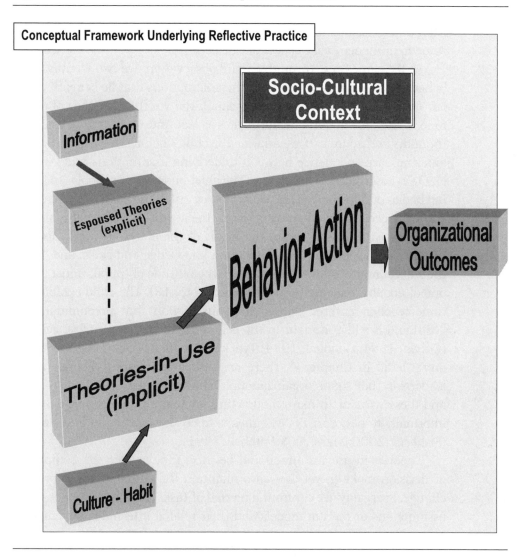

begin their experience with school culture in infant day care. Others begin in nursery school or kindergarten and may continue, as a learner or professional, until retirement and beyond. Through this lengthy and relatively consistent experience, complex sets of knowledge, assumptions, beliefs, and behaviors are ingrained in us so deeply that we are no longer aware of them, yet they guide even minute details of our daily work.

Because of this deep acculturation, we act in very consistent and predictable ways, but we may be unaware of what we do or why. Margaret

Mead commented if fish were learning about their culture, the last thing they'd discover is water. Like that water, these theories-in-use disappear from our conscious foreground and become background, but they continue to influence every aspect of our behavior.

At the same time, through careful observation, we can identify these behavioral regularities and detect the assumptions that lie beneath them. For example, when children play school, the youthful teacher, through tone, words, and actions, demonstrates a clear understanding of teachers' thoughts and actions. If we analyze the child's behavior, we often find an amazing correspondence between underlying assumptions and Dewey's (1938a) description of schooling: The chief business of school is to transmit bodies of information and skills worked out in the past to the new generation. Accordingly, learning is largely the acquisition of what is already incorporated in books and in the heads of the elders. Toward this end, teachers are agents for communicating knowledge and skills, and "since the subject matter is handed down . . . the attitude of 'pupils' must . . . be one of docility, receptivity, and obedience" (p. 18). The child exhibits the same teacher-centered approach to instruction that predominated in 1890 and is still dominant in the beginning of the twenty-first century (Cuban, 1984; Goodlad, 1984; Tyack & Cuban, 1995). As we explain in more detail in Chapter 4, there are also predominant theories about leadership that shape organizational behavior in very predictable ways, and these ways of thinking and acting are communicated formally and informally to new recruits as a means to ensure continuity and stability (Fishbein, 2000; Marshall & Mitchell, 1991).

Theories-in-use are functional because they reduce the complexity of decision making, yet they also maintain the status quo and prevent change. Every day, we confront a myriad of tasks. Like an autopilot, these assumptions or mental models and their related internal rules guide us as we deal with routine and more complicated tasks. However, our theories-in-use can also be dysfunctional as they direct us to act in similar ways, even when those actions may be ineffective or counterproductive. Our theories-in-use keep us lecturing to students, teaching math in the same way regardless of new methods and materials, and acting in non-collaborative ways as group leaders. Quite clearly, we learn to do things the way they are usually done. But, unfortunately, the way they have always been done is not necessarily the best way or the way we might choose if we really thought about it.

The key to change, then, is identification and assessment of these theories-in-use or mental models. Because these beliefs and assumptions are so ingrained, they are difficult to identify, but, by carefully examining behavior, it is possible to develop a profile of these action theories. By observing how teachers teach and how administrators enact their roles, for example, we can come to a deeper understanding of why they do what they do.

If the goal of professional development is improved practice, success can be achieved only by modifying existing theories-in-use. This is the goal of reflective practice and what differentiates it from other change strategies: It aims to achieve deep and meaningful change by uncovering, exploring, and eventually modifying these basic assumptions that lead us to act in predictable, but often ineffective, ways.

Double-Loop Learning

Reflective practice, then, is designed to facilitate identification, examination, and modification of the theories-in-use that shape behavior. Using terms drawn from organizational literature, we are seeking to create second-order changes (Cuban, 1988; Fullan, 1991) through double-loop learning (Agyris & Schon, 1974). In our traditional approach to reform, we introduce changes in procedures but fail to examine—and change— underlying beliefs. While some changes may lead to temporary improvement, these first-order changes have no effect on basic organizational processes, including the way people perform their roles. Second-order changes, in contrast, "seek to alter the fundamental ways in which organizations are put together, including new goals, structures, and roles" (Fullan, 1991, p. 29).

To create fundamental change requires changes in the underlying theories-in-use, or what Argyris and Schon (1974) described as double-loop learning. In this form of learning, change in action is accompanied by change in these underlying assumptions and beliefs. The traditional approach to problem solving follows a rational decision model: a problem is observed, alternatives are generated and considered, a decision is made, and the change is implemented. This analytic process Argyris and Schon (1974) characterized as single-loop learning. Although new strategies may provide symptomatic relief, because assumptions and basic organizational processes remain unexamined and unchanged, the changes are likely to be short lived. Single-loop learning leads to first-order, typically transitory changes.

Double-loop learning begins at the same place, with an observed problem, but it goes further. Instead of simply asking "What next?" double-loop learning involves two additional questions: "What are we doing now?" and, most crucial, "Why?" In double-loop learning, we personalize the problem. We attempt to develop a more objective perspective on our behavior and consider not only what we do but also the way in which personal or organizational behavior (or both) contributes to the problem.

We then begin to develop an understanding of why we act as we do. In this critical process (reflective practice) the taken-for-granted and often unspoken assumptions not only become explicit but also often give way to a new and different perspective. Popular organizational literature refers to new paradigms or metanoia, a shift of mind (Senge, 1990). This new set of ideas, beliefs, orientation, or perspective, the new theory-in-use, leads to an often-radical transformation in behavior. Double-loop learning leads to second-order changes; reflective practice facilitates double-loop learning.

REFLECTIVE PRACTICE: A DIFFERENT APPROACH TO PROFESSIONAL DEVELOPMENT

While reflective practice shares a common goal of improved practice with other more traditional approaches to professional development, its approach is noticeably different. In traditional professional development, for example, there is an assumption that changes come about through access to new information. Reflective practice, in contrast, views professional development as a more complex process that requires change in deeply held action theories. To confront this task, reflective practice is grounded in constructivist learning theory. These assumptions and related practices sharply differentiate it from more traditional approaches to professional development, as we show in the following illustrations.

If we observed a typical professional development session in a university classroom, a school district, a teacher center, or a corporate headquarters, we might see this scene: The instructor, often an outside expert, is clearly identifiable and occupies a central position at the front of the room, accompanied by handouts and visual aids. The presentation usually focuses on a single concept, program, or model that—if implemented—will lead to positive change. Although some are longer, many of these offerings run from a few hours to a day. The instructor has a carefully outlined plan intended to convey information. Although the learners may have an opportunity to ask questions and experiment with new skills, for the most part they sit facing the instructor and listening. Questions tend to be infrequent, and presentations are seldom interrupted. Although ostensibly geared to "success" in the professional context, professional education consists primarily of transmission of knowledge. Knowledge is the province of outside experts, and learners have access to it through the instructor. The instructor's role is to convey that information in a clear and concise manner; the learner's role is to absorb it.

While reflective practice may occur in a classroom setting, it is an approach to professional development that can and should be integrated into educational practice. In a postobservation conference, an administrative supervisor or peer mentor uses data to facilitate reflective practice. Elementary students in a circle of friends use reflective practice as they consider their own role in shaping a supportive school community. A teacher engages in reflective practice while preparing her portfolio to apply for certification by the National Board for Professional Teaching Standards. An action research project or a disaggregated analysis of student test scores may be the entree to reflective practice for teachers and administrators. In some schools, reflective practice is the standard operating procedure as administrators and teachers regularly critique their own practice, whether in staff meetings or in the lunchroom. At its best, reflective practice is not a separate activity but a way of doing business that broadens the notion of professional development and takes it into the mainstream of organizational life.

From these brief descriptions, we see distinctive differences between these two learning models. In the following section, we extend this analysis, discussing how its purpose, assumptions, and strategies distinguish reflective practice from other forms of professional development.

Purpose

The ultimate purpose in the traditional model may be improved performance, but, as illustrated in Figure 1.2, the directly observable purpose is knowledge acquisition. The instructor spends most of the available time in these sessions transmitting information to generally passive recipients and testing the acquisition of that information. In reflective practice, the learning goal is not merely acquiring knowledge but creating and applying knowledge in effective and appropriate ways. Specifically, the purpose of reflective practice is the improvement of professional practice through behavioral change.

Assumptions About Learning and Behavioral Change

The traditional model reflects an assumption that knowledge acquisition leads to behavioral change. It focuses exclusively on changing espoused theory based on an assumption that when espousals change behavior will also change. This is a very simple but widely held theory of behavioral change, tenaciously held in both general education and professional development. In reality, there is little evidence that it leads to significant, lasting change in professional practice (Bredeson, 1999; Firestone & Corbett, 1988; Sarason, 1971, 1990).

Figure 1.2   Contrasting Approaches to Professional Development

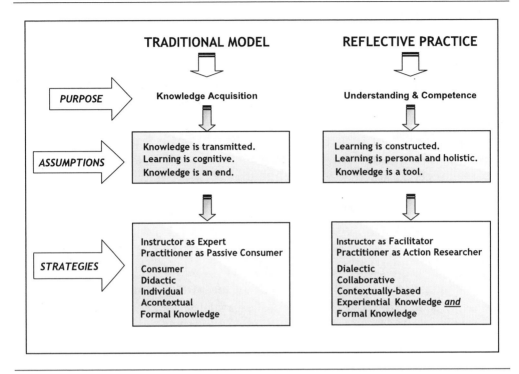

In contrast, reflective practice seeks to identify, assess, and change the underlying beliefs and assumptions, the theories-in-use, which directly influence actions. While espoused theories play an important role in learning, behavioral change depends on change in these deeply internalized ideas. To confront this task, reflective practice adopts a very different set of strategies incorporating key principles drawn from constructivism, experiential learning, and situated cognition (Osterman, 1990, 1999):

- Learning is an active process requiring involvement of the learner. Knowledge cannot simply be transmitted. For learning to take place, professionals must be motivated to learn and have an active role in determining the direction and progress of learning. Meaningful problems engage people in learning.
- Learning must acknowledge and build on prior experiences and knowledge. Accordingly, professionals need opportunities to explore, articulate, and represent their own ideas and knowledge.
- Learners construct knowledge through experience. Opportunities to observe and assess actions and to develop and test new ideas facilitate behavioral change.

- Learning is more effective when it takes place as a collaborative rather than an isolated activity and in a context relevant to the learner.

As the following discussion illustrates, the application of these principles clearly differentiates reflective practice from traditional approaches to professional development.

Learning Strategies

Engaging the Learner

Reflective practice adopts several strategies to engage the learner. Since learning begins with a personal desire to learn, reflective practice begins with problematic experience drawn from personal professional experience. Awareness of a problem, a discrepancy between a goal, or preferred situation, and the current reality, creates a need to know, or the motivation to learn. Consequently, as detailed in Chapter 2, reflective practice often begins with the articulation of the professional platform or goal statement as well as an identification of troublesome problems of practice. The question confronting the reflective practitioner is a personal one: What is my role in this situation, and what can I do to make a difference?

While reflective practice begins with a question or a problem, traditional professional development usually begins with a solution, typically one that is drawn either from the formal knowledge base or from expert experience. In the traditional model, the instructor assumes the dominant role. Whether university professors, consultants, or other external experts, instructors control the nature and direction of the learning process, establishing expectations and providing expertise. In Dewey's (1938a) words, they "start with knowledge already organized and proceed to ladle it out in doses" (p. 82). In contrast, the learner adopts a subordinate and passive role as a consumer of knowledge, complying with expectations and comprehending (or ignoring) what is offered.

In reflective practice, teacher and student roles change. The learner is active, establishing the agenda and guiding the search for solutions. "The practitioner becomes a researcher . . . and engages in a continuing process of self-education" (Schon, 1983, p. 299). Similarly, the instructor's role shifts from expert to facilitator. The main task is no longer to provide answers but to raise questions and guide personal inquiry and professional growth, providing support and resources. Reflective practice is a collaborative search for answers rather than an effort to teach a predetermined response to a problem.

Exploring Personal Beliefs, Knowledge, and Experience

Reflective practice, like constructivism, maintains that ideas influence action and that learning builds on prior experiences and knowledge. Accordingly, an understanding of experience is a basis for development. Since so much of our thinking and related action occurs at a subconscious level, reflective practice begins by scrutinizing experience to gain deeper understanding of practice and personal action theories. Essentially, reflective practice is a critical assessment of personal and organizational practice relative to personal, organizational, and social values and goals. It requires an examination of our behavior and its consequences. To understand behavior, we focus not simply on observable actions and outcomes but also on the unobservable—our thoughts and intentions, our feelings, and the feelings of others.

Reflective practice is also grounded in a sociocognitive understanding of behavior, namely, that the social context affects emotion and behavior. While we may begin with the current situation, the inquiry may also explore prior experience in the family, community, schools, and workplace. This contextual analysis may help to identify important conditions influencing our behavior. It may also help to identify contextual constraints or supports for change. The ultimate objective is to identify key leverage points to facilitate change (Senge, 1990).

The preliminary stages of the learning process, then, require careful observation of many dimensions of practice before new learning can take place. It is through careful examination of our own work that we begin to identify areas for improvement and opportunities for change. Through this examination, we develop a conscious awareness of our behavior. We begin to understand more clearly what we do, the consequences of our actions, and the ideas that shape our action. Awareness is the basis for change, yet this important step is often omitted in traditional professional development.

Constructing Learning: Reconceptualization and Experimentation

In reflective practice, the definitive test of learning is competent performance, enacting new and more efficacious strategies. Toward this goal, reconceptualization is an essential step and a distinguishing feature of reflective practice. To be enduring, changes in practice must be accompanied by changes in thought. Attention to reconceptualization and experimentation represents integration of theory and practice. Too frequently, professional development efforts fall on either end of the continuum: Theory is isolated from practice or practice is unconnected to theory.

Administrative preparation programs, for example, have been soundly criticized for concentrating exclusively on theory unrelated to practice. Conversely, criticism is just as intense with respect to programs relying exclusively on war stories devoid of a relevant conceptual framework. Reflective practice takes a middle ground and recognizes the interdependent and integral nature of theory and practice. Since ideas affect our behavior, it is important that we know not only what to do but why.

Reconceptualization is important. It is equally important to test new ways of thinking. Through analysis, the learner develops new ideas about what needs to be done and why, but, given the intractability of the theory-in-use, learning is not yet complete. The challenge remains to directly confront the former theory-in-use and introduce behavioral strategies consistent with the new espousal. Experimentation tests the feasibility of the new ideas in action; it also develops new competencies. Success confirms and reinforces change. Failure, in a supportive learning environment, becomes an opportunity for reassessment with encouragement for renewed effort.

Information

Like Dewey, Schon (1983) recognized that professional development relied almost exclusively on information drawn from the formal knowledge base, ignoring and even denigrating experiential knowledge. Too often, the focus of traditional professional development is detached from the real concerns of educators and fails to build on their experience and knowledge, relying instead on externally generated information. Consisting of ideas, information, skills, perspectives, facts, or ways of knowing, this "specialized, firmly bounded, scientific, and standardized" knowledge (Schon, 1983, p. 23) is assumed to be truth and can then be given to others (Berlak & Berlak, 1981). In the traditional model of professional development, the formal knowledge base is both the beginning and end of the process. Consequently, Schon's model of reflective practice shifted attention back to the practitioner and assigned a conspicuous, explicit, and central role to experiential knowledge. If learning is constructed, it is essential to establish and examine prior knowledge. In addition, the knowledge gained from personal experience can provide valuable insight in the search for improved understanding and better solutions.

At the same time, however, formal knowledge plays an important, if different, role in reflective practice, serving as a tool to support inquiry and learning. The goal of the educator is not simply to absorb externally developed information but to use knowledge to develop understanding and competence. Educational research has changed dramatically in the last twenty years, with far more school- and classroom-based inquiry and attention to important problems of practice. Much of this work is very relevant to educators and may be useful to identify areas of inquiry, to challenge prior assumptions, or to provide a critical perspective on professional practice. When educators realize that previous beliefs and strategies no longer provide meaningful explanations or generate predictable outcomes, formal knowledge may be a source of new ideas to enrich and expand their conceptual and strategic repertoire. By emphasizing both forms of knowledge, reflective practice expands the types and sources of information available to support professional growth (Hart, 1990).

Dialogue and Collaboration

Because behavior is so habitual, we often lack a full awareness of its many dimensions. For this reason, dialogue and collaboration are critical for reflective practice and learning. Traditional models of education frequently rely on didactic instruction. Reflective practice, in contrast, relies more on dialectic learning, involving dialogue, discussion, and a critical, open analysis of competing ideas. Dialogue and discussion enhance the learning process. As learners ask questions, challenge ideas, and process learning verbally, they clarify their thinking and deepen understanding. They learn more. Dialogue is even more valuable when it incorporates intellectual conflict (Fullan, 1999). Contrasting, opposing ideas or alternate explanations stimulate engagement and further challenge learners to assess and refine their thinking.

Collaboration, too, is an important aspect of reflective practice. The reflective practitioners—and facilitator—are united by a common concern and share responsibility for their professional growth, each bringing knowledge and expertise to the situation. Sharing insights and observations facilitates learning (Fullan, 1999; Johnson & Johnson, 1989). The emotional support from colleagues as professionals identify, analyze, and resolve problems also helps to motivate and sustain commitment throughout the difficult change process (Fullan, 1999).

REFLECTIVE PRACTICE: CREATING A CONTEXT FOR LEARNING

Research and experience demonstrate that solutions are not necessarily interchangeable. What works in one situation may not be successful in another. Reflective practice addresses this by exploring problems in context. Professionals who engage in reflective practice work on issues relevant to them in the settings where they work. At the same time, context also affects individuals' ability to engage in reflective practice and implement change.

Reflective practice is a professional development strategy; it is also a problem-solving strategy. It is about individuals working with others to critically examine their own practice to resolve important problems. To engage in reflective practice requires an environment of support. It requires an organizational climate that encourages open communication, critical dialogue, risk taking, and collaboration.

As we explain in Chapter 4, many organizations adopt bureaucratic procedures that restrict and tightly regulate communication. Problems are hidden, and changes come in the form of directives, developed by upper echelons of the hierarchy. Bosses make the decisions; workers implement them. Everyone knows his or her place, and people are expected to mind their own business, often ignoring blatant problems. In such an environment, reflective practice is difficult but still possible. At a minimum, reflective practice requires a sense of security. Individuals must be assured they may speak freely, without fear of retribution. In addition, they need organizational support: time to work with others and encouragement to assume the difficult work of change. A school leader, in whatever role, can create the conditions necessary to support reflective practice, if only on a small scale. The experience with reflective practice can be important in challenging existing norms, breaking down boundaries, and creating a more positive culture.

In contrast, there are other organizations where hierarchy, depersonalization, and standardization play little part. These organic structures are characterized instead by flexible working arrangements, shared responsibility for decision making, and open communication (Burns & Stalker, 1961; Mintzberg, 1983). Rules are flexible and worked out to meet the needs of workers and clients. Responsibility and authority are widely shared. Members take initiative to resolve problems and introduce improvement, often going beyond the boundaries of their roles. Organizations like these empower people and enhance individual and organizational effectiveness by distributing leadership.[1] In these organic systems, the focus is on the goal and the goal is consistently defined as student learning. Accordingly, people work together to examine, assess, and revise their individual and collective practice to better achieve this goal. These organizations, "where people continually expand their capacity to create the results they truly desire, where new and expansive patterns of thinking are nurtured, where collective aspiration is set free, and where people are continually learning how to learn together," are "learning organizations" (Senge, 1990, p. 3). These communities of professional practice are organizations where reflective practice thrives as an integral part of the culture.

Our goal is to create learning organizations. While organizations certainly exert powerful influences on the people who inhabit them, they remain human creations guided by human intentions and decisions (Greenfield, 1986, 1991), and individuals have the potential to shape them to their purposes. While not the norm, outstanding schools frequently operate like this (Fullan, 1999, 2001; Leithwood, 1993; Leithwood & Jantzi, 1990; Marks & Printy, 2003; Murphy & Louis, 1994). Many have developed this culture of reflective practice under the direction of exceptional leaders, transformational leaders, who have both a vision and the skills to enact this vision. Whether intentional or not, this vision incorporates reflective practice. Because we believe that these mental models or action theories are so important in determining how we enact our roles, as we proceed through this book, we continue to discuss not only the strategies involved in reflective practice but also the assumptions, the beliefs—the mind-set—that lead individuals to be reflective practitioners.

In this chapter, we explored the conceptual roots of reflective practice and considered its role in educational reform. Specifically, we proposed that reflective practice is an alternate approach to professional development. Building on constructivist learning principles, this approach facilitates change in ideas and practice. It is an approach to school reform that begins with individual change. While reflective practice is suitable for individuals, it works best as a collaborative process. In effective school organizations—learning organizations—reflective practice thrives as an integral part of the culture. At the same time, reflective practice can help organizations develop the skills and processes needed to become learning organizations. In the next chapter, we develop a more detailed understanding of how reflective practice takes place.

NOTE

1. For additional information about distributed leadership, see Murphy and Datnow (2003a, 2003b), Ogawa and Bossert (1995), and Pounder, Ogawa, and Adams (1995).

Engaging in Reflective Practice

A Cycle of Experiential Learning

In Chapter 1, we examined reflective practice through a wide-angle lens. We developed a conceptual understanding of reflective practice and considered the promise of reflective practice as a means of overcoming organizational habit and facilitating significant change. In this chapter, we narrow the lens angle and address the more pragmatic questions: How does reflective practice work? What does it look like? How do we begin?

As noted, awareness is essential for behavioral change. To gain a new level of insight into personal behavior, the reflective practitioner assumes a dual stance being, on one hand, the actor in a drama and, on the other hand, the critic who sits in the audience watching and analyzing the entire performance. To achieve this metacognitive perspective, individuals must come to a deeper understanding of their own behavior within the context of their goals, the consequences of their actions, and the ideas or theories-in-use that shape their action strategies. Achieving this level of conscious awareness, however, is not an easy task. Theories-in-use, as we have seen, are not easily articulated. Schon (1983) described this process in the context of professional practice. As he explained, professional knowledge is grounded in professional experience: "Competent practitioners usually know more than they can say. They exhibit a kind of knowing-in-practice, most of which is tacit" (p. viii). Consequently, when asked, master teachers or master administrators are often unable to identify the components of their work that lead to successful outcomes. Similarly, practitioners who want or need to improve their performance are often unclear about how their own actions prevent them from being more successful. So if the purpose of reflective practice is to enhance awareness and understanding of our own thoughts and action as a means of professional growth, how do we begin this process of reflection? How do we develop a critical awareness of our own professional practice? Where do we start?

REFLECTIVE PRACTICE AS EXPERIENTIAL LEARNING

As we explained in Chapter 1, reflective practice is located within the older tradition of experiential learning and incorporates key principles of constructivism (Osterman, 1990, 1999) and situated cognition (Brown, Collins, & Duguid, 1989a, 1989b; Prestine & LeGrand, 1991). Experiential learning theorists, including Dewey, Lewin, and Piaget, maintain that learning is most effective, most likely to lead to behavioral change, when it begins with experience, specifically, problematic experience. Whether described as conflict, discrepancy, perturbation, surprise, dissonance, or problem, some type of unsettling experience is an important stimulus to cognitive growth. From experience and research, we also know that learning is most effective when people become personally engaged in the learning process, and engagement is most likely to take place when there is a need to learn. In professional programs, for example, fruitful learning often doesn't begin until the person is on the job. Situated cognition focuses on both the process and the context of learning. In a view popularized by problem-based learning (Bridges, 1992), situated cognition proponents maintain that learning is best accomplished through an active, social, and authentic learning process. Learning, they argue, is most effective when the learner is actively involved in the learning process, when it takes place as a collaborative rather than an isolated activity, and when it takes place in a context relevant to the learner.

Experiential learning theory further maintains that learning is a dialectic and cyclic process consisting of four stages: experience, observation and reflection, abstract conceptualization, and experimentation (Kolb, 1984). While experience is the basis for learning, learning cannot take place without reflection. Conversely, while reflection is essential to the process, reflection must be integrally linked with action. Reflective practice, then, integrating theory and practice, thought and action, is, as Schon (1987) described, a "dialogue of thinking and doing through which I become more skillful" (p. 31).

THE CYCLE OF REFLECTIVE PRACTICE

Reflective practice engages individuals in this cyclic process. Learning, or the process of inquiry, begins with what Dewey (1938b) described as a problematic or an indeterminate situation: a troublesome event or experience, an unsettling situation that cannot be resolved using standard operating procedures. Prompted by a sense of uncertainty or unease, the reflective practitioner, as researcher, steps back to examine this experience: What was the nature of the problem? What were my intentions? What did I do? What happened? In the process of observing and analyzing this experience, the problem emerges more clearly. The problem—a discrepancy between the current and the preferred, between intention and action, or between action and effects—further stimulates the inquiry and motivates the learner to examine practice more intensely, seeking a deeper and more objective understanding of events as well as the ideas that shape behavior. This awareness of the problem also motivates the learner to absorb new information as part of an active search for better answers and more effective strategies. The final stages of the process involve reconceptualization and experimentation. Having examined and analyzed the experience, the learner moves again into the realm of theory. Now motivated by an awareness of a problem, the learner uses new information to develop alternate theories that are more useful in explaining the relationship between actions and outcomes and to begin the search for strategies that are more consistent with espoused theories and more effective in achieving intended outcomes. This changed perspective becomes a stimulus for experimentation: New theories suggest different strategies that can then be tested through action research. In short, raising questions about practice begins a learning process that leads to behavioral change. Figure 2.1 illustrates the stages of this cyclic process and the section that follows describes each of these stages in more detail.

Problem Identification

Since the intent of reflective practice is to improve the quality of professional performance and because problematic experience plays an important role in learning, the process of inquiry focuses on problems of practice. By one definition (Kelsey, 1993), a problem is a discrepancy, a gap between an ideal or desired condition and the current reality. A problem is also, by definition, relevant. Without personal involvement, there is no problem. As long as existing paradigms satisfy personal needs, there is no incentive to learn and no reason to challenge

Figure 2.1   Reflective Practice: An Experiential Learning Cycle

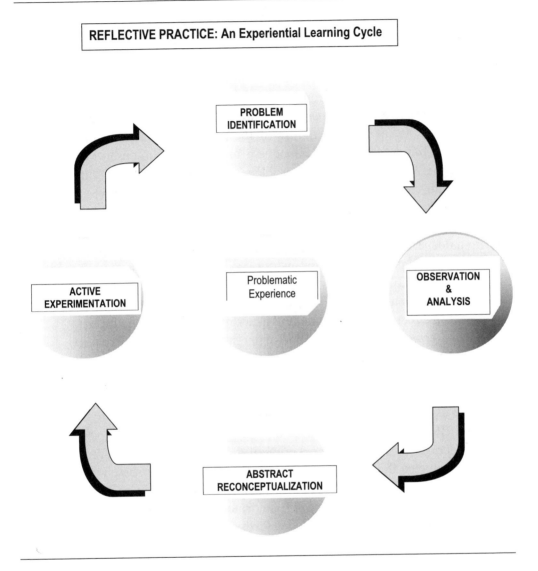

existing perspectives. Why change if it's not necessary? Why learn if you think you already know the answer? A problem, by raising person-ally relevant questions, initiates the learning process and engages the learner.

Identifying problems, however, is not easy. People, and educators in particular, value optimism. In response to organizational problems, discussion turns quickly to solutions, while problem identification and analysis is cut short (Bolman & Deal, 1991; Kelsey, 1993; Leithwood,

Begley, & Cousins, 1994; Leithwood & Steinbach, 1995). Identifying personal problems is even more difficult. Think of children who go to their parents with a problem but cannot bring themselves to disclose it. Once the problem is spoken, what seemed overwhelming becomes manageable, but reluctance is initially great. Adults are not very different. Problems are often seen as indicators of incompetence, and, as individuals, we create defenses preventing problem recognition. Organizations adopt similar behaviors that preclude learning and progress (Argyris, 1990; Argyris & Schon, 1978; Senge, 1990; Senge et al., 2000).

In some cases, problems come from our personal experience. A new principal, for example, enthusiastically assumes the position only to find teachers treating him or her with mistrust. A senior teacher, with 20 years of successful experience, is suddenly unable to engage students. A group of elementary teachers are concerned with the poor performance of a particular group of students in their classes. In these situations, a perceived discrepancy between personal goals and actual accomplishment creates a sense of problem.

Dilemmas can also lead to problem identification. Confronted with the need to establish accountability, educators are conflicted between their perceived need to cover the material and their desire to engage students in challenging and personally relevant learning experiences. Teachers are torn between their desire to address students' emotional needs and their need to teach to the test. As the teachers explore these situations, they realize that there is a discrepancy between what they would like to do (their espoused theories) and their practice. Initially, however, the tension in the situation, the intuitive discomfort, is the signal that this issue requires closer attention.

Organizational concerns may also stimulate reflective practice. An analysis of test scores in a school or district indicates that the lowest test scores occur among students from low-income areas. Reviewing special education referrals highlights the disproportionate number of boys and students of color. Problems also emerge as the professional examines his or her work in the context of theory and research. Research, for example, supports the use of heterogeneous grouping and cooperative learning, but a teacher realizes that he or she relies almost exclusively on direct instruction or homogeneous grouping, or both.

Educators face problems of all shapes and sizes. Some involve a few people; others, an entire school. Some are systemic; some more confined. Some are clearly defined; others are vague. What is important, however, is not the nature of the problem but its significance to the individual. In reflective practice, we seek deep engagement in learning, and relevance produces engagement. A relevant problem rivets attention and arouses the need to learn. In many cases, professionals begin reflective practice because of a personal concern. However, in other cases—staff development activities, university classes, action research projects—the problem may be a presented one. The principal, for example, may be concerned about a growing incidence of student discipline problems in the school and district and hope to use reflective practice as a means to engage other staff members in addressing the issue.

Regardless of the source of the problem, reflective practice invariably focuses on personal experience. Confronting the self, however, may be difficult, particularly in a group situation. Initially, then, it may be more comfortable to begin by focusing on shared issues and gradually move toward examination of personal action and responsibility. Relevance, however, is essential. If the problem emerges from individuals' personal experience, it is more likely to be relevant, but presented problems can also be absorbing, as we show later through specific cases. Although reflective practice may begin in the absence of personal commitment, learning will be greater where involvement is based on personal choice and commitment.

In whatever form and through whatever means, problems arise out of a sense of discomfort or a desire to change, out of a discrepancy between what we perceive and what we consider desirable. In some way, current conditions fall short of the ideal; there is a gap between the current and preferred situation. Regardless of how the problem emerges, its recognition motivates us to develop a deeper understanding of the situation, particularly our own role in the situation. For reflective practitioners, the questions are always the same: What can we do to resolve this problem? What can we do to move closer to the goal? With the problematic situation in mind, the next stage of the process begins.

Observation and Analysis

The second stage of the experiential learning cycle, observation and analysis, is the most critical and complex of the four. In the first step of the process, we identify a problematic situation as a meaningful focus for inquiry. In this second step of the process, we gather and critically examine information about that experience to develop a deeper and more complex understanding of our own behavior —and perhaps of others as well. Initially, our goal is to develop a descriptive picture of the problematic experience. To do this, we take on the role of researcher, gathering comprehensive data about this situation. Metaphorically speaking, we become like theater critics watching and analyzing our own actions on stage; we become both subject and object. We stand back from the experience itself and assume a detached stance to describe it fully and critically. The ability to engage in reflective practice requires an ability to see events and actions in new and different ways. To be a reflective practitioner, then, requires finely honed observational skills. Clear and careful description of experience (observation) becomes the basis for the later phases of the reflective practice cycle: analysis, reconceptualization, and experimentation.

Observation

Observation is important because how we interpret situations shapes our actions, but, too often, those interpretations are quite removed from actual events. In theory, every decision involves a series of steps. Argyris (1982) described this process as the ladder of inference. (See Figure 2.2.) Initially, there is an experience; something happens. The participants observe the experience, interpret what they have seen, and come to certain conclusions about what happened and why. These conclusions form the basis for future decisions and action. In reality, however, the process is highly subjective, and interpretations digress from the actual events. Over time, people tend to skip steps in the process, jumping quickly from experience to conclusions, relying on previous and faulty interpretations.

Figure 2.2   The Ladder of Inference

Ladder of Inference

Top Rungs: I take action

7. I take **ACTIONS** based on my beliefs.

6. I adopt **BELIEFS** about the world.

5. I draw **CONCLUSIONS**.

Middle Rungs: I add meaning and make assumptions

4. I make **ASSUMPTIONS** based on the meanings I add.

3. I add **MEANINGS** (cultural and personal).

Bottom Rungs: I observe data

2. I **OBSERVE** selectively. I see what I want to see.

1. I **EXPERIENCE** a situation.

Because we are all different, with different experiences and interests, we notice different things; we remember different things. We observe, but we do so selectively (Stone, Patton, & Heen, 1999); eyewitnesses tell different stories. Over time, we shorten this process even further. With experience, we develop different interpretations of how the world works, how people act, and how things are. With these mental models, our perceptions become increasingly selective; we absorb confirming and ignore challenging data. We see what we want or expect to see—to the point where believing is seeing (Bolman & Deal, 1991). In time, we accept assumptions as facts, and our actions become increasingly predictable. We think about the experience, but in an idiosyncratic fashion. We have recorded information about what has actually taken place—the events— but we observe selectively, seldom inquiring about those hidden aspects of behavior (assumptions, intentions, feelings) that may help us to understand the events in a more complex way. With limited information, we then interpret through our own perceptual lenses, and we make assumptions about what we observed, often without further discussion with others and with no attempt to confirm our interpretations. From these observations, we draw conclusions that affirm our assumptions. The actions we finally take, the decisions we make, reflect these conclusions. In brief, we see the world as we want to see it and act accordingly. These self-constructed perceptions become our mental models (Senge, 1990; Sergiovanni, 1991, 1992).

Unfortunately, our lens on the world is often clouded or distorted. Not all of us have access to the same data, and we interpret those data that we do share differently. As a result, the assumptions we draw may not be accurate, and the decisions we make may be flawed.

The observation stage of reflective practice short-circuits this unminded, reflexive cycle. It slows down the process of experience, leading quickly to an automatic, unexamined behavioral response. It leads us to take one careful, analytically examined step at a time. We do this by consciously and intentionally gathering additional information about situations, by opening the lens to develop a more comprehensive picture of events, including the tacit assumptions and feelings that color and shape our perceived reality. The observation phase of the process, then, requires us to visit or revisit situations, observing them carefully, taking care to gather more detailed information before we make judgments and rush to action. To do this, we stand back from the experience, striving to achieve a detached perspective like that of the drama critic. We become researchers carefully scrutinizing our own work. By gathering data, we begin to uncover the fundamental elements in our thinking that have created the problems we experience. From that point, freed from a state of unawareness and unminded action, we can examine our behavior more critically and develop a readiness for new ways of thinking and acting.

When we observe, what data do we gather and how? In the observation phase, our purpose is to develop a comprehensive description of the problematic experience. In Chapter 1, we presented a conceptual model illustrating the linkages between espoused theories (our intended goals and the action strategies that we consciously advocate), behavior (our professional practice), and outcomes (effects or consequences of our behavior). These are the elements of reflective practice, and we intentionally gather information about each component as a basis for analysis. We also gather detailed information about the situation itself. With these data in hand, we can then begin to analyze and assess our practice in the light of our goals, beliefs, intentions, and accomplishments. Through this analysis, we also begin to identify the theories-in-use that directly shape our behavior.

From our experience, observation may begin in different places. In very early phases of our administrative preparation classes, for example, students develop educational platforms or vision statements that include educational goals as well as ideas about how to achieve those goals (espoused theories). These statements, then, become standards by which they assess their practice. In other cases, including those we document here, data gathering begins by looking at practice. A problem arises and focuses our attention. Regardless of where the process begins, at some point, reflective practitioners will have examined all these dimensions of their work. Because observation plays such a critical role in reflective practice, in Chapter 3 we provide more specific information on methods of gathering data.

Problematic Experience. The cycle of reflective practice typically begins with a problem. While we understand this problem at one level, because of the habitual nature of our behavior as well as the subjective aspects of our perception, closer examination may yield new insights into the nature of the problem. In this initial stage, then, our goal is to compile a descriptive and comprehensive profile of this problem in the context of our experience. We step back and, with a more objective stance, take another look. As part of this examination, we look closely at our own behavior, but we are also interested in taking a closer look at the entire situation. What is happening in the classroom, the school, the community, or the family that may influence the situation? Who is involved and what are their thoughts, feelings, and actions? In the classroom, we may stand back and watch students to see what they are doing and how they're feeling. In a committee meeting, we may listen carefully to the other constituents' perspectives. As an administrator, we may take another look at the teachers' workday as we assess scheduling problems, or we may arrange a time to talk.

Behavior: Actions, Thoughts, and Feelings. Since our goal is to improve performance, it is important to gather a comprehensive and deep understanding of our own professional behavior in the context of the particular problem. The term *behavior* often refers only to observable actions: "I stood at the front of the room and began the lesson." Here, however, we use a broader definition, to include not only observable acts but also the thoughts and feelings that accompany our own actions. Consequently, we also examine our reactions to and understanding of those events: What were our intentions? Our feelings? How did we interpret what we saw? "When I began the lesson, I was intent on covering the material I had developed for the day, and I was distracted and annoyed by Anthony, a persistent troublemaker."

This is not a simple task but an important one. We have explained the difficulty in discovering theories-in-use. It is equally difficult to develop a conscious awareness of our own behavior. We offer espousals quite easily, but because we lack an objective perspective, we may fail to detect discrepancies between what we say and what we do. A person may denounce prejudicial behavior but fail to recognize his or her own discriminatory actions. A school administrator may espouse the concept of collaborative management but not recognize autocratic aspects of his or her own behavior. A teacher may agree wholeheartedly on the importance of high expectations for all students yet not see the inconsistency in adjusting expectations for students with learning or behavioral problems. These discrepancies are often quite obvious to an outsider but invisible to the practitioner. We simply do not see that words and actions are not aligned. Careful observation of action helps to reveal these inconsistencies, and this awareness prompts reflection.

Espoused Theories: Goals and Intentions. Theories, as we explained, are statements of cause–effect relationships. Our espoused theories, then, incorporate both a vision (where we want to go, what we want to accomplish) and a perception of the appropriate way to achieve these goals (our ideas about the right or best way to do things). Reflective practice facilitates learning by fostering a critical assessment of practice. That critical assessment is not possible if goals are not clearly stated. Articulating goals, whether in the form of a mission statement, educational platform, or specific objectives, serves as a benchmark or a rubric. Similarly, in describing our perspective on best practice—whether in teaching, leadership, or parenting—we make a statement about our intentions: the way we believe we act or hope to act.

Outcomes. We also gather information about the consequences or effects of our actions. Again, to establish a deeper understanding of our practice, we look for different indicators. To assess learning, for example, educators look at test scores; they may also gather information about students' engagement in learning or their sense of belongingness. Similarly, leaders interested in their effectiveness may want to know about parent involvement, teacher commitment, and organizational climate as well as various indicators of student learning.

Analysis

In explaining reflective practice, we refer to observation and analysis as a single step because they are integral processes that depend on and enrich one another. Data are powerful, and gathering information about any aspect of performance almost immediately catapults the reflective practitioner into analysis. Analysis flows naturally from observation; at the same time, it may generate the need for additional information. Through this dynamic process, the problem emerges more clearly and sets the stage for reconceptualization and experimentation.

Reflective practice fosters learning by creating opportunities to become more aware of our practice. Specifically, with the information that we have gathered about events, actions, espoused theories, goals and outcomes, we begin a critical analysis focused on discrepancies among intentions, action, and outcomes.

Comparing Goals and Outcomes. Since our focus is on problematic experience, the analysis may begin by contrasting actual with intended outcomes. When we examine the results of our actions, are we pleased? Were our actions effective? Did they lead to the goals we had in mind or were there unanticipated and undesirable consequences? For example, through observation, it has become very clear that, aside from his frequent misbehavior, Anthony is lonely and uninvolved in any class activities. In her analysis, his teacher begins to contrast this situation (outcome) with her preferred situation. She is a good teacher, and, like other teachers, her ideal is to have every child in her classroom actively involved. She wants her students to be happy about coming to school, but through observation it becomes apparent that she is not achieving her goals with Anthony.

In another situation, a principal examines the success of a recent initiative to standardize curriculum and instruction but finds that the anticipated improvement in instruction and student learning did not occur. Further, the principal has encountered a serious drop in teacher morale.

Contrasting Espoused Theories and Action. Another inquiry strategy is to examine action relative to espousals. Was our action consistent with our intent? Did our behavior (thought, feeling, and actions) reflect the espoused theory we articulated in our personal platform? Did we act as we wanted to act, in a way consistent with our values?

Given dissatisfaction with outcomes, there are several types of discrepancies that practitioners may discover. In some cases, actions are not aligned with espousals. At one level, Anthony's teacher knows that misbehavior in the class often signifies the student is experiencing difficulty. As his teacher, she believes it's her responsibility to regain his attention. By watching her own interaction with Anthony, she realizes that she has been isolating him in the classroom instead of trying to find ways to support him. She has caught herself glaring at him every time he comes near her and assigning consequences that seem to aggravate his behavior. In this situation, the teacher discovers her action is not aligned with her espoused beliefs. She has also begun to see that her actions may be contributing to the problem. Her task, then, will be to align her actions more closely with her espoused theory and also to identify the theory-in-use that prompted the nature of her response to Anthony.

In the case of the principal, actions are aligned with espousals, but, as a result of the analysis, it becomes apparent that the action theories are flawed. They simply don't yield the intended results. In discussing his actions, the principal explained that he wanted to standardize curriculum and instruction to ensure uniformity for students and also to make sure children spent sufficient time in important areas of the curriculum. He believed that these actions would lead to his goal. His actions were directly aligned with his espousals, but the theory was flawed. By examining the situation through observation, shared experience, and formal research, the principal became aware that standardization may also deaden teachers' sense of professionalism, stifle creativity, and breed resentment and antagonism (Cohn & Kottkamp, 1993; McNeil, 1986; Wise, 1988). His task then is to develop a theoretical framework and action strategy that enable him to realize the vision in a more complete way.

Theories-in-Use. Since enduring change requires modification in the theories-in-use that shape behavior, our ultimate goal in the observation and analysis phase is to develop an understanding of our personal theories and to assess them critically. As Griffiths and Tann (1992) so aptly put it, "The action research cycle goes round smoothly and elegantly.

However, unless sufficient attention is paid to the hub of all this activity (the theories that shape behavior), the cycle can become a mere hoop without a hub, careening along, giving enjoyment and excitement, and often going a long way before keeling over" (p. 73).

As we explained in Chapter 1, because these beliefs are so elusive, so hidden, and often unpalatable, individuals can rarely articulate them. They know the theories at a tacit level but may not be able to express them in words. Whether trying to explain how to ride a bike, to use Schon's (1983) memorable example, or describing the process of revitalizing a school culture, it is often difficult for skilled professionals to explain how they are able to accomplish what they do. It is equally difficult to detect personal action theories when the performance is less successful.

Because of this phenomenon, eliciting theories-in-use requires a different tack. Because it is so difficult for people to articulate the assumptions behind their actions, we construct a portrait of these theories by observing behavior. Even this part of the process is complicated because it is often difficult for us to see ourselves in a realistic manner. By gathering information about behavior, we stop the action so that the actor and others can stand back and look more carefully at what was done. By examining actions, it is then possible to detect those precipitating assumptions.

It is also possible to explore these mental models directly. In Anthony's situation, for example, we infer from the teacher's response that her theory-in-use differs from her espoused theory. She consciously knows that student misbehavior is frequently a cry for help (espoused theory), but her gut reaction is an angry one. This response may reflect a deeper assumption (theory-in-use). As she reflects on her thoughts and feelings, she realizes that she interprets Anthony's misbehavior as his disregard for learning and for her as a teacher. When Anthony acts out, she assumes that he's doing it intentionally to annoy her.

When the principal considers his action, he realizes that he ignored his teachers' feelings about the problem and made a unilateral decision, conveying disregard for the staff. This insight led him to think more about his leadership beliefs, and he realized that, even though he views himself as a progressive leader with a respect for teachers, he assumed he alone was responsible for student performance. He detected a theory-in-use that affected his approach to problem solving and led him unilaterally to adopt a counterproductive solution.

Examining Personal Experience in the Context of Theory and Research. Looking for disequilibria between personal practice and what we know from research can also facilitate personal understanding and growth. Anthony's teacher, for example, may review research on teacher expectations and student engagement, whereas the school principal might explore work on leadership and school change to identify strategies that have been effective in engaging teachers and facilitating student learning.

The process of inquiry begins with a problematic or indeterminate situation. In the initial stage, understanding of the problem may be little more than an intuitive sense or a gut feeling that something is wrong or could be better. As Figure 2.3 indicates, through a series of steps, reflective practitioners complete a critical analysis of their practice. They describe their espousals, gather information about their practice, contrast espousals with practice, assess their work and reveal theories-in-use, and perhaps examine their personal practice in the context of theory and research. Through these integrally linked processes of observation and analysis, professionals come to see discrepancies. In the case of our teacher and

Figure 2.3 Finding Discrepancies: Developing a Critical Perspective on Practice

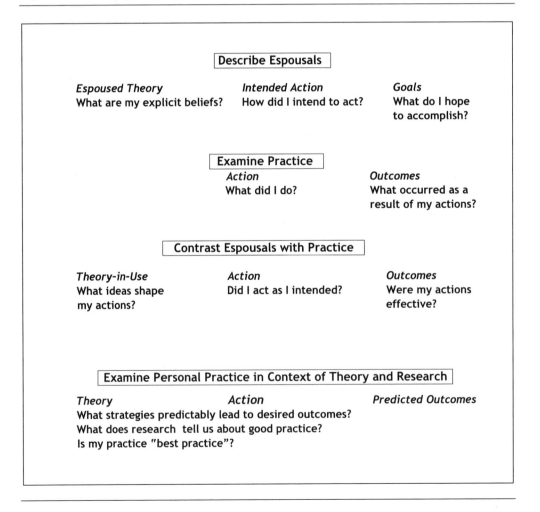

principal, outcomes fall short of goals, actions are either inconsistent with espoused values or ineffective, and the elusive theories-in-use emerge as powerful perspectives influencing actions in ways that are inconsistent with espoused values. Through analysis, the problem emerges more clearly, and the professionals come to a more finely tuned appreciation of their own role in the problem. With this new comprehension, they are now ready to explore other ways of thinking.

Abstract Reconceptualization

Although we describe reflective practice as a four-step process, in reality, the stages often merge together. This is also true with respect to reconceptualization. At this point in the process, the professional has identified a problem or problem area and, through observation and reflection, has developed a deeper understanding of the experience: the events themselves and their impact, the personal interpretation of those events and the theory-in-use shaping the practice. A clear understanding of the problem prefigures the solution. Through observation (gathering data) and analysis comes a more complex understanding of behavior: what we did, why we did it, and the consequences. Much of this understanding is completely new; we have seen things that we didn't see before, and we understand the situation in a very different way. Through this detailed analysis of the problematic experience, the roots of the problem have begun to emerge and the process of reconceptualization has begun.

At this point in the cycle, the reflective practitioner engages in an active search for new ideas and new strategies. There is strong motivation to find new information and ideas to address the problem. At every stage of the cycle, the nature of the learning has been personal and engaging. The problem is self-defined and relevant, and the process of observation and analysis in focusing on the individual role in the problem context generates a felt need to improve, change, or reinforce effective behaviors.

Personal reflection in itself often yields new directions. This is one reason why reflective listening is such a powerful communication strategy. Given the opportunity to talk about an experience, to process it verbally, people often find they easily discover solutions to situations that had previously overwhelmed them. This is one of the main arguments for reflective practice: It enables professionals to use their own experience to address problems. It is not always necessary to go to outside experts to find valuable expertise. At the same time, educators may find great value in working collaboratively with colleagues as they attempt to develop solutions to the same or similar problems (Fullan, 1999, 2001; Miller, 1990). By drawing on the diverse experience and expertise of colleagues, we increase greatly the pool of available ideas and resources. As one participant in a reflection group said, "I have available to me many lives I have not lived." For this reason, reflective practice relies heavily on the professional knowledge gained through education and experience in the university, the home, the workplace, and the community.

Personal experience, however, may be limited, and professionals may also find it valuable to turn to formal knowledge. In an action research project designed to stimulate reflective practice among student teachers, for example, faculty withheld insights from their own experience, thinking that it was important to support students' autonomy and encourage them to trust practitioner-derived knowledge (Carson, 1995). The students, however, were unable to go beyond recognition of the problem. As one lamented, "I know critical reflection is important to teaching, but if you have no ideas regarding the strategies to be used in teaching, the reflection becomes almost useless. We have no actual teaching experience, so we are desperate for strategies" (p. 155). This situation clearly illustrates the important role that information can play when motivation is strong. It also confirms the validity of an important constructivist principle: Information will be integrated readily when there is a strong need to know.

The first stage of the learning process was a time for consciousness raising, developing an awareness of problems and exploring and assessing our experience. With this information in hand, the process of revising, clarifying, or elaborating our thinking began. Through this dialogic and experiential process, educators confirm or question their existing theories. Through careful examination, some discover that personal theories are effective and consistent with ideas represented in the formal knowledge base. In the case of Anthony, the teacher's espoused theory is consistent with research on student engagement; therefore, the challenge is not necessarily to develop an entirely new way of thinking but to align actions more closely with this theory. For her, that becomes the challenge in the experimentation phase of the process. For another teacher without this conceptual framework, personal observation, exploring the research, or sharing experience and ideas with colleagues may lead to a similar conclusion and suggest more positive ways for identifying and resolving Anthony's problems. Through analysis, new ideas emerge, and the teacher may develop an entirely new way of looking at the problem.

If we accept the intractability of the theory-in-use, however, the learning task is far from complete. The goal now becomes one of directly confronting the theory-in-use by introducing behavioral strategies consistent with the new conceptualization. While information can be incorporated into the espoused theory with relative ease, it is more difficult to modify the theory-in-use. We know what aspects of our behavior may have contributed to the undesirable outcomes, and we have ideas about how to get better results. We can say it, but can we actually do it? This becomes the challenge in the final stage of the process—actually changing behavior to realize goals more completely.

Active Experimentation

Active experimentation is an important ingredient in the learning process. While it is relatively easy to explore new ideas, it is far more difficult to change behavior. The opportunity to experience new ideas as effective facilitates this process.

By this point, most professionals are open to new ideas. For some, perhaps because the ideas were so consistent with the perceptions they already held, applying them is relatively simple. They wholeheartedly embrace these ideas and almost intuitively apply them. Others, however, remain skeptical: "Yes, it's a good idea, but . . . "; "Yes, it works for *them*, but . . . "; "It seemed to work in *that* school, but. . . . " Confronted with the decision to act differently, they feel nervous and uncomfortable and begin to identify all of the reasons for not doing it. Underlying the resistance is the theory-in-use: "I don't want to do it because. . . . " For these people, real insight into their own action theories may not develop until they are trying new behaviors. Experimentation, then, is another means to unearth predominant theories-in-use.

Through reflective practice, we develop new ideas or theories about how things work. Anthony's teacher, for example, might decide to replace her glare with a smile, trying to develop a more positive relationship with him as a means to engage him in class. In this stage of the cycle, she tests this assumption. She makes a conscious decision to act in a particular way to test the new hypothesis. She engages in behavioral experiments; she becomes an action researcher. She develops an action plan, deciding what she will do and how she will gather information to assess the effectiveness of this new strategy. In this situation and in most cases, experimentation takes place on the job. In some situations, however, educators may initially prefer to practice new behaviors as part of a role play in the safety of a classroom or professional development activity.

For those who do enact new strategies, there are several possible outcomes. The new strategy may be successful, clearly demonstrating the validity of the underlying action theory and reinforcing the actor's resolve. Where the educator has resisted change, evidence of success may be a critical step in the change process. In other cases, success may not be so apparent. These circumstances provide another entrée into the reflective process as the practitioner once again examines the situation and tries to determine the source of the problem: Was the theory flawed or was the practice flawed, falling short of the intent?

In either case, the experiment produces a new experience, and the learning process begins anew but with one important difference. By now, reflective skills have developed, and self-awareness is acute and focused. Whereas in the first experiences with reflective practice it was difficult to distance ourselves from our performance, at this stage of experimentation we go into the action better able to handle the dual role of actor and drama critic. We are more skilled at gathering information. We are more aware of our own actions, more sensitive to the feelings and reactions of others, and more adept at using a variety of techniques to gather information. At this point, the circular nature of the process is obvious. With data in hand, we analyze the sequence of events to confirm or disconfirm the new hypothesis. Confirmation reinforces the new theory and provides an incentive for repeating what may initially have been awkward or uncomfortable behaviors. Instances when things don't work as intended lead to a renewed search to refine the theory, develop better strategies, or both. Whether the next cycle focuses in a more detailed way on the same problem or addresses another issue, it builds on the earlier cycle—learning and professional development become a progressive and continuing process. Reflective practice may itself become a very functional habit.

In this chapter, we described the stages of the reflective practice as a form of experiential learning and have done so in a linear, segmented fashion. This was done for conceptual clarity but does not adequately represent the process, which in practice is far more fluid and holistic. As the narratives in Chapters 5, 6, and 7 illustrate, when we engage in reflective practice, we move back and forth among the stages. An observation in the early stages of the process may lead immediately to reconceptualization and an idea for experimentation. While analyzing data, we may decide to gather more information. In some situations experimentation both grows out of and enriches reconceptualization. In other cases, the stages may simply merge into a fluid and continuous process. This is more likely as we become more adept because reflective practice, like other activities, becomes habitual. However, for newcomers to the reflective process, whether as participants or facilitators, it is probably good counsel to keep the four stages of the experiential cycle clearly in mind as guideposts to learning and progress.

As we indicated previously, what distinguishes reflective practice and accounts for its power as a professional development strategy is its emphasis on data. Gathering information about different dimensions of practice is the keystone to reflective practice. In the following chapter, we describe different ways to gather information about different dimensions of practice.

The Keystone of
Reflective Practice

Gathering Data

As explained in Chapter 2, observation plays an essential role in reflective practice. Since reflective practice is essentially a critical examination of practice, without data about practice, the process is stymied. Without comprehensive data about practice, the process is limited. The quality of the experience depends on good information. A thorough and accurate description of practice in and of itself often propels the professional through the remaining stages of the process:[1] A clear understanding of the problem prefigures the solution.

In the observation phase, then, we gather information about our experience and about each aspect of our practice. We articulate our goals and espoused theories, the action strategies we believe effective and intend to use. We also gather information about our practice to develop a deeper understanding of the events, focusing not only on observable actions but also on the feelings and thoughts of others and ourselves. To understand practice, we also consider the consequences of our actions. These data provide a more detailed description of our practice; they also enable us to piece together a picture of the underlying theories-in-use that shape our behavior, why we do what we do.

In this chapter, we describe a number of strategies that can be used to develop a comprehensive profile. In the first section, we focus on specific strategies to gather information about espousals. In the section that follows, we describe techniques to gather information about other dimensions of our practice: our behavior (thoughts, feelings, and actions); the consequences of our actions; and the underlying assumptions that shape our behavior (theories-in-use). Some of these strategies focus on observable dimensions of practice and facilitate a close examination of action and consequences in context. Others address thoughts, feelings, and values. Some are used during action; others provide a retrospective analysis.

GATHERING INFORMATION ABOUT ESPOUSED THEORIES

As explained in Chapter 2, espoused theories include the vision or goals as well as the explicit beliefs about the strategies that are most effective in achieving those goals. Exploring this aspect of behavior is relatively easy because espoused theories are reflected in what people say. At the same time, it is surprisingly difficult for people to articulate essential beliefs. Students in our leadership programs, for example, whether prospective or current administrators, often have a great deal of difficulty describing their ideal school or their conception of good teachers. To examine espoused theories—about education, about administration, about supervision—we ask people to think about what's important to them and then to write and talk about these issues. There are a variety of ways to gather this information; the following sections describe several methods that have proved effective in working with educators. (See Figure 3.1 for an overview.)

Figure 3.1   Gathering Information About Espoused Theories

GATHERING INFORMATION ABOUT ESPOUSED THEORIES

- **Educational Platforms**
- **Interviews**
- **Content Analysis: Documents and Statements**
- **Case Studies**

Educational Platforms

A platform is a written statement expressing stated beliefs, values, goals, and, occasionally, the assumptions that guide professional practice (Kottkamp, 1982). It may take the form of a personal vision or reflect the shared vision or mission of a group or organization. While all platform statements fit this basic description, the form may differ depending on the particular context.

Preparation of a vision statement may begin very generally by identifying personal values (Senge et al., 1999) or aspirations (Senge et al., 2000). In the course, "The Reflective Administrator," where students are teachers, administrators, and prospective administrators with different interests and levels of experience, Kottkamp uses an open-ended format. As their initial assignment, students develop a two-part platform. The first part, the educational platform, is about teaching, learning, and its context. In this section, an educator may depict the ideal school. The second part, the administrative/supervisory platform, describes the orientations and means to realize these educational goals. In what ways will the teacher or administrator work to achieve the vision? Students are encouraged to write contextualized platforms grounded in their experiences and to consider this as a realistic rather than a hypothetical exercise. This open-ended approach to platform development allows the professional a great deal of flexibility in determining the structure and the content.

Preparation of the platform may also be more structured. In principal preparation programs, for example, platform assignments may include questions tailored specifically to this administrative role. For example, the statements may address student outcomes, instructional climate, instructional organization, principals' routine behaviors, community, personal beliefs and experiences, institutional context, and personal preparation (Barnett & Brill, 1989). In preparing the platform, the educator describes the types of skills, attitudes, and feelings he or she wants students to possess; the climate needed to support these outcomes; how instruction is organized and delivered to support the desired climate and student outcomes; the activities the principal adopts to ensure that these outcomes actually occur; how parents are involved in school affairs; and the support necessary from the district or other sources.

An even more focused form of the platform is the miniplatform, which is typically used within the context of a particular exercise or activity. For example, after giving the actors the background information in a role play situation, the facilitator asks them to write a brief statement of their goals for the activity (what they hope to accomplish) as well as a brief description of their plan of action (what they intend to do).

The choice of format may be influenced by a number of factors, including the purpose of the activity, the length of time available, and the composition of the group. In Kottkamp's (Osterman & Kottkamp, 1993) reflective administrator course, the purpose is to introduce reflective practice and to provide students with an experiential understanding of the concept and the process. Students who enroll in this course are all educators but bring far different perspectives and experiences—personal, educational, and professional. A relatively unstructured introduction to the platform seems appropriate given the divergent interests and needs of the group. In professional development settings, the objectives of the participants may warrant a structured focus.

Whatever model the facilitator chooses carries an implicit statement of values and assumptions. As the platform assignment becomes more structured, it is more likely to influence individual responses. For example, in a relatively open-ended approach, prospective administrators might discover that they neglected to discuss school governance, reflecting an assumption that this is the sole province of the principal. When the assignment requires a statement regarding governance, facilitator and respondent lose this opportunity to discover and uncover surprises. On the other hand, lack of structure increases ambiguity. Where time is short, more direction may be warranted.

If the platform task is open ended, writers may use various rubrics to assess their work, including those developed by national professional organizations. The Educational Leadership Constituent Council (ELCC), for example, recently developed and approved a set of seven standards to guide leadership preparation (National Policy Board for Educational Administration, 2002). These standards integrate those developed by the Interstate School Leaders Licensure Consortium (ISLLC) and include detailed information about competencies associated with each performance standard. Teachers may use standards developed by various professional organizations to assess their own statements.

While writing a platform or mission statement has reflective value beyond simply attaining a statement of espoused theory, there are other ways of eliciting information needed to construct the basic elements of an individual's espoused theory. With these other methods, a facilitator or event brings forth the needed information.

Interviews

One straightforward method of capturing espoused theory is a direct interview with questions such as the following:

- How would you describe your philosophy as an educator?
- As (name of role), what are some of your most important goals and priorities?
- Of the things that you do, which do you consider to be the most important?

- What are your beliefs about these important areas of your work?
- What do you think are the best ways to accomplish your goals?
- What are the biggest problems you face in your work? How do you believe these should be resolved?

These questions are only suggestions. The important thing is to engage the interviewee in an honest and deep conversation about goals, ideals, beliefs, values, intentions, and desired orientations toward the work. With a little practice, espoused theory can be elicited from most individuals in a fairly short time. The questions and conversation need to be adapted to the individual; the facilitator and the educator can work together to frame questions and seek answers.

Thought provoking questions can also be used to assist an organizational group to develop a shared vision. As examples, Senge, Kleiner, Roberts, Ross, and Smith (1994) offered general questions useful in any organizational setting, and *Schools That Learn* (Senge et al., 2000) included suggestions specifically designed for school settings.

Content Analysis: Documents and Statements

Sometimes espoused theories can be found in statements or documents an individual has prepared for another purpose. Examples include the first speech prepared for the faculty by a new principal, a statement to the PTA on parent's night, a superintendent's annual address to the board of education, articles from a class, a school or district newsletter, regular communication to parents, or journal entries. Such information may prove sufficient to elicit an espoused theory or to serve as the beginning point for gathering more information through interview or a platform or mission statement. To the extent that documents are prepared in a self-conscious way, it is more likely an espoused theory will be presented— as when new principals face faculty members knowing full well they are expected to convey their philosophy and that their words will be carefully scrutinized. Later, we describe how similar documents may be used to identify theories-in-use.

Case Studies

Activities requiring a cognitive response tend to tap espoused beliefs. Analyzing a case study, for example, individuals use cognitive and analytic capabilities; they discuss what others should have done or what they themselves might have done. These analytic responses are not necessarily accurate predictors of behavior. Confronted with a similar situation, they might act in a very different way from what they anticipate. In these typically prescriptive or evaluative responses, we see thinking but not action. Nevertheless, these activities are an important way to capture espoused theory, since the responses reflect conscious values and beliefs. These spontaneous responses translate readily into more general statements of belief, intent, and value.

Espoused Theory: Summing Up

In this section, we concentrated on ways to gather information about espoused theories. Having articulated a philosophy including beliefs, values, and goals, individuals may then begin a conscious process of reflection in which they begin to assess the nature and effects of their own observable behavior. In many cases, discrepancies between actions and stated intentions become readily apparent. These inconsistencies—these surprises—rivet the learners' attention and engage them wholeheartedly in the learning process. We highlighted the platform as a means of eliciting the espoused theory because it is a method that involves the individual to the fullest and because it frequently initiates other aspects of reflection.

Although information about espoused theories may be gathered through dialogue and conversation as well as through writing, because the act of writing one's thoughts seems to have a substantially different and more powerful reflective effect, we recommend that these oral statements be used as stimuli for writing. Being required to name the reality in writing seems to interject another level of reflection beyond that required to express one's thoughts orally. Aside from the value of writing to heighten personal insight and understanding, the written platform serves as a benchmark against which one can measure and assess change. As one administrator explained, the written platform is something to hang your hat on—a reminder of where you stand when the going gets rough.

GATHERING INFORMATION ABOUT PRACTICE

The following section outlines several methods for collecting descriptive information about our practice. Specifically, we look at behavior—actions, feelings, and thoughts—and the consequences. As we gather this information, the theories-in-use that shape behavior also become evident. As we see what we do in certain situations, we come to a deeper understanding of why we act—and react—as we do. Some methods enable educators to gather information about their own practice; others require the assistance of an outside observer. From some, we infer information about the theory-in-use; others explore these ideas more directly.

The methods we outline here vary. Some document observable events, action, and consequences through direct observation of behavior during professional practice or in simulated events. Some use technology; others draw on the perspective of the professional or an outside observer. Others examine behavior from a retrospective stance. There are also a variety of tests, measures, and interview procedures to develop insight into thoughts and assumptions. Finally, we consider briefly some of the many ways to gather information about the consequences of our actions in professional practice. These methods vary in terms of objectivity and subjectivity.

Direct Observation Strategies

Videotaping

Video technology is a highly effective and direct means of gathering information about observable dimensions of practice. Once individuals become desensitized to this strange set of eyes, the video camera provides an unfiltered and true record of events without bias. A first grade teacher, in an action research project, offered an interesting illustration of the impact of this technology:

> The researcher I worked most closely with had communicated to me, in journal entries, about the productive things that were going on in my classroom, but I was not seeing the same things he was seeing until I watched a video of my class. I had begun having my students create their own sentences and stories by using a certain list of words that we formulated together and listed on the chalkboard. One day a week, at reading group time, they came back with their stories to share with other children in the group. I was sitting at the table with them, and I thought I was watching what was happening. What I saw, as I sat there, was fidgeting, what I heard was noise. It did not seem as if anyone was paying attention to anyone reading. Until I watched the video. To my amazement, I saw first graders leaning over the table, pointing to the words on the paper, and asking the reader/writer about the story. I saw interaction among the group members, many interested faces, and a very productive activity. It was quite an insight to realize that what I had valued—or thought that I had valued—as a necessary learning environment was hindering some very important student involvement. I discovered that student activity level and noise were appropriate, productive, and necessary for learning. (Berkey et al., 1990, p. 218)

One outgrowth of this experience, she explained, was a change in the curriculum, with much greater use of student learning centers.

Clarke (1995) also described the value of videotaping to facilitate reflective practice among student teachers and emphasized the importance of observation followed by thoughtful and sustained dialogue. As student teachers watched videotaped incidents, they were able to see not only their own behavior but also the reactions of their students. In one detailed example, Clarke described how Jona's observations of students' confused reactions prompted his dissatisfaction with direct instruction. The example also illustrates how data facilitated analysis and experimentation. Recognizing his reliance on direct instruction and his resistance to alternative methods, he realized that he perceived direct instruction as an easy means to retain control (his theory-in-use). Data also helped him to challenge his own assumptions and reframe the problem. Initially, he felt that students' poor performance reflected their poor note-taking abilities. Through observation, he recognized that direct instruction prevented him from interacting with students and checking for understanding. With this new information and a new conceptualization of teaching and learning, he was encouraged to try alternate methods, and his classroom practice changed. Interestingly, describing the critical and integral role that observation and dialogue (analysis) play, Clarke also noted how the demands of teaching typically preclude these important processes.

Audiotaping

While limited to verbal action, tape recordings can also be very effective in gathering information about individual behavior. The administrative preparation program at Hofstra University places a great deal of emphasis on developing effective group process skills. While completing a major project, one group decided to tape a session. The playback proved particularly enlightening for one group member, who hadn't realized the extent to which she dominated the conversation. For her, hearing how she sounded to others was an eye-opener and an incentive to change.

Structured Observation

In addition to video and audiotapes, there are many structured means to gather information on specific aspects of practice. Some require an outside observer; others can be used by the practitioner. Sullivan and Glanz (2000) and Glanz and Sullivan (2000), for example, provided detailed descriptions of multiple observational methods particularly suited to classroom use. While the techniques are recommended for use in a supervisory context, they may be used by any observer, whether a researcher, peer, or traditional supervisor. All of the methods emphasize the importance of descriptive rather than judgmental information. Each tool enables the observer to gather data about observable dimensions of classroom practice: teachers' verbal behaviors, questioning strategies, and use of space; teacher–student interaction; or peer interaction. Other measures focus on students' experience.

Silva (1998) described a structured approach to kid watching, where the observer gathers information about the experience of a particular child and then organizes data by activity and learning purpose. An observation of a "typical" student, Josh, over five days, showed participation in teacher-directed circles accounted for the largest portion of his time (approximately 30%), while the amount of time spent in small-group activity or learning centers was approximately 1%. The teacher then contrasted these findings with her beliefs about how children should be spending their time in class and began to search for ways to modify the class experience. The case studies presented later also show how gathering information about clients and practice can lead to new insights and understandings.

There are also many techniques useful in gathering information about verbal and nonverbal dimensions of group performance. An interaction diagram, for example, charts the frequency and direction of interaction among group participants (Beebe & Masterson, 1994). Information like this can be useful in identifying power issues in groups. Observation of nonverbal behavior in groups also provides unique insights about experiences and relationships.

Using existing forms provides a good start, but it is also possible to modify these or develop other data-gathering procedures more suited to specific concerns.

Content Analysis

Behavior may also be observed using written materials produced in the course of normal professional activity. We may examine memos, formal correspondence, lesson plans, meeting schedules, supervision and evaluation reports, teacher comments on student papers, newsletters, notices sent to parents, minutes or notes taken at meetings, and other artifacts. An examination of the minutes from an administrators' regular meeting, for example, by showing how much time was spent on various items, provides some information on priorities.

In one situation, an administrator wrote a platform, espousing a humane, open, and democratic orientation toward subordinates. When he made a careful study of his memos over a period of time, he was startled to find that the autocratic tone of many of the documents was the opposite of what he intended. Uncovering the discrepancy led him to change his behavior and gave him a technique for continuing to monitor it.

Role Plays and Simulations

Artificial situations also provide interesting information about behavior. In a role play or simulation, participants receive information about a situation and then respond. The ensuing action can range from developing an action agenda or planning a meeting to taking action—handling a student problem or supervisory matter, deciding on staff or budget cuts, or resolving a conflict. More complex simulations can involve the role players in a school change project to improve student test scores.[2]

Role plays can be done in different ways to achieve different levels of involvement. The facilitator can structure a hypothetical situation designed to examine certain issues. For example, if teachers were concerned about relating to parents, the facilitator might develop a specific situation and ask them to enact an encounter. The experience of the educators also provides material for role plays, and the facilitator may ask the participants to recall a troubling encounter with a parent. Explaining the nature of the problem and the events that occurred, the educators focus specifically on their own actions and reactions. Given this information, they may then reenact the situation with others who, along with the facilitator or other observers, provide feedback about behavior and its effect on them. Computer simulations serve the same purpose: They create an opportunity for action and analysis.

These behavioral incidents help us to detect the theory-in-use. As we observe and analyze the behavior, we can begin to speculate about the ideas (theories-in-use) precipitating the response. We can see what we did, and begin to explore the underlying rationale. Another interesting way of uncovering theories-in-use is to ask individuals to approach the same task from different role perspectives. It is remarkable and eye-opening to see how easily individuals shift their behavior to fit a preconceived notion of a particular role. As they experience these changes, uncovering the assumptions becomes easier. Brookfield (1992) described another activity, scenario analysis, in which learners analyze the assumptions they think underlie the behavior of characters in hypothetical situations. In this exercise, participants are introduced to the process of identifying assumptions but need not focus on their own behavior.

Although artificial in the sense that the action is taking place in the equivalent of a small-group laboratory, role plays tend to be surprisingly effective. In the space of a few minutes, actors become deeply involved in the situation and their characters. The emerging action is far more than a cognitive response; it reflects deeply held assumptions as well as emotions. In the midst of action, habits dominate and the theory-in-use comes visibly into play.

The contrived role play is valuable, but, in our experience, the reenactment of an actual situation is more powerful. In the former, the behavior serves to identify theories-in-use and provides the basis for reflection and learning, but, because of the contrived nature, it is possible for the actor to dismiss the experience as an aberration. Reenactments carry more weight since the person is able to assess the validity of the experience by comparing it with the actual situation, but even in these situations denial is possible. Figure 3.2 provides a graphic summary of ways that direct observation can be used to gather information about practice.

Figure 3.2   Gathering Information About Practice: Direct Observation

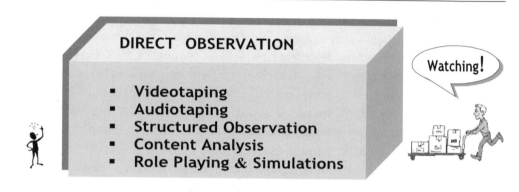

Reflective Strategies: Personal Narratives and Inventories

Reconstructing a particular situation requires the respondent to step back, chronicle events, and describe actions and reactions of self and others. Clearly the most reliable information about behavior is gathered through direct observation; however, narrative also yields important information about practice and facilitates identification of the theory-in-use. The majority of the following methods involve reconstruction of an activity or event from the perspective of the reflective practitioner. The primary goal is to generate a detailed description, and, accordingly, the reports may incorporate different dimensions of behavior: intentions, feelings, assumptions, actions, and outcomes.

In whatever form, narratives serve to contextualize the experience and provide a richer understanding of what has taken place and the narrator's construction of reality (Ershler, 2001; Reagan, Case, Case, & Freiberg, 1993). In examining the story, we see the events as the narrator saw them: We see what was seen and perhaps what was overlooked; we see what was important and what was insignificant. These narratives may be developed orally or in writing; they may be structured or unstructured. Mattingly (1991), for example, described using unstructured oral story-telling, in which professionals told stories about their work and analyzed them for underlying values and assumptions.

Journals

The journal is one form of narrative writing often associated with reflective practice. While journaling may facilitate reflective practice, the mere act of writing entries does not necessarily engage the writer in the full cycle of reflective practice. The journal, however, is an important means of gathering information about events (actions, feelings, and inter-pretations). To the extent that the writer uses this information to assess practice, it can also support reflective practice.

The literature describes two types of journal entries. One, a log, is a running account of important events and interactions occurring in the work setting. The second is a reflective assessment of those events, where the writer raises questions about these experiences and often shares thoughts with others. In some cases, the journal assignment may be more structured. Barnett and Brill (1989), for example, used both a daily and a critical incident journal. The latter has a common format: (1) a brief summary description of a meaningful incident, (2) important questions generated by the event, (3) a list of new terms or concepts, (4) subjective reactions, and (5) what the learners learned and how it might alter their future responses.

Describing his work with adult learners, Brookfield (1995) suggested that students write about whatever seems important but also be provided with a set of questions as initial prompts. The questions focus on what the students learned about themselves and their emotional responses to learning, high and low emotional moments, significant or surprising events, and areas of satisfaction or dissatisfaction. Holborn (1988), speaking directly to student teachers, encouraged them to use journals to describe critical incidents. Recognizing these emotional situations are often problematic, she also urged them to pay special attention to "successes, achievements, and sources of pride" (p. 208).

Kelsey (1993) incorporated journal writing in a course on problem analysis and formulation skills for administrators, requiring that students reflect on at least one class event each day. To stimulate the quality of their entries, he outlined his expectations:

What is necessary is that the entries should show that you have done some thinking about each day's work (why it did or did not turn a light on for you, its relation to something else you have read, or experienced, or learned in another class, or . . . etc., etc.) and that the thoughts provoked are not entirely banal! (pp. 236-237)

Whatever form is adopted, the journal is an effective means to obtain information about professional practice and personal action theories.

Brookfield (1995) also gave special attention to the use of the log, a record of events. Here, too, the emphasis is on events that are most memorable. "By focusing on these events," he argued, "we learn much more about our assumptions than if we just tried to list them. Events that excite or enrage us often do so because they confirm or contradict our assumptions" (p. 72). In keeping a log, then, he recommended regular entries on a weekly basis and suggested students look for moments when they feel most connected or disconnected in their work and situations that cause anxiety or surprise. Over time, patterns emerge that help to identify persistent dilemmas and sources of satisfaction or anxiety. Analysis of these patterns helps to uncover hidden assumptions.

Critical Incidents

Osterman (1991) described the use of the case record to gather and analyze personal experience. The technique, developed by Silver (1986) and modified by Osterman (1991), is a format for creating a structured narrative about a problem situation. (See Figure 3.3.) In addressing a series of questions, the respondent describes the problem and the actions taken to resolve the problem. Several other questions prompt a reflective analysis of the thoughts and intentions that prompted the action and its impact: What did you hope to accomplish? What alternatives did you consider? What actions did you take? What happened as a result of your actions? Were your intended objectives achieved? Why or why not?

While the case record was intended to facilitate individual reflection, Brookfield (1992) described a critical incident analysis in a small-group context. Rather than focusing on a problematic issue, he asked participants to identify a highly emotional situation from their own lives, either positive or not. They wrote the descriptive details of this situation, and, in a three-person group, verbally described the situation. The other two members then offered insights about the person's assumptions.

Personal experience, whether one's own or another's, offers another means of gathering information about assumptions and theories. Recognizing what he calls the "alarming reality of starting to question long-held assumptions," Brookfield (1992, p. 18) outlined an indirect approach to search for assumptions. In an activity called Heroes and Villains, for example, participants identify people they regard as exemplary

Figure 3.3   The Case Record Format

CASE RECORD FORMAT

1. THE PROBLEM
Who was involved?
What was the pertinent background information?
What was your role in the problem?

2. OUTCOME and/or OBJECTIVES DESIRED
What did you hope to accomplish?

3. ALTERNATIVES CONSIDERED
What alternatives did you consider to solve the
problem?

4. STRATEGIES IMPLEMENTED
What action did you take in an attempt to achieve
your objectives?

5. RESULTS
Were your objectives achieved?
What happened as a result of your actions?

6. ASSESSMENT
Did your plan work as intended?
What critical events, decisions, situations influenced
the outcome?
What would you do differently, if anything?

or the reverse and describe aspects of their practice they admire or find distressing. In three-person groups, one tells the story and the detectives try to uncover the assumptions underlying the storyteller's descriptions. After they generate a list of the assumptions, they test their ideas, trying to generate alternative explanations. Brookfield recommended this strategy as a low-risk means of introducing reflective practice: It engages people in thinking about theories-in-use but is not as threatening as discussing personal practice. While it does not directly deal with personal stories, the responses and interpretations draw on personal experiences.

The Good Practices Audit (Brookfield, 1995) is a more comprehensive analysis that draws on multiple experiences to analyze and address common problems. Teachers, individually and then collectively, identify pressing problems encountered in their work. Selecting one problem for attention, they describe their best and worst experiences, as a learner, as a colleague, and as a teacher. After analyzing this information, they draw on their insights to identify potentially useful strategies.

Portfolios

The portfolio is a document with particular relevance in education and a tool with special value in facilitating reflective practice. In theory, portfolios "provide an opportunity and a structure for teachers to document and describe their teaching; articulate their professional knowledge; and reflect on what, how, and why they teach" (Borko, Michalec, Timmons, & Siddle, 1997, p. 345). To test this proposition, the researchers introduced portfolios into a professional seminar course taken concurrently with student teaching. Written guidelines directed the student teachers to include a statement of teaching philosophy; description of teaching situation; entries about planning, teaching, and student learning; and reflections. On completing the project, the majority described the portfolio as a tool for reflection, and approximately half said that it "allowed them to make connections between theory and practice" (p. 351). Preparation of the portfolio, including their philosophical statement, led them to think more deeply about their beliefs, to observe in greater detail, to develop a more realistic picture of their own strengths and weaknesses, and to identify ways to improve.

Brookfield (1995) took a slightly different approach, focusing specifically on growth in learning as well as description and critique of practice. His guidelines requested an overall summary of themes from reflective journals, a description of contributions to various projects, a summary of personal learning, and an assessment of class materials and the course itself. The portfolio concludes with a list of recommendations for incoming students and a reflection on how learning will influence practice.

In a far more extensive fashion, the National Board for Professional Teaching Standards (NBPTS) uses portfolios to determine whether teachers meet specific standards developed for various specializations. The portfolio "is designed to capture teaching in real-time, real-life settings" and enables the reviewer to see "how teachers translate knowledge and theory into practice" (National Board for Professional Teaching Standards, 2001, p. viii). Included are videos of practice and samples of student work as well as detailed commentaries "on the goals and purposes of instruction, the effectiveness of the practice, teachers' reflections on what occurred, and their rationales for the professional judgments they made" (p. viii). In this case, the portfolio includes not only the documentation of the performance but also the reflective analysis of those data.

The Left-Hand Column

This activity was originally developed by Argyris and Schon (1974) as a means of uncovering assumptions and has since been incorporated in many professional development activities (Jentz, 1982; Jentz & Wofford, 1979; Senge et al., 1994; Stone et al., 1999). Again, the activity begins with identification of a specific problematic situation involving one or more people. The reflective practitioner then prepares a script of a verbal exchange with the other person(s). The conversation is usually one that has already taken place but may be one that is anticipated. The dialogue, what is said aloud, is written in the right-hand column. In the left-hand column, the person scripts what is thought and felt but left unsaid. Senge (1990) illustrated the use of this method in a business setting. Stone et al. (1999) discussed it as a means of improving one's ability to communicate effectively in difficult situations, and Jentz (1982) developed a powerful role-play activity that used the strategy to reveal Model I assumptions in administrators' supervisory practice. Figure 3.4 is an example drawn from a typical supervisory situation:

Figure 3.4   The Left-Hand Column

What I'm Thinking	What I'm Saying
Supervisor's *Unspoken* Thoughts	Supervisor and Teacher's *Actual* Dialogue
This class was so dreadful. I hope that he will see all of the problems so that I don't have to raise the issues.	Supervisor: How do you think your class went?
	Teacher: Well, I thought that some of the kids were a little out of order, but overall, I thought that it went very well.
How can he possibly say that? Didn't he learn anything in graduate school? He must be really unaware of what's going on. This person apparently doesn't have a clue. If I tell him all the things that are wrong, it will overwhelm him so I'll tell him exactly what needs to be done and that I will be back to make sure that it is done, if he wants to keep his job.	Supervisor: In general, you're right, but I think there are a few things that I'd suggest for the future.

In this situation, as the left-hand script demonstrates, the supervisor withheld judgment about the teacher's performance, interpreted the teacher's behavior as incompetence, and relied on prescriptive, rather than descriptive, feedback. From this script, we gain insight into the predominant theory-in-use and find, as we will see in Chapter 4, an example of Model I behavior. Without adequate feedback, the teacher may fail to understand what went wrong and why, limiting the possibility for real improvement.

Questioning

From behavioral data, we can infer theories-in-use. It is also possible to explore these underlying beliefs through direct questioning. As noted in Chapter 4, it is important to remember that some types of questions facilitate reflection, while others have an opposite effect. The right kinds of questions are those with no hidden agenda. They are not intended to ascertain truth or fix blame; they are not statements disguised as questions or statements that hide a complaint. Their only purpose is to develop a deeper understanding of the other person's perspective. Open-ended statements or questions that elicit more detail about events, intentions, or feelings are supportive. For example, consider the following: "Tell me more"; "Can you help me to understand this situation a little better?"; "Can you explain a little more about what you were trying to do or why you decided on that particular course of action?"; and "How are you feeling about this?" It's important to remember, though, that in some cases reflection can be painful and even well-intended and well-phrased questions may elicit defensive responses.[3]

Once you have descriptive information about certain events, additional questions can reveal assumptions. The Five Whys, a strategy described by Senge et al. (1994), is a series of "why" questions designed to develop progressively deeper understanding of the personal reasoning behind a problematic situation. The first step is to identify the symptom (an unanticipated or undesired situation) and ask why. The process is repeated another four times. By this time, the questioning process has gone beyond superficial appearances to reveal systemic causes. If this process is done in a group, anticipate multiple answers to each "why." These may be posted and explored as a means of searching for important root causes.[4]

Personal Inventories

Personal inventories and diagnostic, counseling, or research instruments offer another useful perspective on behavior. By providing information on particular attitudes, perceptual or assumptional frames, and other aspects of behavior, such instruments shed light on why we do what we do. The information they generate often leads to provocative surprises and helps direct attention to a search for specific behaviors.

Students in administrative preparation courses have found feedback from the Meyers-Briggs Type Indicator (Myers & McCaulley, 1985) useful in identifying espoused theories and highlighting behavioral areas for observation. Based on Jungian psychological concepts, this instrument provides information on how individuals process information, focus attention, and come to decisions. It focuses on individual strengths and has been used widely in counseling among high school, college, theological, business, and nursing students and for organizational development work in schools, universities, corporations, and social service agencies. Barnett and Brill (1989) used Kolb's (1985) Learning Style Inventory to give principal preparation students information about the particular stages of experiential learning that they are most likely to employ.

Project Implicit (implicit.harvard.edu/implicit), a collaborative effort of researchers at Harvard University, the University of Virginia, and the University of Washington, offers information and tests that "examine thoughts and feelings that exist either outside of conscious awareness or outside of conscious control." The goal is to identify divergence between what people say and what they do. Using reflective practice language, they seek to uncover the theories-in-use. As an example, the site offers tests that measure bias regarding age, sex, and race.

The Learning Connections Inventory (LCI), developed by Chris Johnston (1998), has been unusually effective in stimulating reflective practice. An instrument that gathers data about learning patterns, the LCI determines the degree to which the learner uses each of four basic interactive patterned operations: Sequence, Precision, Technical Reasoning, and Confluence. While everyone uses all operations, patterns of use differ. Confronted with a learning task, some may use one operation first, avoid others, and use the remainder only as needed. Others lead their learning with several operations; some use all four interchangeably. A deeper understanding of these patterns helps learners, whether children or adults, to understand their own strengths and weaknesses in completing various learning tasks. This enables them to develop a metacognitive approach to their own learning and to initiate change in their learning strategies. The information also enables teachers to realize that all students really can learn and helps them to develop appropriate strategies to facilitate learning for students based on their unique arrays. The LCI has been used to gather information about students and teachers in elementary and secondary classrooms, in higher education, and in corporate and industrial settings. Chapter 7 offers a detailed description of the LCI, its conceptual framework, and its application in classrooms to facilitate reflective practice among children and their teachers.

While instruments such as these provide important information to guide self-reflection, they are also useful to facilitate group work. In addition, there are numerous instruments examining different dimensions of group performance to be found within the tradition of organizational development. This section, as noted in Figure 3.5, identified several reflective strategies that reveal important information about practice.

Figure 3.5   Gathering Information About Practice: Reflective Assessment

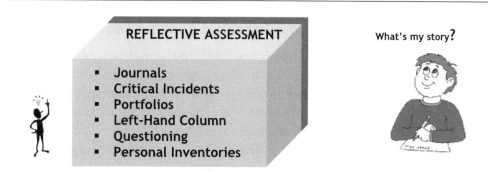

GATHERING INFORMATION ABOUT PERFORMANCE

Reflective practice is potentially useful to educators (and other professionals) in many different roles. Accordingly, the intended consequences of actions vary, depending on the role as well as specific values, beliefs, and the particular situation.

Examining Student Learning

Ultimately, the primary goal for all educational institutions is student learning. In this era of accountability, the test is an important measure of student performance. Under pressure from state and federal legislators, school districts are placing greater attention on the analysis of test score data to identify strengths and weaknesses and to direct school improvement efforts. There is no question that data are a powerful component of school reform. Disaggregated data analysis, for example, enables teachers, schools, and districts to examine their effectiveness in dealing with students who differ in race, economic status, and gender. These data present important information that uncover and challenge assumptions in very direct ways.

At the same time, the test is only one measure of student performance and addresses only one educational goal. Knowledge is important, but, depending on their philosophy of education and specific values, educators may also want to look at other learning outcomes, such as competence, emotional intelligence, or relational skills. Consequently, many educational settings adopt a full range of assessment measures. In the classroom,

rubrics, project-based activities, or other authentic assessments, such as oral presentations or student portfolios, supplement teachers' understanding of what and which children are learning. Examining these assessment data can be a powerful professional development strategy (Falk, 2001).

Organizational Conditions That Support Learning

With information about intended and actual outcomes, educators may then consider factors that affect student performance. Are students engaged in the learning process, and what characteristics of the classroom influence engagement? What is the nature of instruction and curriculum? Do instructional strategies inspire students and enable them to achieve? What is the quality of interaction between teachers and students and among students in the classroom? Are individual needs being addressed and are individual differences respected and valued? Is the climate one of encouragement and support rewarding effort and accomplishment or one fostering competition and rewarding ability? For each of these questions, the observer can rely on different forms of data gathering discussed previously, such as direct observation, surveys, or interviews.

What occurs in the classroom most directly influences student learning, but conditions in the school and district also affect teacher and student performance, and information about these conditions is also an important indicator of organizational effectiveness. Drawn from published and emergent research and leaders' craft knowledge, a recently released report from the Center for the Study of Teaching and Policy (Knapp et al., 2003) identified five areas of educational leadership with potentially powerful effects on student learning:

- *Establishing a focus on learning*: by persistently and publicly focusing their own attention and that of others on learning and teaching
- *Building professional communities that value learning*: by nurturing work cultures that value and support their members' learning
- *Engaging external environments that matter for learning*: by building relationships and securing resources from outside groups that can foster students' or teachers' learning
- *Acting strategically and sharing leadership*: by mobilizing effort along multiple pathways that lead to student, professional, or system learning and by distributing leadership across levels and among individuals in different positions
- *Creating coherence*: by connecting student, professional, and system learning with one another and with learning goals

These pathways lead to student, professional, and system learning. The detailed description of these action areas—strategies and rationale—provides an excellent framework for reflective practitioners to guide and assess their own work and organizational conditions.[5]

In addition to surveys that shed light on individual orientations, attitudes, and assumptions, there are numerous instruments dealing with different dimensions of organizational behavior and climate. As only one example, Leithwood, Aitken, and Jantzi (2001) provided a set of survey instruments as part of a comprehensive monitoring system for schools and school districts.

This monitoring system incorporates five organizational dimensions and thirty specific elements of the school and district. The key components are as follows:

- *Inputs:* the human, financial, material, and cultural resources available to the school and district
- *District and school characteristics, conditions, and processes:* focusing on mission and goals; culture; core tasks of leadership, management, planning, and instruction; structure and organization; information collecting and decision making; policies and procedures; and community partnerships
- *Immediate outcomes:* achievement, engagement, equality, and equity
- *Long-term outcomes:* contributions to individual welfare and the public good, such as preparation for higher education and employment, economic productivity, and quality of life

This orientation is particularly relevant in this discussion because it highlights conditions and processes that support the development of schools as learning organizations. As the authors explained, gathering information about these important organizational indicators potentially leads to changes in thinking and action as members of the organization come to understand their work differently. This resource shows how educational leaders can use existing district data to develop this organizational profile. It also includes a series of survey instruments to measure the current status of individual schools from the perspective of students, staff, administrators, parents, and community members with respect to mission and goals, culture, core tasks, structure and organization, information collection and decision making, policies and procedures, school-community partnerships, student participation and engagement, and family culture.

The Internet is also a source of audits and surveys. For example, the North Central Regional Educational Laboratory offers a participatory management checklist as well as tools for assessing school and family involvement and the connections between school and afterschool programs (www.ncrel.org/cscd). Available from the Association for Effective Schools, Inc., are More Effective Schools Surveys for instructional and support staff, students, and parents (www.mes.org). As Figure 3.6 indicates, there are various means to gather information about important learning outcomes. Information like this is valuable to facilitate reflective practice.

Figure 3.6   Gathering Information About Practice: Assessing Performance

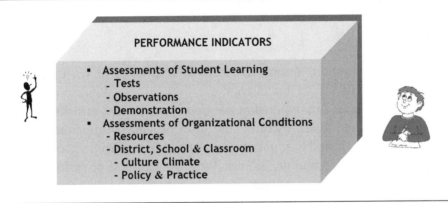

SUMMARY

In sum, the reflective process begins with experience. By examining what is said and done, it is possible to identify espoused theories and the more elusive theories-in-use. While espoused theories can be identified rather easily through dialogue and writing, the identification of theories-in-use requires action. Toward this end, there are a variety of means that can be used to gather data about events and experience, each of which can be adapted in an almost limitless number of ways to meet the special needs and interests of the participants. By carefully observing behavior, theories-in-use become more apparent and the stage is set for reflection.

Valid and reliable information about goals and outcomes is also important. Contrasting performance outcomes with clearly articulated goals and objectives can be an energizing, unifying force and a basis for data-driven decision making to improve school and student performance.

While data are essential, they are only the entrée into the important stages of analysis, decision making, and subsequent change. In each of these stages, the quality of the process depends on the nature of the interaction among the participants. Regardless of the source—standardized tests or behavioral simulations—the value of the information depends on the quality of the analysis and subsequent action decisions. Regardless of size, groups benefit from skilled leadership. The facilitator is the individual who provides opportunity, support, and encouragement for groups of educators to examine data through the reflective practice lens. In the next chapter, we consider reflective practice as a collaborative process and discuss the important role that the facilitator plays in supporting collective efforts to engage in reflective practice. We consider organizational obstacles to reflective practice and identify perspectives and communication strategies that support reflective practice in an organizational context.

NOTES

1. McLaughlin (2001) described research from the Bay Area School Reform Collaborative (BASRC), a five-year reform effort involving schools throughout the 118-district Bay Area region and supported by the Hewlett-Annenberg Challenge. Data-based inquiry was an important component of reform and the authors concluded that the results in some of these schools "demonstrate how knowledge of and evidence about school-level outcomes activates teachers' inquiry into classroom practices and refashions external knowledge into resources particular to the particular school context. The trajectory of inquiry, knowledge use, and change . . . shows how evidence can animate and guide teachers' reflection on and reinvention of their practices" (p. 100).

2. The NETWORK, Inc. (Change@Netwrk.org) offers three leadership simulations, Making Change Happen, Improving Student Success, and Systems Thinking/Systems Changing, which are research based and engaging and can be used effectively in a leadership preparation program.

3. For samples of conversational lines to use in difficult situations, see the section on productive conversations in Senge et al. (2000).

4. From her study of preservice teachers, LaBoskey (1994) concluded that asking "why" questions differentiated what she described as Alert Novices from less reflective Commonsense Thinkers. She also suggested that those involved in the preparation of educators need to devote more time to helping students examine these questions about the roots of problems and the meanings of ideas and actions.

5. *Leading for Learning Sourcebook: Concepts and Examples* and its summary, *Leading for Learning: Reflective Tools for School and District Leaders,* can be downloaded free of charge from the Web site for the Center for the Study of Teaching and Policy: www.ctpweb.org. These materials are specifically designed for the use of educational leaders in schools and districts.

Facilitating Reflective Practice in the Workplace

While reflective practice clearly involves analysis, it is distinctively different from reflection. In contrast, reflective practice involves, as noted, a systematic and comprehensive data-gathering process, not simply a recollection of events. Similarly, while reflection often relies solely on personal resources, dialogue and collaborative effort enrich reflective practice. Analysis may be done alone—while listening to a tape recording of a committee meeting, watching a videotape, or considering the assumptions reflected in memos. Nonetheless, because of the deeply ingrained nature of our behavioral patterns and the tacit nature of our assumptions, it is sometimes difficult to develop a critical perspective on our own behavior. For that reason, the power of reflective practice is greater in a collegial setting when usually private thoughts about observations, assumptions, and interpretations are shared openly. Anthony's teacher or the new principal meets with colleagues to process their experience. A new teacher and mentor meet to discuss a teaching episode. After a daylong shadowing experience, an intern meets with a principal, or a group of students meets with their teacher to share observations about bullying behavior in their classroom. These occasions provide an opportunity to gather different perspectives on the situation. Drawing on their own experience, other participants may share observations, offer different interpretations, or ask questions leading to greater recall or new insight. For that reason alone, analysis in a collaborative environment is likely to lead to greater learning. Dialogue also plays a significant role in learning, by enabling learners to clarify and deepen their understanding. When people have a chance to ask questions, to challenge ideas, and to process their learning verbally, they learn more.

By sharing observations and ideas with others, and through the resulting dialogue, we are better able to assess the validity of our initial observations and interpretations. Do we have a full and reasonably accurate description of the events, or did we neglect important points? Is our interpretation consistent with what we saw, or are there other more reasonable and powerful explanations? Including different voices and different perspectives in the analysis enriches the process. As questions are raised, the need to revisit the situation, gather more data, clarify facts, and test assumptions becomes very evident.

Experience and research show that reflective practice is a valuable process for organizations, and particularly for schools, whether it occurs as a special activity or is an integral part of the culture. Professional groups meet as collegial circles or critical friends to critique and develop their work. Effective supervisors—whether administrators, mentors, or peer coaches—use reflective practice to foster professional growth. Outstanding schools and districts invariably have educational leaders who use data-driven decision making and assessment to facilitate reflective practice throughout the organization. To support self-directed learning, good teachers support reflective practice among their students. A skilled assistant principal uses reflective practice to deal with an irate parent or a troubled student. In an effective organization, reflective practice takes place in faculty and grade-level team meetings, supervisory conferences, parent and board meetings, child-study teams, or any problem-solving situation.

Reflective practice should be an integral part of organizational life in educational settings, but frequently that isn't the case. Before considering ways to support reflective practice, it is important to understand some of the obstacles.

As a professional development strategy, reflective practice engages individuals and groups in a critical analysis of problems and examines how individual and collective ideas and action patterns help to cause or maintain these patterns. To engage in reflective practice requires trust and openness of communication. It requires people to be willing to analyze their own behavior and explore thoughts, feelings, and actions. Years of research, however, demonstrate that these types of behaviors are atypical. Organizations resist identifying and analyzing problems and may actively work to suppress problems (Argyris, 1990, 1993). Think of organizational reactions to whistle-blowers. Organizations exert a powerful influence on human behavior, and people comply with expectations and maintain a conspiracy of silence about troublesome matters. These organizational norms make it difficult to initiate reflective practice. Nonetheless, we believe that reflective practice can be learned and integrated into professional practice on an individual and collective basis. Administrators, teachers, counselors, social workers, and other educational personnel can learn to be reflective practitioners, and this way of thinking can become a part of the school or district culture. One of the purposes of this book is to encourage reflective practice in educational settings to facilitate problem solving, professional development, and organizational change. In this chapter, we consider some factors that help and hinder reflective practice, discuss the important role of the facilitator, and identify important action theories and strategies to facilitate reflective practice in the workplace.

RESISTANCE TO REFLECTIVE PRACTICE: MODEL I

Based on extensive organizational research in the United States and developed countries throughout the world, Argyris and Schon (1974, 1978) identified a common pattern of behavior reflecting an internal set of rules. Described as Model I, this meta-theory-in-use, they maintained, is a pervasive part of society and shapes behavior in almost every domain of our personal and organizational lives.

Two values most highly prized in organizations are personal determination and rationality. Those values are then reflected in predictable behavioral patterns. Personal determination, for example, is often apparent in actions to ensure unilateral control. The decision-making process is primarily an internal dialogue based on assumptions about other people, their intentions, their feelings, and their likely behavior. To maintain control, assumptions are not shared or tested; options are not explored. As Argyris (1993) explained, "Model I tells individuals to craft their positions, evaluations, and attributions in ways that inhibit inquiries into them and tests of them with others' logic" (p. 52). In sum, we withhold information. We assume that retaining control and keeping our own counsel will further our personal agenda while avoiding distractions, challenges, or complaints.

To act in a rational manner is to suppress emotion. To avoid emotional reactions, organizations adopt protective strategies. The pattern of withholding particularly applies when information might create conflict or hurt others. People keep things quiet, cover up, or push things to the back burner in an attempt to protect self and others, prevent emotional outbursts, and maintain an appearance of calm: Don't ruffle feathers; keep things on an even keel. Underlying these strategies are other hidden assumptions and action theories: Problems are indicators of personal weakness or failure, and discussion of problems is personally demeaning and unlikely to have positive effects.[1]

People learn how to behave by watching others. As students, teachers, and administrators, they observe these strategies in the workplace and learn the expectations.[2] The result is that these patterns predominate. Consequently, few organizational environments offer the conditions necessary for reflective practice. Rather than an environment of open communication and collaboration focused on problem solving, organizations tend to be highly bureaucratic, where authority figures exercise unilateral control, regulate behavior by directive, rigidly restrict communication, and criticize imperfection. As a result, people in organizations typically avoid discussing problems, refrain from expressing emotions, and withhold information, particularly when it might be threatening to themselves or to others. Students in the classroom, for example, are reluctant to express opinions different from the professor for fear of jeopardizing their grade or the chance of a strong recommendation. Teachers or principals in school settings run the risk of alienation by their peers and sanctions from superiors if they offer different or challenging views. Teachers experiencing discipline problems won't ask for advice or assistance because they feel they'll be judged incompetent. Administrators unsuccessful in implementing site-based management use the same ineffective strategies because they're afraid to admit they aren't succeeding.

The norm of silence prohibits sharing critical information about self as well as others. We don't share our own shortcomings, and we don't provide critical information to others. Consequently, even when we may see troubling policies and practices, the conspiracy of silence precludes discussion because we're afraid of making waves or hurting others' feelings. As a result, while opportunities for reflective practice abound, it is uncommon to find students, teachers, or administrators engaged in deep and sustained conversations about individual and mutual problems of practice. Even less likely are situations where problem analysis crosses hierarchical lines, engaging teachers in dialogue with principals or principals with central office administrators. Confronted by problems, we avoid conflict.

Unfortunately, this Model I theory is flawed. While some recommend masking feelings to ensure organizational survival, we argue that the result of attempts to avoid conflict and maintain equilibrium is the loss of trust. When we adopt Model I strategies, we do so because we anticipate certain outcomes. Exercising unilateral control and withholding information may have short-term benefits in terms of expediency and stability, but in the long term, the organizational costs—defensiveness, passivity, resistance, and diminished creativity and commitment—are substantial.

According to Argyris (1990), Model I beliefs are deeply embedded in organizational behavior throughout the industrialized world. There is also evidence that these beliefs are pervasive in school settings (Fishbein, 2000; Fishbein & Osterman, 2000; Hargreaves, 2002; Hargreaves, Beatty, Lasky, Schmidt, & James-Wilson, in press). As a result, educators, like those in other organizations, reluctantly share information and avoid delving deeply into those aspects of personal belief and practice that are the substance of reflective practice. How then does one begin to challenge these norms and develop an environment that will support the open communication essential for reflective practice?

CREATING A REFLECTIVE PRACTICE ENVIRONMENT: MODEL II

Breaking this conspiracy of silence requires different actions and action theories. To engage in the reflective process, individuals need to be confident that discussion of problems and feelings will not be interpreted as incompetence or weakness. People will not talk about problems—personal or organizational—unless they feel safe, secure, and able to take a risk. In essence, engaging in reflective practice requires trust. Without trust, educators are unlikely to admit having problems or discuss them openly. Where reflective practice occurs, people are willing to share sensitive information about their work with their colleagues and discuss those areas of their practice where they may be weak or at least not as strong as they would like. How does this sense of trust develop?

Reflective practice depends on what Argyris and Schon (1974) described as a very different organizational model. Model II, in contrast to Model I, is based on an antithetical set of values and assumptions. A Model I environment emphasizes unilateral control; a Model II environment, focuses on collaborative problem solving. A Model I environment values private thought; Model II organizations value open communication and open access to valid information. Interestingly, these Model II strategies very predictably develop an organizational climate characterized by trust and creative problem solving, while Model I strategies foster defensiveness, passivity, and resistance (see Figure 4.1). How then do we establish the Model II conditions necessary to encourage reflective practice?

In the following sections, we discuss the need for a facilitator to serve as an organizational buffer and change agent and then identify some assumptions and strategies that predictably support the development of trust and collaboration in organizational settings.

Figure 4.1 Contrasting Model I and Model II

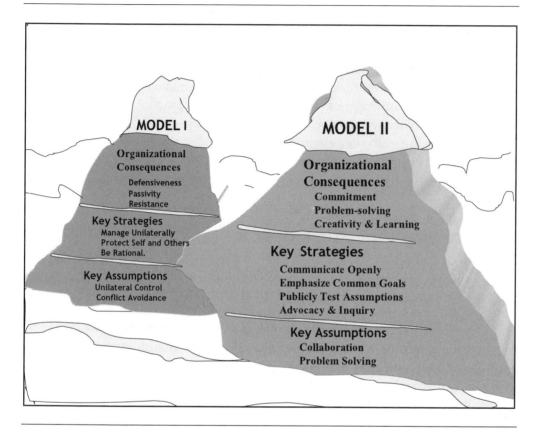

THE FACILITATOR

As the work of Argyris and Schon (Argyris, 1990, 1993; Argyris & Schon, 1974) have demonstrated, organizations do not encourage or support open communication, and sharing critical information about self or others poses certain risks. To engage in reflective practice, people need a sense of security. They need to trust that they can communicate openly without fear of retaliation (Cambron-McCabe, 2003). Consistent with organizational norms, people in organizational settings typically adopt Model I communication strategies that restrict the flow of information and create misunderstanding, defensiveness, and mistrust. So, while people need support to engage in a new form of dialogue, they also need to develop new strategies to communicate sensitive information openly and effectively. Given the defensive norms and patterns of communication in most organizations, accomplishing this goal is unlikely without the assistance and support of a facilitator. The role of the facilitator is an important one in any group (Doyle & Straus, 1982; Straus, 2002) but particularly so for reflective practice.

The facilitator is not restricted to a particular role. In schools and other educational settings, for example, the facilitator might be a principal, supervisor, or teacher; an outside consultant; or a university faculty member.[3] Certain criteria are important, however.

Because trust is an essential ingredient in the process of reflective practice, one of the facilitator's first responsibilities is to build trust. But how does that happen? Regardless of the role, because of the potential risk involved in problem analysis and critical reflection, it is essential that the facilitator have the authority and power to ensure safety. Reflective practitioners need assurance that openness is accepted and valued and will not lead to unpleasant consequences in the group or the organization. Individuals must trust one another, and the facilitator, to maintain confidentiality.

There are several effective techniques to establish trust and facilitate reflective practice, but by now it should be clear that actions are directly influenced by underlying theories-in-use. Consequently, in the following section, we first outline some of the key beliefs essential to reflective practice and then discuss those communication strategies that facilitate reflective practice. These beliefs and strategies influence reflective practice in two ways. They engender trust, a basic precondition for reflective practice. They also facilitate communication, encouraging and enabling participants to share information as well as ideas and feelings in a nonthreatening manner. Because the facilitator's interaction with the group is critical in determining the level of trust within the reflective group, these beliefs and methods are an important part of the facilitator's conceptual framework and repertoire of skills.

KEY ASSUMPTIONS AND BELIEFS

To serve as an effective facilitator, actions have to be grounded in a certain set of beliefs that reflect a deep commitment to the potential for human change and development. These beliefs about professional development constitute a credo for reflective practice. (See Figure 4.2.)

The facilitator in the reflective process must be someone who strongly accepts these beliefs about professional development at the level of espousal and action. We know a great deal about the importance of expectations. If teachers have high expectations for students, students learn. If principals have high expectations for staff, staff members rise to the occasion and lead the school to high levels of success. To communicate high

Figure 4.2   Credo for Reflective Practice

Credo **for Reflective Practice**

1. Everyone needs professional growth opportunities.

2. All professionals want to improve.

3. All professionals can learn.

4. People can change.

5. People need and want information about their own performance. All professionals are capable of assuming responsibility for their own professional growth and development.

6. Collaboration enriches professional development.

expectations requires more than speeches and awards assemblies; it depends on deeply rooted beliefs that, if given the opportunity, individuals can actually meet high expectations. An interesting experimental study illustrates this point.

In the first phase of this study, teachers were videotaped while they talked for several minutes about two students from their class-rooms, one strong, the other weak. In the second phase, the two students were called into the classroom and taught by the same teacher for two to five minutes. In both situations, the video- and audiotapes captured facial expressions, body language, and speech. At a later point, a group of fourth graders (along with groups of older students and adults) viewed ten-second clips from the tapes and rated the aca-demic ability of the students and the feelings of the teachers toward the students. Although the teachers tried to disguise their feelings, even young children could easily detect the level of student performance and the extent to which the teacher loved the student (Babad, Bernieri, & Rosenthal, 1991).

In other words, true feelings are conveyed in very subtle ways and difficult to disguise. Unless the facilitator has a deep commitment to these beliefs about professional development—or at least can suspend doubt—she or he will be unable to disguise real feelings. The facilitator has to be a person who not only espouses this educational philosophy but also models it. Although these beliefs are common espousals, as the following discussion suggests, they are not always evident in practice.

1. *Everyone needs professional growth opportunities.* The effective facilitator views professional growth as a normal and necessary part of life for all members of the organization. The facilitator understands that all professionals experience situations where they are not as competent as they would like and confront problems in their daily work that require new and different strategies.

Problems of professional practice are the norm rather than the exception. Few people experience no difficulties in the work setting, but the system conveys a very different set of signals about problems and those who admit to them. Teachers having difficulties controlling student behavior are deemed deficient in classroom management, particularly if they refer these students to the principal. Administrators unable to contain parent complaints or minimize teacher grievances are viewed as incompetent by the central office. The educational system by its very nature constantly generates new and changing problems, and teaching and administration should be viewed as problem-solving occupations. Yet, typically, problems are viewed as the exception rather than the norm, as a sign of incompetence rather than the everyday reality of organizational life. In other words, there's an inconsistency between espousal and theory-in-use.

2. *All professionals want to improve.* Reflective practice is based on an assumption that all professionals want growth opportunities. Some motivational theorists (Connell & Wellborn, 1991; deCharms, 1968, 1976, 1984; Deci, 1980; Deci & Ryan, 1985; Deci, Vallerand, Pelletier, & Ryan, 1991) view competence as a basic psychological need: Individuals need to experience themselves as capable of producing desired outcomes and avoiding negative outcomes. They need to feel effective. This means that teachers unable to reach at-risk students and administrators who fail to maintain a safe, secure, and clean environment experience frustration at their inability to realize their goals.

This belief is not always evident within the school community. To the contrary, we seem to assume that educators, whether teachers or administrators, are unconcerned about their performance and resist efforts to improve. Consistent with this assumption, schools and districts implement various procedures to ensure attendance, from the sign-in sheet to threats and fiscal penalties. Although research and experience demonstrate that change in professional practice is, in fact, hard to achieve, some of this resistance may reflect problems with the nature of professional development rather than a lack of intrinsic motivation. As Bredeson (2003) explained, professional development is often piecemeal, fragmented, narrow, and incoherent, having little relevance to teachers' work and unlikely to lead to actual changes in teacher practice. Rather than assess professional development, however, the tendency is to criticize the professional.

Reflective practice maintains that professional growth is as important to the individual as it is to the organization. While professional development appropriately meets organizational needs, organizational needs are best met by meeting the professionally oriented needs of individuals.

3. *All professionals can learn.* This is probably one of the most difficult facets of the reflective practice credo. Despite what we say, few educators truly believe that professionals with unsatisfactory performance can improve, particularly when the professional is a seasoned teacher or administrator. We talk about people being set in their ways and conclude you can't teach an old dog new tricks. At a general level, we may espouse optimism, but on a personal level, confronted by a real person whose performance falls short of expectations, we are pessimistic about even the possibility of change. This is probably a clear example of how the ladder of inference functions to reinforce assumptions. We observe burnout and make assumptions about these behaviors. Often, the behavior is interpreted as intentional—they don't care about their work; they don't care about kids; they've given up. This interpretation shapes the action strategy—typically one of control and avoidance (Manzoni & Barsoux, 1998). This action strategy, in turn, generates the predicted response, reinforcing prior assumptions. What is true is that organizations—schools or others—seldom support learning and, in many cases, offer working conditions and environments that actually deaden people's desire to learn. What is not true is that individuals are incapable of growth and development.

4. *All professionals are capable of assuming responsibility for their own professional growth and development.* Historically, supervisory practices in schools and in other organizations have reflected bureaucratic assumptions,

including the notion that expertise is concentrated in the upper echelons of the hierarchy. Subordinates, in contrast, are incompetent and require close supervision. Supervisors are responsible for performance, and their job is to detect and eradicate error by regulating behavior. While researchers and professionals decry autocratic approaches and proclaim the need for more collaborative and democratic approaches to supervision, theory and practice still diverge. While conceptions of supervision have changed, the practice of supervision still relies heavily on the use of external assessment and external prescription.[4] While modern theories describe supervision as a process of helping teachers to engage in self-assessment and assume responsibility for their own professional growth, in practice, someone other than the teacher determines both the problem and the solution.

Reflective practice is a professional development process incorporating a very different set of assumptions. It assumes that professionals are competent and able to assume responsibility for detecting and addressing weaknesses in their practice. When the facilitator deeply believes that individuals are committed to improving their own performance, willing to assume responsibility for their professional growth, and able to learn, it is likely that she or he will interact in a positive, constructive, and nonthreatening way with the other participants. If the facilitator trusts the participants, they are more likely to return that trust. Trust engenders trust.

Assuming that others are able to take responsibility also requires the facilitator to respect the participants' autonomy. Requiring reflective practice is as inconsistent as mandating site-based decision making. While reflective practice may be difficult, voluntary participation, indicating an intrinsic motivation for change, combined with often-dramatic rewards, minimizes stress. In fact, as later examples show, the risk of reflective practice often goes unnoticed.

5. *People need and want information about their own performance.* If we accept that people are willing and able to assume responsibility for their own professional growth, how, then, does growth come about? One of the key issues in reflective practice responds to that question.

Literature on adult supervision identifies performance feedback as a critical aspect of the supervisory process. Information about performance—strengths and weaknesses—is essential to continued learning and professional growth. Nevertheless, in practice, school administrators, teachers, or students seldom receive meaningful feedback about their performance (Bridges, 1986; McGregor, 1960; McLaughlin & Pfeifer, 1988; Natriello & Dornbusch, 1984; Osterman, 1994).

From a reflective practice perspective, changes in behavior are inextricably linked with growing awareness of one's own performance.

Consequently, it is important to examine this discrepancy between the espoused theory and the theory-in-use. What accounts for the breakdown in the supervisory process? Why are professionals so reluctant to share performance information with one another?

As explained previously, organizational behavior is often shaped by bureaucratic principles emphasizing hierarchical control. The teacher in the classroom develops instructional management techniques to make sure that the class doesn't get out of hand. The administrator takes no actions that upset parents, teachers, or the board of education. One of the primary ways to stay in control is by withholding information. This strategy increases unilateral control in several ways. First, withholding information precludes others from active involvement in decision making. If the administrator keeps information from staff, knowledge needed to analyze problems, develop strategies, and make decisions remains the exclusive property of the administrator. If the supervisor withholds information about a subordinate's performance, the supervisor retains the right to make decisions about the subordinate's work and progress. Second, withholding information, particularly critical information, presumably reduces the likelihood of conflict. Administrators are reluctant to confront teachers with complaints because they fear the teachers' response. By withholding information, we keep things calm and under control—our control.

Withholding information also responds to a protective need, a well-intentioned but misguided sense of social responsibility to others. We hold back critical information because we believe it hurts other people's feelings and perhaps reduces our own ability to remedy the situation. Teachers reward students with a gold star even though the work falls far short of standards for fear of destroying self-confidence. When we withhold information, we assume responsibility for the other person's well-being. Obviously, no one likes to hear their work isn't up to expectations; at the same time, how can they address the problem if they're not aware of it? Unless we believe people want to be competent, want feedback about their work, and will use the information to improve, there is little incentive to engage in what is likely to be a difficult conversation.

How we define professional problems affects our attitudes toward feedback. When we observe positive actions and effects, we assume these actions and outcomes are indicators of professional competence, dedication, or commitment. When we observe marginal or unsatisfactory practice, we often make judgments—not simply about the act but also about the person. Conversations about the senior teacher whose performance has been slipping gradually or even precipitously often lead to a decision to do nothing, or to recommend a transfer, because we assume that the problem lies with the person. We believe that the person doesn't care or is incapable of changing. With this theory-in-use shaping actions, it becomes difficult if not impossible to raise certain issues. When we talk about the problem, if we do, we will likely speak in a circumspect way, rather than confronting the problem directly. Information is withheld; the problem is kept hidden.

We withhold critical information and avoid discussing problems or concerns because we believe that in so doing we will keep things under control, protect ourselves, and keep others from being hurt. In reality, however, this action strategy does not yield the predicted results. In contrast with what we might expect, these bureaucratic strategies generate defensive relationships and mistrust (Argyris, 1990, 1993; Argyris & Schon, 1974). Further, these efforts at unilateral control are disincentives to innovation, organizational commitment, and risk taking. In short, Model I beliefs and action strategies do not support the development of a community committed to professional growth and development; they do not help to build a learning organization (Argyris, 1990; Senge, 1990; Senge et al., 2000).

By comparison, Model II encompasses very different beliefs about people and their motivation, suggests very different strategies, and predicts very different outcomes. In Model I, the desire for unilateral control leads to withholding information. In Model II, the belief in the efficacy of collaboration is associated with an open flow of information. The outcomes associated with each of these action theories are very different. Model I behaviors predictably lead to defensiveness, passivity, and resistance. Conversely, open sharing of information leads to improvement in the quality of interpersonal relations, stimulates professional growth, and enhances organizational effectiveness.

There is a growing body of research confirming that Model II strategies are more likely than their counterpart to create organizational conditions that encourage trust, collaboration, and effective problem solving. Sharing goals, information, ideas, and authority fosters collaboration and encourages the development of a sense of community. These organizational characteristics, whether in the classroom, the school, or the district, affect morale and are associated with better performance of teachers, students, and the organization as a whole (Fullan, 2002; Leithwood et al., 2001; Little, 2001; Louis, Kruse, & Associates, 1995; Murphy, Beck, Crawford, Hodges, & McGaughy, 2001; Murphy & Datnow, 2003a, 2003b).[5] Nevertheless, there is still a great deal of resistance to open communication, particularly when the message involves critical feedback. Reflective practice requires Model II assumptions and strategies. To engage in reflective practice requires that we rethink Model I assumptions that counsel us to exercise unilateral control and withhold information. If we assume that problems reflect a lack of motivation or personal weakness, there is no rationale for providing information. On the other hand, if we believe that problems exist because people may not be fully aware of the problem or because they lack information, resources, or support needed to design and implement other strategies, we are more likely to engage in those difficult conversations and name the problems openly.

From this perspective, information about performance, whether strengths or weaknesses, is welcome because it gives professionals the knowledge they need to begin to see their own performance clearly and to create change. "When a practitioner becomes a researcher into his [or her] own practice, he [or she] engages in a continuing process of self-education. . . . the recognition of error, with its resulting uncertainty, can become a source of discovery rather than an occasion for self defense" (Schon, 1983, p. 299).

6. *Collaboration enriches learning and professional development.* Because of the deeply engrained nature of our behavioral patterns, it is sometimes difficult to develop critical perspective on our own behavior. As Brookfield (1992) explained, it is "extraordinarily hard to analyze one's own assumptions using the same frames of interpretation and understanding within which these assumptions are embedded. It is like trying to catch one's perceptual tail" (p. 18). For that reason alone, analysis occurring in a collegial environment is likely to lead to greater learning:

> When people gather to do this in small groups, . . . they find that other members of the group serve as reflective mirrors; they reflect back to each learner an image of his or her practice that is partly recognizable, yet at the same time oddly unfamiliar. . . . Viewing one's practice through another's eyes is a powerful trigger to becoming a more critically reflective practitioner. (p. 18)

Aside from individuals' access to more information and different perspectives in a group setting, there are other reasons to recommend collaborative approaches to reflective practice. The focus of reflective practice is professional practice. The social environment in the workplace influences individuals' practice. When other professionals participate in the effort, this collaborative process helps to develop a culture supporting learning and growth. From a more general perspective, Johnson and Johnson (1991) concluded that change—in action theories and behavior patterns—is easier and more likely to be permanent when it occurs in a group because the group provides needed emotional support, encouragement, and consensual validation of changes.

These findings apply to professional development in general and to reflective practice in particular.

For these reasons, collegial reflective practice in the workplace can enrich the process. Creating an environment to support reflective practice is a challenging task, however. Reflective practice in and of itself is a difficult process. It is difficult to develop new insights into behavior, and seeing these new perspectives can be a painful experience that creates stress among the reflective practitioners (Argyris, Putnam, & Smith, 1985; Clarke, 1995). Engaging in reflective practice and sharing sensitive information with others promises richer insights but also increases personal risk. It is additionally complicated in an organizational setting where widely accepted norms seriously constrain the ability of individuals to engage in the open and critical dialogue about actions, feelings, and thoughts that constitutes the core of reflective practice.

Every semester when we begin group problem-solving activities in administrator preparation courses, students experience discomfort. Many have little experience working in task groups; others remember unpleasant situations where the group was unable to accomplish its goals or struggled with members who dominated the process and ignored other members. Based on these experiences, their underlying beliefs about the importance and effectiveness of collaboration are weak, and many prefer autonomous work settings where they directly control their own work.

These pressures toward unilateral action and against collaboration are intensified in the school setting. Despite the rhetoric about collaboration, teachers have few opportunities to work together, particularly in problem-solving situations (Fullan & Hargreaves, 1996; Johnson, 1990; Rosenholtz, 1989). The situation is similar for administrators, and situations where teachers and administrators cross their role boundaries to work together are even less frequent.

How the facilitator works with participants is shaped by beliefs about the value of group effort. Particularly important is the extent to which the facilitator can relinquish individual control to share leadership and learning decisions with the entire group. Through actions and words, the facilitator must model these beliefs to establish an open atmosphere of trust in which people may communicate openly and freely.

KEY STRATEGIES: COMMUNICATING FOR REFLECTIVE PRACTICE

While beliefs provide the underpinning for facilitating, far more is required. Reflective practice requires open communication about thoughts, observations, and feelings. People's ability to communicate effectively, however, is also influenced by the organizational environment. Unfortunately, the communication patterns most of us learned reflect Model I assumptions and, rather than supporting reflective practice, preclude it.

In the earlier section, we described the predominant values and action strategies pervading bureaucratic organizations. These action strategies are themselves reflected in certain communication patterns. To maintain control, we rely on directives and prescriptions: We tell people what to do and how to do it. To ensure compliance with our goals, we rely on manipulation, persuasion, coercion, rewards, and rationalization (it's the right thing to do). To avoid conflict, we assure others that everything is all right: don't worry about it. We avoid communicating critical information; we don't talk about problems. We strive to achieve rationality and avoid any emotionality. As we show later, even when well meaning, all these strategies reflect a hierarchy of power and expertise. As such, they serve as obstacles to communication (Bolton, 1979) and preclude reflective practice. Confronted with these behaviors, people withdraw from dialogue and become wary of others whose language fails to hide ulterior motives. Unfortunately, because these bureaucratic strategies are so pervasive, we learn these patterns of communication through our interaction with superiors, whether parents, teachers, or administrators.

While these communication strategies have a deadening effect on people's ability to engage in collaborative reflection and problem solving, other communication strategies facilitate dialogue and support reflective inquiry. It is our belief that these strategies can be learned, and using them helps to create a supportive environment for reflective inquiry.

Defining Communication

Reflective practice benefits from the availability of multiple perspectives. To facilitate dialogue, it is important to understand communication as a two-way process, involving inquiry (learning about others' positions) and advocacy (stating one's position). Far too often, we equate communication with the ability to frame ideas and information in an interesting or persuasive manner. With the primary focus on the speaker, too little attention is paid to the listener. Theoretically, then, we are defining communication as a shared message: One person sends a message, and the other person interprets that message. Communication is more or less effective depending on the quality of the exchange. To the extent that the message is interpreted as intended, the communication is successful. Interestingly, what we know about communication tells us that this shared understanding seldom takes place—on the first try. In the party game called Rumor, as the whispered message goes from person to person, we watch the transformation. Because of differences in experience, interest, or values, each person provides a slightly different interpretation, and the end result is often a very different message from the one intended. Because of these predictable gaps, communication is often described as a dual process of advocacy and inquiry.

Through verbal and nonverbal behavior, one person communicates information and ideas (advocacy). The other person attempts to establish a clear and complete understanding of the message (inquiry). Only through this mutual process of advocacy and inquiry do people develop a valid shared understanding. Once the listener confirms understanding, the dialogue continues with the sharing of ideas. In response to the message, the listener now becomes the advocate, sharing his or her ideas while the other shifts roles to become the listener. Through this continuous process of advocacy and inquiry, people share ideas, information, and feelings (see Figure 4.3).

What seems like a simple process in theory is extremely complicated in practice. Communication is far more than words. Through our expressions and movements, we powerfully communicate information that adds a great deal of meaning, often different from our words. Developing shared understanding involves attention to words and meaning.

Messages are complex, and what we hear is filtered through experience. "What we notice has to do with who we are and what we care about" (Stone et al., 1999, p. 31). We interpret things idiosyncratically, making sense of what we're hearing by drawing on our own experiences. Because we define communication as talking, few people have well-developed listening skills. We also interpret listening as a silent process. Instead of

Figure 4.3 Communication: Advocacy and Inquiry

Speaker A	**Advocacy**	**Statement**
Speaker B	**Inquiry**	**Clarification/ Confirmation Response**

carefully clarifying and confirming our impressions, we climb the ladder of inference, leaping to conclusions based on untested assumptions. In framing our responses to what we think was said, we often rely on forms of communication that block rather than support continued dialogue.

Reflective practice requires skill in both advocacy and inquiry. Communication is difficult under normal circumstances, but even more so in reflective practice as individuals try to articulate thoughts, ideas, and feelings that are not clearly defined. A goal of reflective practice is developing deeper understanding of dimensions of behavior not readily apparent, even to the self. As individuals share information about their own practice, others facilitate personal understanding through inquiry and advocacy. As listeners, they seek to clarify their understanding and confirm shared understanding. As reflective practitioners respond to questions and hear the interpretation of others, they usually develop a clearer understanding of their own experience. As advocates, the facilitator and group members provide feedback, raising additional questions or offering suggestions about the theories-in-use underlying behavior. Through this dialogic process, where colleagues, in essence, serve as intelligent mirrors, individuals come to see their work in new ways.

Communication in traditional organizations reflects Model I beliefs. Consequently, skills of inquiry and advocacy, while essential to reflective practice, are not well developed. While learning new behavior is always difficult, there are specific inquiry and advocacy strategies that facilitate sensitive communication, and they can be learned.[6] In a reflective practice group, the facilitator must assume responsibility for establishing communication norms and helping the group members to develop skills in using these strategies. The following section introduces basic strategies to facilitate communication and contrasts them with typical but less effective practices.

Inquiry Strategies

To reiterate, the purpose of inquiry is to develop a deep and accurate understanding of what others are trying to communicate. We are interested in words, but we are also interested in parts of the message that may be unsaid: thoughts, intentions, desires, and feelings. The essence of inquiry is listening, but listening is far more than being silent. A focused activity, in which the listener pays close attention to verbal and nonverbal dimensions of the speaker's message, listening includes verbal and nonverbal behaviors designed to grasp the intellectual and emotional content of messages.

In many instances, listening facilitates the articulation of ideas. In administrative preparation classes, for example, students have no difficulty identifying a problematic situation, but when they try to explain the problem, many experience difficulty. They can easily describe the situation and express their feelings about the issue but often have difficulty explaining the reasons for their distress. A good listener will help bring these issues to the forefront. Listening is also critical for developing social awareness and empathy and building strong interpersonal relationships, key components of emotional intelligence (Goleman, 1998, 2000; Stein & Book, 2000). Attending, reflecting, and questioning are three key listening strategies (see Figure 4.4).

Attending is the most basic listening strategy. Through a combination of posture, gestures, eye contact, nods, and murmurs, the listener tells the speaker that she or he is being heard. This sense of being heard has a powerful impact on the course of future conversations (Belenky, Clinchy, Goldberger, & Tarule, 1986). Attending, therefore, conveys interest—and acceptance—and encourages the person to be more forthcoming.

Reflecting is another important listening strategy that involves repeating or paraphrasing the meaning of the message to verify the listener's perception. Because so much of communication is a process of interpretation, as the listener seeks to develop a deep understanding, the reflection includes different dimensions of the message, content and emotions, things said and unsaid.

Figure 4.4   Inquiry Strategies

Through this process, the listener checks or confirms understanding. This is particularly important because so much misunderstanding—and consequent mistrust—occurs simply because we make assumptions about meaning and intent without ever testing our interpretations. Typically, conversations move quickly from one voice to another: One person makes a statement or takes a position, and the next person reacts, expressing his or her own position. In these conversations, however, we seldom check the assumptions or attributions we make while we listen.[7] We hear the words a person says, and we assume we understand what the person meant to say and why. The reality though is that people don't always say what they mean, and, even when they do, words are not always interpreted as intended. It is difficult to understand words, difficult to understand others' intentions, and impossible to be sure unless we ask.

Argyris (1982, 1990, 1991, 1993), Argyris and Schon (1978), and others (Bolton, 1979; Senge, 1990; Stone et al., 1999) cautioned us to slow down the communication process, clearly articulating and testing unspoken assumptions. Reflective listening is a strategy that enables us to do that. By reiterating what we think we heard, we are testing our own understanding. In doing that, we give the other person the opportunity to clarify his or her own meaning. This process of reflection and confirmation is important for effective communication and essential for reflective practice.

In an organizational setting, the facilitator and group members are technical assistants. They tilt the mirror so that it reflects from a different angle, focus the microscope so that an undistinguishable entity comes into view, turn the prism, or change the lens from telescopic to wide angle so that the observer sees the same phenomenon from many different perspectives.

Questioning can be another way of listening that helps to shift the perspective and encourage reflective practice. Reflective practitioners and facilitators ask questions. Doing this, they strive to deepen their own understanding of the other's message. The use of questions also helps the reflective practitioners to explore their own behavior in deeper and different ways. Researchers who use teachers' stories to encourage reflective practice, for example, talk about how they respond "with questions about why the story was told in the way it was. By answering the researcher's question, the participants may penetrate more deeply to other experiences" (Clandinin & Connelly, 1991, p. 268).

A teacher involved in a four-year collaborative project involving university researchers, teachers, and principals described the questioning strategies the university researchers used and their importance in facilitating reflective practice:

The researchers did not come into our classrooms to recommend changes or to tell us how we might improve. Instead, they approached us with a deep respect for what we knew, a desire to learn what we saw as troublesome in our own teaching, and a methodology that encouraged us to become aware of and to question our own assumptions about our practice. The researchers came into our classrooms to observe, take field notes, share with us what they had found, and ask questions about what they had observed. The questions were non-judgmental, non-critical, accepting, and supportive. We answered the questions, and, in the process, became more aware of our own knowledge. They asked us questions that we knew the answers to; but, until they had asked us the questions, we hadn't thought about the answers. That began to get us to question more things for ourselves. The researchers were not suggesting changes we should make, but by being asked questions and reflecting on them, we discovered ways that we wanted to change. Reflecting on these questions was a real breakthrough for us because we began to question our own assumptions. Why had we not asked ourselves those questions before? We had been overwhelmed by the complex task of teaching in the traditional style that did not include opportunities to observe or experience reflection. (Berkey et al., 1990, p. 213)

Another study (Sagor, 1991) showed how principals used questions to facilitate development of an environment of critical practice in their schools. By asking "probing questions which go to the heart of the teaching/learning process" (p. 15) and by gathering information about professional practice, principals established a norm of inquiry and experimentation. By acting as facilitators rather than experts, by providing information and support, they helped teachers in these schools to experience empowerment and efficacy in developing new and more effective instructional policies and practices on an individual and schoolwide basis.

Not all types of questions are appropriate, however. Questions likely to foster reflective practice are those reflecting openness to ideas and information and a desire to develop a deeper understanding of events and meanings from the other person's perspective: Would you tell me more? Can you help me to understand your meaning a little better? What was your reasoning here? Questions that have the opposite effect are those that try to place blame, lead the respondent to a predetermined answer, or interrupt and distract rather than complement and enrich.

These listening strategies facilitate reflective practice in many ways. They explore different dimensions of meaning—feelings as well as cognition—and slow down the process to check assumptions and confirm understanding. Unlike typical conversations, in reflective practice, exploring what is usually unspoken becomes a priority concern to examine assumptions and reveal theories-in-use. The listening strategies facilitate this analysis. They also tell the speaker the message was important enough to warrant close attention. This implicit message of care and concern encourages the speaker to probe a little deeper.

Listening also supports reflective practice in another important way. Often as we listen, our thoughts jump ahead to our own response. We begin to make assumptions and interpret what is being said; we think about what we will say and about how we will address these issues or concerns. In contrast, the mode of listening we describe here requires full attention to the speaker. As the facilitator and group members actively attend to what the speaker is saying and try to understand the speaker's point of view and feelings, there is less opportunity to think about their own response. By concentrating fully on the other person, we become rooted on the ground floor of the ladder of inference, and we avoid the tendency to make unwarranted assumptions and judgments or to take control.

Advocacy Strategies

Supported by careful listening of the facilitator and group members, the reflective practitioner has provided a detailed description of events and actions. Through attending, reflecting, and questioning, the listeners have developed and confirmed their understanding of what happened as well as the feelings and thinking surrounding the events. At this point, the dialogue shifts. The listeners now engage in advocacy. As inquirers, the primary focus is to develop an understanding of the other person's message. As advocates, the objective is to communicate one's own thoughts and feelings about that message.

Consistent with Model II values, communication should be open. Reflective practice builds on problems and incorporates the assumption that awareness of problems is an important stimulus to professional growth. As the narrative unfolds, the listeners may observe inconsistencies—between the espoused theory and action, for example. Examining practice, they may also develop alternate explanations of the behavior (the theories-in-use) from those presented by the reflective practitioner. In the spirit of professional growth, the facilitator and group members must be prepared to communicate this critical information. Even more important, they must be able to communicate, so the listener is able to hear it.

While most people are comfortable giving positive feedback, most find it very difficult to convey critical information. The logic behind this withholding strategy is this: People feel vulnerable in the face of criticism, and conditions of safety and trust are conducive to learning. To create a sense of trust we need to be supportive; that is, we need to emphasize the positive, minimize criticism, and take responsibility for meeting others' needs. Confronted with the need to convey critical information or ideas, then, the facilitator and group members experience a dilemma. On one hand, the espoused theory (reflective practice) maintains that feedback is important. On the other hand, fears of providing critical information (based on the Model I theory-in-use) create anxiety and cause them to shy away from these situations.

Unfortunately, this rationale is based on faulty logic and untested assumptions. If we look at evidence, gathered through formal research and experience, we arrive at very different conclusions. People do feel vulnerable in the face of criticism, and it is important to develop a sense of safety and trust if learning is to occur. Contradicting the Model I perspective, the literature on communication and supervision provides ample evidence to support a very different perspective. Sharing even critical information has positive effects on trust and learning, while withholding information creates mistrust and reduces learning. Additionally, the problem with critical feedback is not information but the way the information is conveyed.

Typically, when we offer feedback, our statements are evaluative. We observe certain events, interpret those events, and draw conclusions. Often those conclusions include attributions about the intent or capability of the other person. When we provide feedback, our statements usually incorporate those judgments; we share our conclusions, but we bypass the other steps on the ladder of inference and often fail to explain the logical process we used to arrive at the judgment.

What's missing from such judgmental statements is a description of what was observed and an explanation of how those actions or events were interpreted. Both stages are important because of the selective nature of our perceptions and the idiosyncratic nature of our assessment. As we explained previously, what we see and how we interpret what we see are affected by who we are. Because we all differ in many important ways, these descriptions are important to facilitate mutual understanding.

Evaluative statements—whether positive or negative—are problematic for important reasons. While we avoid conveying critical opinions, we are far less reluctant to offer praise. Unfortunately, criticism and praise, as judgmental statements, are two sides of the same coin. As we observe events, we interpret what we see and make judgments using criteria that may or may not be clearly defined and articulated.

To the extent that participants develop a comprehensive picture of the many dimensions of their own behavior and develop a deep understanding of that behavior, the process is richer. Because these evaluative or judgmental statements exclude important descriptive information and obscure meaning, they do not contribute useful information or facilitate learning. Further, judgmental statements have a negative effect on interpersonal communication. Rather than supporting open dialogue, they block communication, create mistrust, and evoke defensive reactions. Regardless of our words, intentions show through.

Judgments take different forms. The most direct and obvious are straightforward evaluations of performance: "You certainly didn't handle that well," or, on the positive side, "you're a fantastic teacher." Judgmental statements also appear in messages as untested assumptions about the intentions of the other person and frequently convey blame: "You were just making excuses again." Prescriptions can be a more subtle way to express judgments: "If you ever have to do that again, I'd suggest . . . " Statements like these implicitly and sometimes explicitly communicate the sender's desire to change the other. They also imply that the sender knows what the change should be and how it should come about. Messages like these, although intended to help, merely reinforce the recipient's sense of subordination, helplessness, and incompetence.

Even praise can convey a status message: I, the expert, am using my standards to assess your performance. In either case, the sender of the message makes a unilateral decision for or about the receiver and assumes responsibility and authority to interpret, assess, or direct the other person's behavior. Because they lead to unilateral control and preclude collaboration, judgmental messages are Model I messages. As such, they block communication and generate defensive behavior. Judgmental messages are unlikely to be heard and unlikely to encourage reflection.

Unfortunately, our use of judgmental messages in our daily communication is extensive. While it is not difficult to appreciate that techniques like ordering, directing, commanding, warning, admonishing, and threatening convey and maintain status inequalities, it may be surprising that apparently innocuous communication strategies such as moralizing, preaching, advising, suggesting, solving, persuading with logic, and even consoling and praising also have a negative effect on interpersonal communication (Bolton, 1979; Gordon, 1980; Johnson & Johnson, 1991; Kohn, 1999; Kottkamp, 1990).

In summary, when we examine practice, we find that when people provide feedback to others—whether adults or children—they generally rely on judgmental or prescriptive statements that provide no clear information about the quality of the performance itself. Secondly, while people are very comfortable providing positive feedback (praise), they avoid giving negative feedback and rely, instead, on prescription. The absence of descriptive information prevents recipients from gaining clear information about how others view their work. For those whose performance falls below acceptable standards, this is a major handicap. In a study of student feedback during alternative assessment projects, for example, Baaden (2002) described an incident when an eighth-grade student approached the teacher following a failure on a quiz. "I want to know what I did wrong," the student said. "Everything," the teacher responded. Similarly, the supervisor tells the student teacher what to do or how to do it but, by not offering a clear explanation of what went wrong, limits the student's ability to self-assess and self-correct. Prescriptive and exclusively judgmental statements like these reinforce status differentials and block communication. Intentionally or inadvertently, these statements convey a sense of superiority and diminish the recipient's sense of personal agency.

How do we resolve this tension? On one hand, we say that reflective practice requires open communication. On the other hand, many of the strategies we use to communicate have a negative effect and close the door to further discussion. If we can't communicate our assessments, how can we be open? How can we share our ideas and our thinking?

Descriptive Messages

Although we tend to rely on judgmental and prescriptive feedback, particularly with subordinates, whether children or adults, there is an effective alternative: the descriptive message. Because habits of communication are difficult to change, using descriptive feedback is challenging initially but leads quickly to competence and mastery.

Bolton (1979) used the term *I-message* to explain the unique focus of the descriptive message. In contrast with judgmental messages, which convey interpretations of the other's behavior, the descriptive message is a personal one that provides information about the speaker's own perspective. Excluded are attributions, inferences, or interpretations about the other person. Emphasis on personal perspective also acknowledges the highly subjective nature of observation and interpretation. While I can provide my interpretation of what happened, it would not be possible to arrive at a full understanding of the situation until we share perspectives. And, in fact, that is one of the interesting and valuable insights emerging from reflective practice experience: as we share observations, we begin to see the world in different ways. As we gather more data about a situation, our interpretations often shift in dramatic ways. We begin to appreciate that it is not easy to predict what the other person was thinking and that human behavior is indeed complex.

The descriptive message is also unique in the information it includes. Rather than conveying only the judgment or the prescription, the descriptive message provides information about each step in the decision process. While these steps on the ladder of inference are normally bypassed in verbal communication, the descriptive message offers insight into one's own thinking. Only when this information is open to public inspection can differences be identified and examined. Since we observe selectively, observations may differ. Interpretations also differ, even in homogeneous groups. Unless we explain our thinking, there is no opportunity to clarify differences, and opportunities for misunderstanding abound.

Framing the Descriptive Message

What does a descriptive message look like? While authors approach the issue differently, most agree that the message should incorporate three components: a description of the particular situation, an explanation of how you felt about the situation, and your interpretation of the situation or the consequences for you. A fully developed message, then, consists of three parts: behavior, feelings, and interpretation (see Figure 4.5).

Figure 4.5   Components of the Descriptive Message

Descriptive Message ⇨ Behaviors **+** Feelings **+** Interpretation

Description of the Behavior/Situation. This part of the message describes the behavior and the situation that you observed. Constructing the descriptive message is like developing a picture in words so that the other person can see the situation as you saw it. The picture becomes clearer to the extent that the language chosen is concrete, graphic, and nonevaluative.

Feelings. The second part of the message describes your feelings about the particular incident. Is the situation upsetting, surprising, or pleasing? Confronted by this situation, are you tense, angry, concerned, or hopeful? This is an important part of the message for several reasons. First, sharing your feelings helps to personalize the conversation. You are speaking not simply from perspective of your role (as parent, teacher, principal) but as a human being with thoughts and concerns.

Emphasis on feelings also recognizes the important role of emotions in communication—and in learning. Emotions run high when important beliefs or values are involved. Anxiety, tension, anger, or other deep feelings indicate personal involvement and can be a stimulus for learning. Often times, when events trigger strong emotions, feelings precede cognitive understanding. We know we're angry or depressed but have difficulty explaining the rationale. Since emotional reactions often indicate underlying action theories, recognizing and exploring these feelings helps to articulate these beliefs and assumptions and complete the next step of descriptive message.

Interpretation. The third part of the message explains how you are interpreting the event. It provides the rationale for your emotional reaction: I'm concerned or pleased *because . . .* It explains your understanding of the consequences. An emotional reaction reflects assumptions about the consequences of the action or events. The identification of these action theories and subsequent analysis is an important step in the reflective practice process.

To illustrate, consider the parent dealing with the soon-to-be condemned teenager's room. If the parent were to construct a descriptive I-message for that situation, it might look like this:

Description of the Behavior/situation:	Your room looks like a disaster area. There are no clothes left in the closet or the drawers: I haven't been able to find the floor or the furniture in months; the dust is building up to a dangerous level; and the dirty dishes, glasses, and half-filled soda cans are a health hazard.
Feelings:	I'm really upset about this
Interpretation:	because . . . a. You have allergies and are close to an attack; b. I enjoy having a neat and clean home, and the sight of your room drives me nearly insane; and/or c. I'm worried that you aren't developing the habits that you need to be a responsible adult.

The verbal sketch of the room is vivid, and, while the parent's perspective is very explicit, there is no effort to place blame or denigrate the child. This nonjudgmental format and the personalization of the communication minimize the other person's defensiveness and set the stage for open communication and dialogue. While it may not always lead to a successful resolution, the use of this form enables people to express feelings openly without attacking the other person or creating an adversarial, win-lose situation. Equally important, by reducing the need for defense, this communication form enables the other person to hear the message.

When this technique is introduced in class, students then try it in their homes, classrooms, or professional dealings. Typically, they experience difficulty constructing the message. They struggle to describe the problem so that another person can see the situation as they do; they also have difficulty articulating how they feel about the situation and identifying meaningful consequences. Take, for example, the teacher who is repeatedly late for class. After preparing the descriptive message, the administrator is able to state clearly that he is concerned about this pattern of behavior because of the effects on student learning. In retrospect, this may appear obvious, but before framing the message it may not have been so clear. The format of the message requires you to think things through in ways that can be shared. As one administrator explained, the descriptive message "forces you to look at yourself. When you have to give a descriptive message, there's a degree of honesty about yourself that you have to have." It encourages you to articulate and examine the assumptions and beliefs you bring to different situations. It requires you to decide how you really feel about things and to determine if what's bothering you really does have important consequences: Are you upset because the teacher's actions affect students, or are you upset because the teacher's actions are a challenge to your authority? If the consequences are important and the link between the behavior and the effect is plausible, it is more likely that the listener will be able to hear the message and accept the importance of change.

At the same time, after using descriptive messages, students invariably return with success stories. Whether addressing a problem involving a student or colleague, typically, they report a sense of surprise on the part of the other person, who was anticipating criticism and was somewhat startled at the very different nature of this message. In most cases, even difficult situations gave way to dialogue where there had been none before, and often resolution.

Dealing With Defensive Reactions

The descriptive message is an effective way to communicate, particularly with troubling information. While the descriptive message increases the accessibility of the information, it does not preclude defensive reactions. Reflective practice may explore sensitive areas and examine problems that are frequently unspoken. Even though conveyed in a nonjudgmental fashion, the listener may interpret the message as criticism and respond defensively, whether in icy withdrawal or a heated attack. Unfortunately, such reactions usually bring conversation to an abrupt end and preclude dialogue. The recipient of the attack immediately moves back into the Model I stance, reacting defensively or withdrawing to protect self. The attack confirms Model I beliefs about the importance of withholding information ("Now look what I've started") and reinforces the intent to avoid conflict now or in the future.

Initially, we described the importance of identifying a problem as a stimulus for reflective practice and learning. We talked about the importance of identifying discrepancies as a means to growth. On a cognitive level, that language is easy to accept. As we engage in dialogue, however, we develop an emotional understanding of those words; we *feel* the tension. As the cognitive and emotional experiences are linked in dialogue, we begin to understand why reflective practice is difficult. When we engage in reflective practice, when we turn a critical eye on our practice, we engage fully as thinking and feeling people. It is only then that we understand that contrasting intentions and actions can be upsetting. And here again, we begin to feel what was described previously in cool language: Our behaviors are often so habituated that we are literally unaware of either the reasons or the unintended effects of our actions.

Only as we engage in dialogue do we realize that reflective practice involves and requires conflict. By conflict, we refer not to hostile attitudes but to an interaction between individuals, addressing differences in opinions or beliefs. Reflective practice is a process designed to uncover these underlying differences, and, because organizational and interpersonal norms seek to minimize conflict, direct confrontations are uncomfortable.

To extend dialogue and to move toward deeper understanding, the facilitator and group members must be prepared to respond to predictable defensive reactions. When conflict emerges, the facilitator and group members must be prepared to accept, understand, and cope with emotional reactions—their own or their colleagues'.

Empathic Listening

Listening involves hearing words, thoughts, and feelings. Initially, a person who receives critical information is likely to feel inadequate or hurt. If a dog is hurt, almost everyone knows that the animal might bite if you try to approach. When we encounter an angry adult, however, we seldom consider that anger may represent personal pain, and we take it personally. We make assumptions about the behavior and seldom frame this anger as an effort—however unsuccessful—to reflect or deal with a personal problem.

The appropriate response is listening. By depersonalizing the response and recognizing the legitimacy of the person's reaction, the intense emotions are rapidly diffused, once again setting the stage for continued dialogue. This accepting response is an important step in establishing trust. Emotions are okay.

Self-Disclosure

Several studies (Blase & Kirby, 1992, 2000; Sagor, 1991) found that principals able to create a culture of professional learning shared a number of characteristics. Foremost among these was not knowing it all. These principals were willing to admit they didn't have all the answers and to ask for help in understanding problems and developing solutions. By admitting to their own fallibility, they generated a sense of openness among their subordinates. The principals made it possible for teachers and staff to discuss problems and created an atmosphere where people were able and willing to pool ideas and resources. They created environments where reflective practice was the norm; they created cultures of reflective practice.

Self-disclosure—the deliberate communication of information about oneself to others—is an important way to establish and maintain trust (Beebe & Masterson, 1994). If the facilitator is willing to engage in reflective analysis of his or her own ideas and to share his or her own imperfect processes, trust is more likely to develop (Belenky et al., 1986). Seeing behaviors modeled by others is also critically important in encouraging reflective practice among others (Brookfield, 1995). Recognizing the importance of the organizational context, it is unlikely that teachers will engage in reflective practice unless administrators do the same. Similarly, reflective practice in a classroom setting—whether with student teachers or prospective administrators—is unlikely unless the instructor sets an example through critical self-examination. Brookfield (1995), for example, described the "need to constantly say out loud what we're thinking . . . to explain our actions laying bare our pedagogic reasoning" (pp. 92, 108). This "continuous full disclosure by teachers of their expectations, guiding agendas, and evaluative criteria," he explained, "is an important sign of authenticity" (p. 109). At the same time, it's important to remember that, in a Model I world, these attempts at openness and flexibility may be interpreted by some as weakness. Your ability to persist in your efforts to align your actions with your beliefs and intentions may depend on the strength of those values and your level of commitment. Effective advocacy, then, requires a combination of descriptive messages and reflective listening. (See Figure 4.6.)

Figure 4.6 Advocacy Strategies

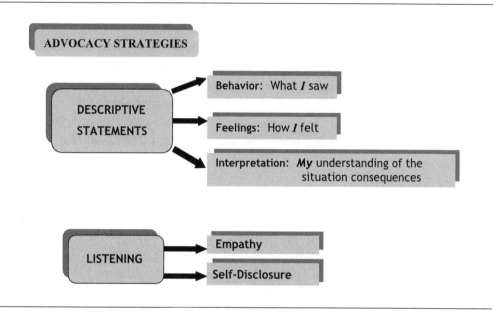

Communication in a Small Group

It is important to remember that reflective practice often takes place in a group context. While the skills described previously are important for facilitating interpersonal communication whether one-to-one or in a small group, the facilitator needs additional skills to work effectively with a small group.[8] One reason for describing reflective practice as a collaborative activity is the belief that professionals can learn more by sharing with others. The facilitator's role is not to provide content expertise but to create an environment that supports cooperative learning. To the extent that other professionals contribute their knowledge and experience, the process will be richer. Consequently, the facilitator must be skilled at developing an environment where participants feel comfortable enough to contribute actively (safety) and an environment in which they have opportunity to participate (equity). Furthermore, the facilitator must attend to the task and socioemotional needs of the group members, addressing personal feelings and ensuring that the group experiences a sense of accomplishment.

This is not an easy task. As Argyris et al. (1985) explained, the process is not necessarily an equitable one at the outset. The facilitator, by virtue of knowledge and experience, may have greater facility in detecting theories-in-use that characteristically shape practice and may assume responsibility for guiding participants as they develop their own under-standing. Information also plays an important part in reflective practice and the facilitator may bring skills in observation and analysis to assist the group and also support the search for relevant information drawn from research as well as experience.

The goal of reflective practice is improvement; therefore, discovering areas of weakness is an essential aspect of the process, but these discoveries can trigger distress and anxiety and generate hostility toward the facilitator. As later examples show, however, this is not always the case. Use of the communication strategies described previously, as well as an emphasis on equity, is important to ensure group productivity and satisfaction.

SUMMARY

In sum, one of the most important elements in the reflective practice environment is trust. Without authorization and support from organizational superiors (the buffer), it is unlikely that reflective practice will take place, let alone flourish. Once organizational permission is secured, the role of the facilitator is vitally important in creating an environment conducive to reflection. In keeping with the experiential model of learning, which was described in Chapter 2, the successful facilitator is distinguished by an ability to engage individuals in a challenging learning process. Emphasizing professional development beliefs and communication skills, an advertisement for a facilitator might look like the one in Figure 4.7.

Figure 4.7   Position Announcement: Facilitator

Position Available: Facilitator for Reflective Practice

A person who has great confidence in others' desire for and capability for learning and trusts them to assume responsibility for their own learning, the facilitator will be sensitive to the needs and feelings of others and, at the same time, be able to anticipate and provide information and resources to support learning. The facilitator will be inherently curious; someone who doesn't have all the answers and isn't afraid to admit it; someone who is confident enough in his or her ability to be able to accept challenges in a nondefensive manner, secure enough to make his or her own thinking public and therefore subject to discussion, and a good listener. Experience desirable but not as important as the ability to learn from mistakes.

NOTES

1. For a detailed discussion of the importance of emotions in school settings and their effects on the quality of relationships among teachers, administrators, students, and parents; their performance in the workplace; and their emotional health see work by Beatty (2000), Hargreaves (2001), Hargreaves et al. (in press), and Osterman (2000).

2. A recent study by Fishbein (2000), for example, described how these norms of silence are conveyed to administrative interns by administrators and teachers and the negative effect they have on the quality of relationships between these two groups.

3. It is important to remember, however, that the principal plays a critical role in determining whether an innovation is adopted and thrives in the school setting (Murphy & Datnow, 2003a, 2003b).

4. Texts by Sullivan and Glanz (2000) and Glanz and Sullivan (2000) attempt to bridge this gap between theory and practice and use reflective practice as a means to develop the communication skills necessary for supportive supervision.

5. There are many important works that examine the role of community in schools. For additional information, see Fullan (1999, 2001), Furman (2002), Hargreaves (2002), Lieberman (1988), Louis et al. (1995), McLaughlin and Talbert (2001), and Wehlage, Rutter, Smith, Lesko, and Fernandez (1989).

6. For some excellent samples of inquiry and advocacy statements, see the section "Productive Conversation" in Senge et al. (2000).

7. One technique for examining these unspoken thoughts is the left-hand column technique, described in Chapter 3.

8. There are numerous guides to facilitating dialogue in small groups. One of our favorites is the classic *How to Make Meetings Work* by Doyle and Straus (1982). A more recent text by David Straus, *How to Make Collaboration Work* (2002), focused exclusively on group facilitation. Senge et al. (1994) offered several suggestions suitable for any setting, and Brookfield and Preskill (1999) devoted an entire book to the tools and techniques for stimulating discussion in teaching.

The Problematic Student

In this chapter, we describe a classroom-based strategy for engaging educators in reflective practice. In these examples, the reflective practitioners are teachers enrolled in a university-based administrator preparation program. The introduction to reflective practice is a field-based project in problem framing and analysis with a focus on the problematic student, the child who is a persistent thorn in the teacher's side.

This chapter is important for several reasons. The problem itself is significant. There are few teachers who haven't experienced the persistent behavioral problem. Having a difficult student in the classroom can have serious effects on teacher morale and performance. Teaching is a demanding and often difficult profession. Until recently, financial compensation was universally poor, and working conditions, for many, are still less than desirable. Even under the best of circumstances, the primary reward that teachers seek is their sense of accomplishment. As Lortie (1975) discerned and as Cohn and Kottkamp (1993) reaffirmed nearly twenty years later, "Knowing that I have 'reached' students and they have learned" (Lortie, 1975, p. 105) is the essence of this psychic satisfaction. Problematic students undermine this sense of accomplishment: They wreck the good days; they steal psychic rewards. Unfortunately, this problem may be increasing with evaluation systems that narrowly judge teacher merit on the basis of test score results.

The students in these stories are troublesome from the perspective of the teacher; more important, they are also children who fail. They are not engaged in learning; they fail tests, and they fail to learn. Without an effective intervention, the problematic child in kindergarten will be the dropout in high school. Unfortunately, research tells us that intervention is not easy.

Engagement is an important prerequisite to learning. Not all successful students are engaged, but students who are engaged are more successful learners. Teachers play the most important role in student engagement with a contribution that may be more significant than that of family or peers. At the same time, there is also substantial research demonstrating that teachers behave very differently with students, depending on their behavior and performance in the classroom. Problematic students have the greatest need for teachers' attention and support, but, because of their behavior, they are least likely to get it (Osterman, 2000).

The chapter is also important in understanding different dimensions of reflective practice. In this situation, the problem is a presented one and illustrates the potentially important role of the facilitator in bringing an issue to the forefront. These problematic children are often taken for granted. Without outside intervention, the problem might not appear on the teachers' agenda. While this problem has solid roots in theory and research and important consequences for children, schools, and society, it is also one that has deep personal meaning for individual teachers. It is a situation that affects their sense of themselves as teachers, their desire to remain in the profession, and their own ability to remain engaged. As a result, it is one that should be engaging.

These stories also illustrate the ladder of inference, the way professionals develop action theories and corresponding action strategies on the basis of often-inaccurate assumptions. We see very graphically the power of observational data to interrupt this mindless cycle, and we also see how academic resources may be integrated into reflective practice to support learning. This activity is also interesting because even though it does not require the final stages of the cycle, namely reconceptualization and active experimentation, it seems to lead naturally into these stages in a way that is intensely personal and meaningful. This activity is also one easily adapted for use in a school setting.

THE ASSIGNMENT

The assignment consists of three steps. The first is to identify the student and explore perceptions and assumptions. The second is to conduct a careful observation of the student. The final step is to analyze the information and describe the learning.

Step 1: Identify a Problematic Student

Think of a student who is problematic to you, that is, one whose current behavior presents a gap with some image of how you would like this person to behave in the role of student. Before doing any observation—and don't cheat on this—write down a description of the problematic behavior, as you perceive it. Also indicate how you would prefer the student to be.

To engage the learner, it's necessary to personalize the problem. The first step of the assignment, then, very simply asks the teacher to identify a student who is problematic, that is, a student whose performance is not consistent with the teacher's notion of appropriate. This definition is purposely vague to accommodate different conceptions and to permit teachers to begin to define the problem for themselves. The teachers prepare a written statement outlining their perception of the students' behavior as well as a description of the way that the teacher would like the student to act, the preferred behavior. These descriptions establish a contrast between the current situation or the outcome and the teacher's preferred situation or the goal. They also usually include information revealing the educator's assumptions about the student and students in general.

Step 2: Observe

Observe carefully the student's actual behavior in as many settings for as much time as you can arrange. Aside from the classroom, good places to observe include the playground and the lunchroom. Extracurricular activities offer another opportunity to observe behavior. For classroom observations, you may gather information about the student in your own class, but it is better to observe in someone else's classroom. It is also informative to observe in classroom settings that differ from your own, in method or subject area. Record as accurately as you are able the actual behaviors you observe. These should be as close to facts as you can get. Facts are those descriptions that a group of reasonable and carefully observant individuals could agree on.

Recognizing the selectivity of our perceptions, this aspect of the assignment pushes the observer to take a new look at the situation, gathering more complete information about the student. While reflective practitioners can gather information through various means, this assignment uses only direct observation. Under normal conditions, the teacher's attention may be drawn in a hundred different directions, but here the telephoto lens focuses exclusively on a single child, not just for the moment when the child attracts attention but throughout the day and under different conditions. In preparing the write-up, the participants are reminded to rely solely on descriptive language, simply writing what they observed or heard while excluding interpretation or judgment.

Step 3: Analyze

Describe the learning that you came to about the student, yourself, and your mental models. Look for discrepancy between what you knew about the student and what you saw. Wrestle with what this tells you about yourself, especially your mental models. (If you want to be really reflective, go back to your platform statement and take a look at what you intend to do.) Indicate any other learning you came to in the process of moving toward enhanced personal leadership and ability to model new ways of thinking and doing that lead toward improving education for kids.

In Steps 1 and 2, the educators gathered information. They described the situation, exploring their perceptions about the current situation as well as their goals, and they gathered additional information through direct observation. With this information in hand, they begin their analysis. They compare their perceptions of the situation with the information they gathered in Step 2. They contrast prior perceptions of student behavior with the observational data and assess their prior assumptions. Typically, the observation data introduce very new information about the student and challenge prior assumptions. Before the teachers thought that they knew these students; they're no longer so sure. They also look very carefully at the assumptions they made about the students in light of this new information, and they begin to see their mental models. The theories-in-use become very evident.

As part of their coursework, these teachers have read Senge's (1990) *The Fifth Discipline* and have an understanding of mental models. When they compare their initial descriptions with descriptive behavioral data stripped of inference and judgment, they begin to see the mental models that have been shaping their action. They are also introduced to the ladder of inference. Through their analysis, they can see the practical implications of this conceptual framework in their own behavior. They see how observations of behavior are selective and quickly become overlaid with inferences. On the basis of what we see (or don't see), we make assumptions about what is happening and why, and we take action on the basis of these assumptions. These assumptions and related strategies then perpetuate a self-fulfilling prophecy, and our sense of reality is based on assumptions rather than actual events. Our assumptions determine what we see, and, over time, we only see what we assume.

THE PROBLEMATIC STUDENT

The following example of experience with this assignment comes from Wafa, a third-grade teacher.

Problem Identification

My most problematic child is a handsome eight-year-old, Daryl. I have known Daryl for three years. His kindergarten teacher described him as the most obnoxious child she had ever met. She often complained to me about his behavior, explaining how he always pushed and shoved other children for no apparent reason, often disrupted class by calling out, deliberately fell out of his chair, and stole items from other children. His first- and second-grade teachers made similar complaints.

Before Daryl became my third-grade student, I several times caught him running and screaming down the hall and asked him nicely to walk quietly in the halls. He insisted he was walking quietly, and several times our confrontation led to him serving detention for talking back to me. Other times, I saw him fighting with other children. Each time I confronted him, he denied wrongdoing and at times used inappropriate language with me, leading to more detention. He had a poor reputation, and I cringed when I saw him on my roster.

I hoped he would mature into a respectful, well-mannered, responsible, obedient, and cooperative young man over the summer. I was disappointed when he returned to school the "same old Daryl" in September. For the past month, Daryl has served detention for incomplete homework, fighting, calling out in class, and acting disruptively in music, art, and other classes.

Wafa's description of Daryl portrays him as a child who offers a sharp contrast with her ideal student. While she envisions a child who is "respectful, well-mannered, responsible, obedient, and cooperative," she perceives Daryl as disrespectful, ill-mannered, disobedient, uncooperative, and irresponsible. Although she doesn't provide much detail on her own personal feelings about having to deal with him, she conveys some sense of how she feels when she notes that she "cringed" when she learned he would be in her classroom. It is also apparent from her description that Wafa has accepted the judgment of other teachers about Daryl, and she cites examples from their experience and her own to support their judgment. They have gathered data about Daryl's behavior to confirm their assumptions about him. Repeated references to various forms of punishment also give us information about the action strategies Wafa and her colleagues have used with Daryl. From this information, we infer the theory-in-use: Disruptive children require confrontation and consequences.

The project helped to move Wafa into the next stage of the experiential learning cycle of reflective practice by guiding her to observe very carefully Daryl's behavior and—unlike the record detailed previously—describe it with all her judgment, inference, and attribution about Daryl stripped away. Her own emotional response to what she observed highlights the discrepancy between the first description and the second.

Observation

To make an accurate analysis of his behavior and my own, I observed Daryl in several situations. The first was recess on the playground. He first played on the monkey bars with several children. I heard him telling jokes and could not believe how jovial he was and how he got every-one's attention. Other children seemed to be having a wonderful time listening to him and were totally attentive to him. I was amazed at how agile he was. (Most of the time he seems lethargic and solemn, yet eas-ily irritated, in class. He often gives me "dirty looks" when I reprimand him or don't give in to his demands.)

Later, I observed him shooting hoops with several peers and noticed that the other children were excluding another boy, Andrew. I was completely astounded when Daryl took the ball and gave it to Andrew. He told the others to give him a chance. The children did not argue with him. Daryl also showed Andrew the proper way to shoot a basketball, and when he shot successfully, Daryl said, "I knew you could do it."

The second observation was during physical education class. They were playing soccer, and a boy tripped over Daryl's foot and accused him of doing it on purpose. Without investigating, the teacher told Daryl to sit against the wall and remarked, "I knew you couldn't control yourself for the entire period." She refused to listen when he tried to defend himself. He cried for the rest of the period.

The third observation was in science class. The children were in a lesson weighing objects to determine their mass. While the teacher was explaining the lesson, Daryl was restless and distractible. Several times the teacher told him to pay attention. He insisted he was being attentive. The teacher sternly told him if he talked back she would send him to the principal's office. He gave her the same dirty look he gives me. But once he was involved in the activity of weighing, Daryl was like any other child. He was so focused that he barely noticed me. When he and Andrew were finished, Daryl went to assist classmates who were having difficulty. The teacher yelled at him and told him not to bother others. When he tried to explain he was helping, she continued to yell at him and threatened to call his parents.

I sensed that things were getting ugly and asked the teacher if I could take him out of the room to help me. I think she was relieved to be rid of him for fifteen minutes and agreed with my request. I used the time to speak with Daryl to try to understand him better. He asked me if he was in trouble. I asked him why he thought that, and he said, "Because Mrs. A yelled at me."

The way other teachers treated Daryl literally made me sick because it opened my eyes to the fact that I was treating him similarly. When he was wrongfully accused of tripping a child in gym, I wanted so to intervene on his behalf—but did not—not wanting a confrontation with another teacher. Whenever Daryl confronted another child, I took the other child's word and forbade him the chance to defend himself. He was automatically guilty because of inferences I made long ago. He looked so innocent and helpless on the floor crying that I wanted to hug him and ask him to forgive me for the numerous times he had tried to explain himself, but I would not let him. I ached for him.

As she observes, Wafa sees aspects of Daryl's behavior not apparent to her before and not part of the student profile that teachers shared. While she does see Daryl's misbehavior in the classroom, she also sees very positive aspects of his behavior. Where before the only observations of Daryl dealt with his misbehavior, there is now evidence that Daryl has good interpersonal skills and qualities and, in certain situations, functions quite well in the classroom. Where prior observations recorded Daryl's attitudes and reactions toward teachers, in this observation, Wafa also sees how teachers, including herself, react to Daryl and how those actions affect him. She begins to see another side of the picture; she begins to see Daryl's perspective and develops empathy.

In the next section of the assignment, Wafa analyzes the data and describes her own learning about Daryl and herself; she also reports how this learning affects her action strategies. She learns new things about Daryl that undermine her previous assumptions, and we see that she is already adopting new action strategies as she begins to interact with him in a different way.

Analysis

I learned that he is very sensitive, intelligent, humorous, lonely, and sad. He is starved for attention. I had recognized that he sought more attention than the average child, but I discovered some of the reasons why. He told me that when he goes home he has a baby-sitter until nine o'clock at night. Since she does not speak English, he completes his homework on his own and watches TV alone. She reads books in Spanish but doesn't converse with him. He misses his Mom and Dad but only spends time with them on weekends. (Throughout our conversation, I used the reflective listening skills I learned in Karen Osterman's class to understand better what he was telling me.) I asked whether he had expressed his feelings to his parents. He has tried, but they will not listen. She is a cheap baby-sitter, and they cannot afford more.

The next day, I spent more time speaking with and listening to Daryl. I discovered that he is extremely intelligent. . . . We discovered that we share a common love for all types of music.

Watching Daryl with Andrew on the basketball court and in science made me realize that he is very sensitive and compassionate toward others. He recognized Andrew's struggles and enjoyed helping him. I realized that Daryl had leadership qualities I did not see. Other students allowed him to take full control during shooting practice and complied with him when he told them to give Andrew a chance. I used to think Daryl bullied others into giving in to his demands, but he is not a bully at all. Other children are not afraid of him; they genuinely like and respect him. The more I learned about him, the more I liked him.

Realizing I had been unfair to Daryl, I felt angry with myself because I consider myself a good teacher. I usually know my students better than many teachers because I take the time to learn about them. But I did not give Daryl a chance. I have mental models I did not think I had. I made inferences about Daryl based on past confrontations and other teachers' descriptions and conclusions. I "jumped" on him every time I thought he was doing something wrong. I was afraid that if I were not very tough on him from the beginning, I would lose control over him. I was afraid the other children would follow his lead, that he would become the authority in the class. I am more insecure than I thought.

I climbed the ladder of inference in relation to Daryl. I had convinced myself that my inferences about him were obvious and true (after all, previous teachers all felt the same way I did about him). I am guilty of jumping to conclusions. Like the science teacher, I accused Daryl of bothering other students when, in fact, he was trying to assist them.

Reconceptualization and Experimentation

This assignment did not require a separate discussion of reconceptualization or experimentation; nonetheless, as the following sections show, new action theories and new action strategies emerged very naturally as part of the critical analysis of the new data.

I also learned from Senge (1990) that I cannot be a linear thinker; I have to look at Daryl as a whole person. Knowing him better, I see him more holistically. I recognize his good qualities and his weaknesses; previously, I concentrated on his faults. I kept trying to change his negative behavior in the way I wanted him to behave, as opposed to understanding why he behaves as he does. To close the gap between what I saw and what I want, I have to give up some of my idealistic expectations of Daryl (i.e., being a "perfect student") and allow him to be himself. I have to accept him the way he is and not try to change him into who I want him to be. I wanted him to be a robot complying with my every command (Frederick Taylor's philosophy). I did not want him asking any questions because I felt his questions had an ulterior motive to them. I realize I am more of a controller than I previously cared to acknowledge. I wanted total control of the class, Daryl included. That was surprising because I often include student input in many classroom decisions.

I feel somewhat disappointed in myself as a teacher. When I read Martin Haberman's Star Teachers of Children in Poverty, I felt proud to consider myself a "star" teacher. In the past, I was successful with empowering students by developing mutual rapport, being open and honest, and making learning meaningful to them. But with Daryl, I made a prejudgment. I was almost afraid of him—not in the physical sense—but afraid of him challenging me and winning. This subconscious fear prevented me from seeing him as a lonely, confused child who needs me to understand him. It prevented me from seeing his true potential and tapping into his multiple intelligences. I always felt one of my strengths was building up a student's self-esteem, but with Daryl I achieved the opposite.

With my eyes open to the real Daryl, I recognize I contributed to his misbehavior. He probably acted out because I expected him to. Rather than taking a proactive stance (Senge, 1990, again) to his behavior, I reacted to it. I acted under the notion that by aggressively reacting to his behavior, I could control him. What I learned is that the more I reacted to his behavior, the more he misbehaved. It became a continuous power struggle between us.

Daryl and I have now established an open line of communication. I have gained his trust and have allowed him to see me as more than just his teacher. We have gotten to know each other better and have built up a relationship that will, hopefully, be long lasting. I no longer react to his misbehavior; therefore, he is misbehaving less often. We have successfully broken the control cycle between us.

I realized that I tend to be less gentle with students like Daryl because of my assumptions about them and my own insecurities. I feel a sense of relief in discovering my own weaknesses because I can now strengthen them. I feel relieved in becoming more conscious of my mental models and in not making inferences about people. I am confident I will be able to overcome these weaknesses because I have already changed how I interact with Daryl. I have a better time in class since making these changes, and Daryl tells me he enjoys school more now.

I actually look forward to seeing him, whereas before I dreaded dealing with him. He knows that if something is bothering him, he can talk to me about it.

Although facing the truth about ourselves is a very difficult thing to do, I truly believe that this project has opened my eyes; it has been a mirror into my soul.

Although Wafa doesn't use our specific terms to explain reflective practice, these concepts are embedded in her reflective analysis. Using these labels, we can see that she discovers the incongruity between her espoused theory and her actions. She perceived herself as a fair and kind teacher who "knows [her] students better than many teachers." Where she prided herself on "taking the time to learn about them," she now realizes that she "did not give Daryl a chance." While she thought of herself as a teacher who "empowered students by developing mutual rapport, being open and honest, and making learning meaningful to them," she recognizes that she did not use these strategies with Daryl. She espoused openness, building up students' beliefs in themselves, empowerment, and real personal understanding of individual students but finds that her mental models, at least with Daryl, resulted in prejudgment, refusal to listen, physical and psychic isolation, fear, and, at the bottom of it all, control.

As her thinking expands, she generalizes and concludes that her "less gentle" strategies extended not only to Daryl but also to students like Daryl. Now, however, she understands that her actions were influenced by a theory-in-use that had not been apparent to her and begins to recognize the Model I assumptions affecting her behavior. She realizes she felt she "needed to be tough with him or else [she] would lose control—over him and over the class." She thought "by aggressively reacting to his behavior, [she] could control him." This theory-in-use influenced her action strategy: Being tough meant "jumping" on him for everything he did wrong.

When she considers the relationship between her actions and Daryl's behavior and contrasts these outcomes with her goals, she realizes her action strategy didn't work. She wanted students who were "respectful, well-mannered, responsible, obedient and cooperative," but she learns she was personally responsible for her inability to achieve her goals: "the more I reacted to his behavior, the more he misbehaved." Actions have consequences, and they may be "intended or unintended, productive or counterproductive" (Argyris et al., 1985, p. 85). As Wafa discovers through the reflective process, her efforts to bring Daryl under control created "a continuous power struggle," a consequence both unintended and counterproductive.

She identifies her theory-in-use and finds it flawed. She also finds errors in her assumptions about Daryl. Where she once perceived him solely as an antagonist, she now realizes that he is a child with difficulties and gifts in need of nurture and support. With this new understanding, she begins to rethink her practice. While she does not explicitly refer to reconceptualization, her changing perspective is apparent in her narrative and becomes more visible as she begins to align her actions more closely with her espoused theory.

In this final stage, experimentation, she tries to work with Daryl in a different way, building a relationship with him and eschewing her former critical and punitive stance. Instead of assuming she knows all about him and making attributions about his intent based on others' reports, she now observes and engages in direct conversation with Daryl to establish valid understanding. She begins to listen. She substitutes a demand for perfection with more realistic expectations, based on more complete and accurate information about Daryl's needs and talents. Rather than withdrawing from him and isolating him in the classroom, emotionally and physically, she draws closer to him and establishes a caring relationship. In short, Wafa reconceptualizes her role.

As she experiments with this strategy and begins to see its positive effects in Daryl's behavior, her espoused theory will gradually supplant the existing theory-in-use. The ultimate test of this, however, is her ability to integrate this way of thinking and acting as she works with other students like Daryl.

THE LADDER OF INFERENCE

In her report, Wafa refers to the ladder of inference. As students work on the Problematic Person Project, we provide information on this analytic framework developed by Argyris (1982) and find it of great value in helping educators become aware of their mental models and theories-in-use. The ladder of inference illustrates how we use observations to make meaning of our experience and how that meaning shapes our action strategies. Typically, we draw on prior experience and leap from observation to conclusion without examining or disclosing our assumptions. Through reflection, we try to develop a conscious awareness of each step of the process. In Figure 5.1, we illustrate how Wafa used observation and analysis to develop a detailed profile of her own ladder of inference with respect to Daryl. We begin at the first rung on the ladder, with observable data, and climb up, step-by-step, to taking action.

When Wafa began the Problematic Person Project, she had a three-year history with Daryl. During this time, she developed an understanding of him based on other teachers' reports as well as her own direct experiences. Here we see that her observations were already shaped by assumptions she had developed before Daryl entered her class. Because these assumptions remained unexamined and untested, she saw the Daryl she expected to see and no more. Articulating these assumptions, observing the connection with her intentions and actions, and then testing this thinking in the light of new observational data motivated rethinking and change in her teaching practice. As Argyris (1993) explained, "learning occurs whenever errors are detected and corrected" (p. 49).

Figure 5.1 Wafa's Experience With the Ladder of Inference

Rung 7: I Take **ACTIONS** Based on My Beliefs
I yell at Daryl, glare, give him detention, or send him to the principal's office.

Rung 6: I Adopt **BELIEFS** About the World
Daryl and others like him must be stopped. I must exercise total control over those who disrupt the learning of others and threaten to wrestle control of the class from me.

Rung 5: I Draw **CONCLUSIONS**
Daryl is always disrupting: he threatens my control of the class.

Rung 4: I Make **ASSUMPTIONS** Based on the Meaning I Added
Whenever Daryl is out of his seat and interacting with others, he is disrupting them and causing trouble.

Rung 3: I Add **MEANINGS** (his reputation and my experience)
Daryl must be bothering the students and distracting them from engaging in the lesson.

Rung 2: I Select **"DATA"** From What I Observe
The two students are looking at Daryl rather than the materials for the lesson.

Rung 1: I **EXPERIENCE** a Situation
During a lesson done in pairs, Daryl is out of his seat, away from his partner, and interacting with another pair of students experiencing difficulty with the lesson.

DOUBLE-LOOP LEARNING AND THE PROBLEMATIC STUDENT

Wafa's experience also provides a good illustration of double-loop learning. Before encountering the Problematic Person Project, as Daryl's classroom teacher, Wafa struggled to figure out how to handle him. When Daryl behaved in unacceptable ways, she tried different strategies. None of these efforts worked for long. Confronted with students like Daryl, teachers have little choice but to try to find some way of minimizing disruption and maintaining order. To achieve that goal, there are a number of options. In a small study, Osterman and Pace (1999) presented student teachers with a scenario describing Albert, a typical problematic student, not unlike

Daryl. An analysis of responses found that the majority recommended behavior modification or removal from the classroom, often to a special education setting. Their immediate goal was either to gain compliance or to remove the problem. While these solutions may provide temporary relief, they fail to address "the more basic problem of why these problems existed in the first place" (Argyris, 1990, p. 92). This symptomatic approach to problem solving constitutes single-loop learning.

In this case, Wafa engaged in double-loop learning. As we explained in Chapter 1, double-loop learning explores the underlying reasons for problems, including our own values, beliefs, and actions. Through her involvement in this project, Wafa arrived at a total reframing of the problem and in so doing answered the fundamental *why* underlying her difficulty with Daryl. She shifted the problem focus from his behavior to her behavior and her underlying theory-in-use. She discovered her own desire for control and realized that she had interpreted many of Daryl's actions as threats to her. Through the full experiential learning cycle of reflective practice, Wafa raised to conscious awareness her tacitly held theory-in-use. From this reframing of the problem, she realized that it was she, not Daryl, who kept the cycle of conflict in play between them. To break the cycle she would have to act differently toward Daryl. Accordingly, she reaffirmed her espoused commitment to empowerment, and she began to shift responsibility to Daryl, giving up her efforts to control him. She believed that students had the capacity and the motivation to be reasonable partners in their learning, and she now enacted these beliefs in her interaction with Daryl. With the assistance of a reflective practice process, Wafa engaged in double-loop learning, and it made the world of difference for Daryl and for her. She identified the dominant theory-in-use and the related action strategies. She saw the negative consequences of these teaching behaviors, and with this new reconceptualization she began to align her actions more closely to her espoused theory.

Double-loop learning is not properly applied to every problem. In fact, Argyris and Schon (1974) cautioned that "single-loop learning enables us to avoid continuing investment in the highly predictable activities that make up the bulk of our lives" (p. 19). What distinguishes one problem from another and determines the need for deeper analysis is its pervasiveness and significance. With these criteria in mind, we would argue that the problematic student is one area of educational practice demanding deep attention and double-loop learning.

Wafa's story is merely one of hundreds of examples we have gathered over the years. While the names and ages differ, problematic students have remarkably similar profiles, and teachers respond to their behavior in very predictable ways. Like Wafa, teachers make similar assumptions, adopt the same unsuccessful strategies, and thereby perpetuate a prophetic and counterproductive cycle that further alienates the child from the teacher, the classroom, and learning. A formal analysis of thirty-eight of these written cases prepared by students in our administrative preparation program confirmed these patterns (Kottkamp & Silverberg, 1999a, 1999c) as did a later study by Silverberg (2002).

The problematic students described in these cases were predominantly male (81%), 21% were minorities, and 29% had limited English proficiency or special education classifications. The behaviors that warranted the problematic designation were quite common. The students were disengaged. They were the daydreamers who spent their time gazing out the window. They were the students who did not stay on task. Unprepared for learning, they failed to do their homework, complete assignments, or bring necessary materials. They were the clowns, the students who laugh out loud and interrupt the class with wise guy comments. They resisted authority by defying or ignoring rules. They lacked social skills and bothered others by invading their space, physically or verbally. They were verbally abusive or whiny, belligerent or apathetic. Regardless of their style, they were all annoying. They distracted other students and interfered with teachers' ability to teach.

Like the student teachers described by Osterman and Pace (1999), the majority of the often very experienced teachers completing the Problematic Student Project attributed these behaviors to emotional, social, or physiological deficits in the students or their families. These students, their teachers thought, didn't care about learning. They were intentionally disruptive, manipulative, devious, calculating, malevolent, antisocial, lazy, or sneaky. One seven-year-old was described as a con artist. Students were also criticized for trying to get too much attention, for selective hearing, or for trying to prove their manhood.

These profiles once again provided a sharp contrast with their preferred students. Invariably, the ideal student was actively engaged in learning, responsible for his or her own learning, and self-reliant. This was not a child who needed or demanded attention. Preferred students had well-developed social skills and were willing and able to conform to the rules and work cooperatively and positively with others. While the majority of the respondents expressed their ideal in terms of active engagement, others would settle for compliance: They wanted the child to stop the disruption.

In response to these behaviors, a substantial majority of the teachers relied on isolation. They physically removed the child from the room or distanced the student from classmates: Desks were moved, or children stood against the wall, were sent to detention or the principal's office, or suspended. Teachers also reported psychological isolation. They dismissed or ignored students and avoided interacting with them. As one reported, "It's the way I cope with them. Rather than let them bother me, I'll dismiss them as having some personality flaw and try to totally ignore them . . . try not to get too . . . worked up and avoid the person as much as possible." Another reported her problematic student doesn't bother the other students, so she "just lets him be." Judith permitted Jon to sleep in her class so that she could teach those students who were "willing" to learn: "I used to call on him a lot to jostle him, but now I do not make any effort to get him involved during group lesson time. I am quite relieved not to have his disruptions." Graphic descriptions of children who are literally ignored for the greater part of the school day, despite their obvious noninvolvement in the process of learning, are prolific.

The data we present here are consistent with other research. Engagement is an extremely important phenomenon directly influencing teachers' perceptions of students and affecting the nature of their interaction with them. Engaged students receive more positive attention. Disengaged students receive less support from teachers and are frequently subject to more constraint as teachers try to control their behaviors. This pattern of interaction has serious consequences because teacher support is one of the most important predictors of student engagement (Connell, Halpern-Felsher, Clifford, Crichlow, & Usinger, 1995; Connell & Wellborn, 1991; Osterman, 2000, 2002). When teachers withdraw support from students and restrict their autonomy in the classroom through restrictive and punitive strategies, this further reduces the students' sense of self and reinforces the problematic behaviors. Stated more simply, "the 'rich get richer'" and "support is withdrawn from those who need it most" (Connell et al., 1995, p. 59). By virtue of their behaviors, these problematic students, frequently male from low-income disadvantaged families, become at risk and are more likely to drop out from school before completion (Connell et al., 1995).

This contrast between empirical research and action strategies adopted as accepted teacher practice highlights the significance of the theory-in-use. The consistent descriptions of problematic students, the attribution of blame to the student, and the reliance on these counterproductive strategies suggest that these patterns are embedded in teachers' socialization. Wafa learned about Daryl's behavior from his previous teachers:

> I remember Daryl's kindergarten teacher describing him as the most obnoxious child she had ever met. . . . He always pushed and shoved other kids for no apparent reason; he often disrupted the class by calling out and deliberately falling out of his chair. . . . His first and second grade teachers had the same complaints.

Many, if not all, of the other cases also mentioned reputational reports sent from one teacher to another as troublesome students moved to their next class assignment. These reports, starting from the child's earliest days in the school system, follow the child and shape teachers' assumptions, perceptions, and interactions. When the teachers see the "bad" behaviors they learned to expect, their beliefs about the incorrigibility of the child are affirmed.

These reputational tales and the assumptions about the children were accepted as valid, never challenged or tested. There were no instances where, prior to the reflective exercise, teachers actually approached the student to gather information. They approached the student to moralize, persuade, and scold but not to listen. Teachers not only shared their perception of these children (usually judgmental), but they also shared their craft knowledge. While the research may suggest more effective ways to address these behaviors, teachers learn from one another the best way to deal with the problem, often in their first few days as new teachers. Unfortunately, these strategies involving isolation, coercion through punishment or reward, or constraint further alienate the child from the learning situation and create more problems (Glasser, 1997; Osterman, 2000; Ryan & Powelson, 1991). Unfortunately, these interpretations and responses are the norm.

An examination of teachers' strategies permits us to infer the theory-in-use, and again we see evidence of Model I assumptions. Consistent with other research, classroom management is a key issue for teachers, particularly so for new entrants to the field, with legitimate reason. From a pragmatic stance, the teacher's ability to keep the class in order influences evaluations and tenure decisions. At a deeper level, however, our society's conception of teaching prescribes a didactic and autocratic role for the teacher. The teacher is the expert; the teacher is responsible for directing how and when learning will take place. The role of the student is to follow directions. Further, schools are organized around the expectation that children learn in a lockstep, age appropriate manner (Berliner & Biddle, 1995). These regularities in the organizational structure—the age-graded classroom, the standardized curriculum, and the now omnipresent testing system—permit little variation, and this structure reinforces teachers' need to maintain control. To a certain extent, the system expects it, and teachers have come to expect it of themselves. Achieving this sense of control contributes to their sense of satisfaction: "I like the feeling that my class is '*controlled*,' when they are all working at the same pace, and everything is going smoothly."

In these project reports, we see what research asserts, but we also see that through reflection, teachers were now able to see how their need for control determined their actions:

All my experiences/mental learning models (elementary school, my student teaching experience, my college roommate, and personal thoughts—which have unfortunately turned into anxiety and panic attacks) are about *control.* All of these people and ideas have fostered my own personal thought of "being in total control." I think subconsciously these ideas have created mental models of (regardless of the situation) "I must be in control."

They also developed an understanding of how their assumptions about their students shaped their behavior. Amanda, a fifth-grade teacher, reported the following:

My ladder of inference began with observing Danny glancing around the room during the lesson. After the lesson, Danny would talk with a student rather than completing his class work. I selected data and added meaning: Danny isn't really focused or engaged, and he really isn't trying. Next, I drew the conclusion that Danny doesn't care about learning. Finally, I took action based on my belief, which was that other students would benefit from my assistance, and that Danny doesn't need as much of my attention as his classmates.

With this new understanding of their own patterns of thought and action and with new information about the problematic students, they began to think and act in different ways. Sophia illustrates how she, like the other participants, reframed the problem and redefined her role:

It was as if a light bulb went on as I analyzed the behaviors I observed and compared them to my mental models of children who have been classified ADHD. . . . I found myself becoming quite fond of Matt. . . . Given the chance, he has an interesting sense of humor, which others can appreciate. . . . Initially, I think I allowed myself to see Matt's disability as my problem because of how it affected my class. . . . In reality, the problem was always Matt's, not mine, and I realized I was there to help him find a way to deal with the repercussions they had on his life.

Amanda describes how this new understanding translated into a new action theory and strategy:

I need to give Danny more recognition when he participates in class discussions, as well as to provide opportunities for his involvement. . . . I am now aware of the need to provide Danny with assistance when he has difficulty completing assignments. This new awareness may also require inquiry to determine why Danny is not completing an assignment or working independently.

While not all of the students who completed the project completed the entire cycle of reflective practice, many (68%) described strategies they intended to use, and 42% actually changed their practice. Those who did were pleasantly surprised at the changes they observed. Sophia, for example, saw her relationship with Matt change and Matt's relationship with the other children also improved:

Last week, the children were choosing small groups among themselves. . . . Matt sat quietly as this went on, anticipating he would be partnered with me as usual. . . . Then, Alex and Greg walked across the room and stopped at his desk. . . . "Let's work on this, Matt," Alex said. Matt glanced at me and flashed a huge smile!

Through this reflective practice exercise, teachers began to see options where before they saw none. As their understanding of the problem changed and their own role in the problem became clearer, they discarded prior assumptions about the intentionality of these students' behaviors and began to extend care to these students, as they had to other students in their classes. Because they were acting in ways more consistent with their own concepts of good teaching (their espoused theory) and because they could see the positive effects on their students, they began to feel better about themselves as teachers. As Wafa explained earlier, she thought she was a star teacher, but through this activity she became the star teacher she hoped to be. Another participant framed the outcomes in an equally meaningful way: "These interventions are only part of the beginning of a long and continuous process for this student to receive an equal opportunity to learn—without being classified as special ed."

We believe this reference to special education as an option for dealing with the problematic student is an important one. A recent study of 4,151 school districts serving twenty-four million students found, like previous studies, that students classified as learning disabled, particularly those with the greatest stigmas, are disproportionately male, impoverished, or members of minority groups, and some have more than one of these characteristics (Coutinho, Oswald, & Best, 2002). While there are many children for whom a special education classification and placement is highly appropriate and an invaluable service, it is also possible that many placements are the end result of this cycle of interaction between problematic child and teacher. Kottkamp and Silverberg (1999c) suggested that any child perceived as problematic by the teacher is at risk. We also argue that children from these at-risk groups, by virtue of differences in race, culture, or prior learning, are more likely to be defined as problematic by teachers because of their failure to meet social, academic, and behavioral expectations. Whether behavioral problems are the chicken or the egg is moot; nonetheless, the resulting lack of support from the teacher invariably contributes to growing alienation (Osterman, 2000). Without involvement, there can be no learning.

This chapter identified some of the important cognitive, emotional, and social factors perpetuating this destructive pattern of behavior we believe is linked to disproportionate special education referrals, lost opportunities for learning, and emotional distress among children and teachers. More important, it showed that these patterns, these regularities, can be broken. In the next chapter, we continue this theme by describing a school-based action research project designed to support another type of problematic student: the bullying victim. In this case, we see more clearly the effects of teachers' changing practices.

Bullying and Victimization in the Classroom

Drawing on a study of the National Institute of Child Health and Human Development, a recent report noted that more than 3.2 million children in Grades 6 through 10 are victims of bullying each year, while 3.7 million bully others (Fight Crime: Invest in Kids, 2003). The problem is also serious in elementary schools. While incidence varies, a recent study conducted by the Committee for Children reported that 78% of children in Grades 3–8 experienced bullying within the previous month, with approximately 5% to 6% experiencing severe bullying (Walls, 2000).

While commonplace, harassment has serious consequences. Rejection by peers and the accompanying emotional distress undermines children's psychological well-being, the quality of their social relationships, and learning and may contribute to violence toward self and others (Osterman, 2000). In Columbine and other school shootings, approximately 75% of those responsible for violent attacks against peers, teachers, and administrators had experienced harassment, rejection, and other forms of abuse by their peers. While not as regularly or systematically documented by the press, incidents of depression and suicide among children and adolescents continue to increase, with many related to the pain of victimization in schools and classrooms.

While the costs to the victims are blatant, there are also costs for the bullies. Bullying itself is often a response to victimization, and there is growing evidence that bullies also experience emotional distress affecting their behavior and learning. Bullying behaviors tend to persist beyond school, and, as adults, bullies are more likely than their peers to have criminal convictions or abusive relationships. Victims, too, may experience depression into adulthood, well after the harassment has ended.[1]

This chapter presents a case study of an action research project designed to reduce the incidence of bullying and victimization in an elementary school. Like reflective practice, action research is intended to improve practice, and, like reflective practice, it begins with problem identification and continues with systematic data collection, analysis, and experimentation. It is possible to develop more effective procedures without changing the underlying conceptual framework. Nonetheless, in this project, data gathering and subsequent collegial sharing and analysis did, in fact, lead teachers to examine and change their underlying beliefs about another group of problematic students.

The project was relatively short, lasting approximately fourteen weeks from beginning to end, yet was extremely powerful in changing teacher beliefs, practice, and, most important, student behavior. In light of the often minimal success of traditional means of professional development as well as the difficulty of linking professional development to changes in student behavior, this is important information for educators considering whether and how to integrate reflective practice into schoolwide professional development. This case is also of particular interest because it illustrates the importance of organizational and collegial support.

ALLEVIATING BULLYING AND VICTIMIZATION IN THE CLASSROOM

As an elementary school principal and doctoral candidate, Karen Siris was concerned about the problem of bullying and victimization. When the time came for her dissertation, she decided to work with teachers to address the problem in individual classrooms (Siris, 2001).

Problem Identification

Dr. Siris began the project with a workshop on bullying offered to twenty-five teachers in the district. She introduced the session with a video, *The Broken Toy*, produced by the National School Safety Center. Drawing on current research, Dr. Siris then presented an overview, developing a profile of bullying. She defined bullying, reviewed its effects, outlined characteristics of bullies and victims, and identified some of the factors that affect behaviors of victims and bullies.

At the conclusion of the workshop, she invited teachers to participate in an action research project to help alleviate the problem of bullying and victimization in their own classrooms. To participate, each teacher needed to identify one student in his or her classroom who met the description of either a bully or a victim. As it turned out, eight of the nine teachers who volunteered for the project selected children who were victimized by peers; the case study focuses on these students.

At the first meeting, Dr. Siris reviewed some of the information about the problem of bullying and victimization in schools and presented the question to guide their work for the next fourteen weeks: In what ways can teachers change classroom practice to help alleviate bullying and victimization? The format was conversational, and teachers shared concerns about situations in their own classrooms as well as their personal experiences as victims in school. One teacher recalled, for example, that as a kindergarten student, "Nobody wanted to play with me, never had a play date. They would take everything away from me. . . . I was so unhappy that my mother stopped sending me to school."

At this first session, teachers also discussed the stages of action research and its purpose—to enable them to reflect on their work systematically and to make changes based on what they discovered from their shared observations. Some authors view using external, expert information as inconsistent with the notion of reflective practice. Carson (1995), for example, differentiated between reflective practice and technical practice noting that "decisions in technical practice are based upon the authoritative application of validated generalizations" while "decisions in critically reflective practice are the responsibility of the participants" (p. 156). We take a moderate stance. We recognize the importance of individual and self-directed learning; we also recognize the importance of integrating research-based knowledge into the learning process.

In this situation, a theoretical framework guided the action research process. Based on extensive research, Connell and Wellborn (1991) argued that children, as well as adults, have three basic psychological needs: competence, autonomy, and relatedness. To the extent that students experience themselves as able to accomplish tasks, free to exercise some control over their own work, and cared for by other members of the school community, they are more likely to be engaged in learning. Addressing children's psychological needs also affects children's emotional well-being and the quality of their relationship with others. Children whose needs are well satisfied have more positive attitudes toward themselves and school and more positive relationships with adults and peers (Osterman, 2000).

These needs are situation specific. Behavior will differ depending on how well these basic needs are met, and characteristics of the specific situation determine how well those psychological needs are met

(Ryan, 1995). In school, for example, learning situations differ, and a child may be highly motivated in band practice but not in math class.

What does engagement have to do with bullying and victimization? By examining characteristics of bullies and victims, it becomes apparent that both groups are disengaged from the learning process. Their behaviors in the classroom differ—bullies are regularly aggressive, while victims may be aggressive, passive, or withdrawn. However, as a result of these behaviors, both bullies and victims become alienated from teachers and peers. The sense of isolation and rejection that accompanies bullying or victimization is antithetical to the sense of belonging and care children need. In addition, research tells us that bullies engage in bullying as a means to experience control that fails to come to them in normal ways. This study tested the theory that addressing the psychological needs of bullies and victims in the classroom reduces the frequency of inappropriate behaviors and facilitates engagement.

As we explained previously, a problem is a discrepancy between the current and the ideal. In this case, the action research project began with an abstract conceptual understanding of the current situation. During initial discussions, this sense of problem became deeper and more personalized as teachers shared their own experiences as well as their observations, assumptions, and feelings about the current situation in their own classrooms. Describing bullies and victims as disengaged students added another dimension to the problem and also established the ideal: academic and social engagement.

Once the problem is identified, action research and reflective practice both incorporate observation. In this project, the teachers agreed that bullying and victimization was a problem, and they identified students in their classes who fit the criteria. The next step in this project, then, involved systematic observation in the classroom.

The original plan was for each teacher to collect observational data and develop a profile of the selected student. In the second session, teachers would share their findings about the students and begin to analyze their practice. During the first session, however, teachers were eager to talk about their students. In light of their enthusiasm, the facilitator (Dr. Siris) deviated from the intended plan, and teachers shared their perceptions of the students and the problem. This was an important step in the learning process. As they began to talk about their students, it became clear they had defined the problem in very specific ways. They had made assumptions about the students and about the reasons for their behavior and rejection. In doing so, they began to articulate their theories-in-use. Initially, when they discussed the problem of bullying and victimization, they had a theoretical but detached understanding. Now they began to discuss the problem in a very personal way.

The initial subjective descriptions of the selected students were quite negative. Of the eight victims, four were girls and four were boys. All four boys were medicated for attention deficit hyperactivity disorder. Academically they were diverse: Four were bright and academically successful, two were average, and two received support services, but all were perceived as troublemakers. While different in some respects, all were lonely, isolated from their classmates, and sad. The teachers were aware of the students' feelings but, at the same time, felt that these students were responsible for their situation. They had trouble forming relationships, they believed, because they behaved in ways that maintained or deepened the rift between themselves and their peers. The victims were simply not likable. Consistent with research, they were either quiet and withdrawn or aggressive. Some kept to themselves; others would start trouble. According to the teachers, the provocative victims were "mean" and "nasty," "quick to tattle," and irritating. They "smirk" and "egg the others on." They "bring out the worst in [other] children."

Teachers felt the victims had "no social skills for life." They wanted things their own way or no way and got upset easily but failed to recognize their own role in the problem. They were too needy, were constantly demanding, and used inappropriate ways to get attention: "She says mean things . . . she's always bossy, getting into other kids' business." The other children in the classroom did not like these victims, and the teachers felt the same.

The teachers also perceived the victims as physically unattractive and unappealing. Five of the girls and boys were thin and frail. Three were children of immigrants. While some of the victims were meticulously dressed, others went "to school wearing the same clothes four days in a row," with hair unbrushed. One looked "like he rolled out of bed." Another looked "like he just arrived in this country," wearing clothes that were "often too large and shirts that [were] buttoned all the way up to the neck."

Ultimately, the teachers attributed the social problems of these children to the quality of parenting: "It all stems from their mothers." The teachers assumed that the parents were overly aggressive and inappropriate role models. They blamed them for providing too little attention or too much, being overindulgent or overly aggressive: "Her mother's a pushy woman"; his "parents have given him no social skills for life."

It is not uncommon for people to attribute victimization to social deficits. Initially, these teachers shared this view and were not optimistic about the students' ability to change or their own ability to make a difference: "By his age, you know he can't cut it with other kids, and you give up." There was little attention to their own role in the problem, but they generally felt that they were doing a good job in providing opportunities for students to experience competence, autonomy, and relatedness in their practice. Some were interested in understanding ways to implement the theory in their practice; others didn't feel that there was anything more they as teachers could do: "there comes a point when there is just so much you can give somebody." Others challenged the basic theory. They questioned the idea that students needed their attention. They felt that students shouldn't need the teachers' approval or attention, and their goal was to make students less dependent on them and more dependent on their peers. They also sensed that it was inequitable for them to single out a particular child for attention.

They were relatively confident in the quality of their practice. Nevertheless, even at this point, some of the teachers began to make connections. As one commented, "When Michael has a choice, he misbehaves the least. . . . The days the kids have more freedom to make a choice, they behave better." Another remarked on how pleased Dina had seemed when the teacher commended her thoughtfulness during a reading lesson. In theory, the group agreed that students needed opportunities to experience competence and autonomy, but they were more reluctant to accept the ideas about the importance of relatedness, particularly between teacher and student.

This discussion, exploring their beliefs about the situation, provided the groundwork for reflective analysis. They had articulated assumptions about these students and about the classroom situation and now began a more systematic observation of their practice. As it turned out, the data that emerged presented a very different picture and challenged the validity of these assumptions. This contrast clearly facilitated change; as teachers' ideas began to change, so did their practice.

Observation and Analysis

Phase I

During the next three weeks, teachers observed their individual students and recorded those instances when the students appeared to feel a sense of competence, autonomy, or belonging. Specifically, teachers looked for active participation in or successful completion of a task, open expression of feelings or preferences, or positive involvement with teachers or students. For each of these instances, teachers also gathered data about the classroom situation that seemed to promote the experience, such as opportunities for paired or group work, positive affirmation, or task differentiation.

Teachers also watched for specific incidents of bullying or victimization and used these experiences to develop a deeper understanding of the situation from the student perspective. Following these critical incidents, teachers recorded a description of what they had observed and then met with the student, sharing the information and asking about his or her understanding of the situation.

Following three weeks of formal data collection, the teachers gathered to present and discuss their observations. With respect to competency experiences, they had found examples of student success in each of the categories listed on the form: successful completion of task and active participation in either class discussion or group activity. They had also observed how important these experiences were to the children:

We had a very challenging "Math Challenge" today. The students were able to work in pairs to solve the problem. The student who finished first and had a correct answer would get a prize. Several children fought over having Michael as a partner. They wanted him as their partner in this situation since he is so good at math. This made him feel wonderful.

Because of their observations, they were already beginning to change their practice. Carol, for example, talked about the effect of positive feedback:

Today, while trying to make a transition from one activity to another, I pointed out several students who had successfully followed my directions. James, being one of the students, improved his posture immediately after I said it. He also maintained eye contact during instruction and raised his hand to participate. He seemed to feel great about himself.

Before the action research project began, she said, she would not have offered public recognition.

When Dina used appropriate listening skills in the classroom, Gail, her teacher, commended her behavior to the class: "I'll know you are reading when you look like Dina." When the class gave Dina a silent cheer for being a great listener, Gail noticed that Dina beamed.

Before the observations began, teachers thought they had a clear understanding of autonomy and felt they provided students with ample opportunities for choice and free expression of opinion. Yet during the three weeks, collectively, they found only four examples, and one of these took place outside of the classroom. In the classroom, all three examples occurred during center time, when the children had the choice of a learning center. The other instance happened during a trip to the zoo:

> When I saw James, he and another child in the group were smiling, moving from animal to animal in an almost skipping fashion. I heard him say things such as "Cool, look at this." The next day, when I interviewed James about his best day at school, he said it was our trip to the zoo because he got to be with his friends and visit any animals he wished.
>
> – I realize now how much James needs to feel he has some control over what he does.

Finding opportunities for autonomy in the classroom was a challenge, but the teachers struggled even more to find examples of relatedness in their practice. For Michael, the opportunity to read to first graders in their Reading Partners project was a highlight in his school day. "Michael's self-esteem in reading," Janice noted, "is especially low due to his difficulties in reading. However, he enjoys this very much [and] has a great attitude during this time." While this example could easily be categorized as an instance where Michael experienced competence, the teacher coded this as relatedness because of the quality of Michael's relationships with the younger children.

During the observation period, the teachers began to see the importance of these psychological experiences. At the same time, however, they were beginning to see deficits in their practice. With respect to competence, for example, the teachers all agreed that it was very important to include practices in their daily plans to highlight their students' strengths. They realized they were providing these experiences haphazardly and extending fewer opportunities to victims. Gail explained:

> When I took the time to examine my own practices in the classroom, I realized I was not calling on Dina as frequently as I was the other children. I saw that even when she had her hand up to answer a question, I tended to call on a child that I knew would have the right answer.

The teachers also recognized their difficulty in finding opportunities for autonomy in their practice. Kristin commented, "Although we claim to be providing experiences that allow autonomy for our students, we didn't bring many back to today's session." Leslie noted a similar problem with respect to relatedness: "We are struggling to find examples of how we are taking a personal interest in our selected students." Carla noted, "It seems that we think we do more than we really do in our daily practice to meet our students' psychological needs. Hopefully, we will increase experiences in all three areas in the plans we are going to create."

Phase II

Teachers continued to gather information about their students through both observation and interview. To facilitate, Dr. Osterman visited the school and discussed communication strategies with teachers, highlighting active listening and descriptive feedback. As explained in Chapter 4, both strategies encourage open communication. Active listening would encourage children to express thoughts and feelings more openly. Descriptive feedback, because it avoids blaming, would also help teachers to discuss critical incidents with their students. Both strategies would help teachers to develop a deeper understanding of their students, but, as noted in Chapter 4, careful listening also empowers others and sends a message of care and concern that helps to establish positive relationships. Although primarily intended as a data-collection method, the use of these strategies would establish a sense of relatedness and perhaps facilitate the students' sense of autonomy by permitting them to express their ideas openly and freely.

During this session, teachers again raised concerns about giving students too much attention or being too caring. They also questioned how to handle the child who is left out. At that point, Dr. Osterman reviewed the theoretical framework, explaining the importance of having a sense of belongingness and encouraging the teachers to develop strategies to make sure all students feel included. As they finished the session, several teachers mentioned they were eager to try the new communication techniques. They now realized that addressing psychological needs was important and saw the need to modify their practice. This sense of discrepancy between their goal (to address children's emotional needs) and their action made them open to new learning and new strategies: "I clearly need to try something to help him feel more cared for in my classroom."

A week later, the teachers met again to review and analyze their experiences. Much of the discussion focused on the new communication strategies. Carla described the following incident:

> Some of the girls came to me, telling me that Farah wants to play games with them but doesn't know how to. Farah was listening. I asked the girls to teach her how to play. I also had a private critical conversation with Farah. I said "I saw you looked sad when the girls said you didn't know how to play. That made me feel badly, too. How can I help you learn to play with the rules the other girls are using?"

Noting that Farah had beamed in response, Carla commented, "I see this new practice as having big benefits. The other girls saw that I cared about including Farah in their games." Farah also received a message that Carla cared about her relationships with the other girls and was willing to help her deal with the problem.

Leslie described a conversation with David and noted her amazement at how he opened up to her:

> I've been asking David to have conversations with me since we started our work. He's usually very short with me, but this time we had a long talk. I said to him, "David, I noticed you were upset today when Steven spoke to you at the computers. I don't like it when you seem so sad. Would you like to talk about it?"

In this situation, Leslie's well-framed door opener seemed to encourage David to be more open in sharing his feelings. David told her that one of the boys had said something to him that hurt his feelings. "I don't like when Steven uses me—he's only my friend when he wants my things." When Leslie asked how she could help, David continued to explain how a lot of people try to use him and make fun of him. "I'm always being bullied," he said. "They bully me and call me a fag and bad curse words. Then they're nice when they want my things." They were not able to arrive at a solution, but Leslie felt the new communication strategies were helping her to gain David's trust, and she hoped to continue these conversations.

Not all of the teachers were successful in using these strategies, but, for those who were, the active listening and noncritical feedback helped to establish a positive and empathetic relationship between teacher and student and seemed to be a critical step in the change process.

Reconceptualization

In practice, the distinction among the various stages of the experiential learning cycle of reflective process is not so clear. As you may have noticed, reconceptualization flowed naturally from observation and analysis. As the teachers observed, their ideas began to change. By the time they began to formalize action plans, their thinking was very different, and, in some cases, their practice had already begun to change. They had a more concrete understanding of the concepts of competence, autonomy, and relatedness and a deeper appreciation of how important these psychological needs were as a part of children's experience in the classroom. They were beginning to construct real and personal meanings of the ideas the facilitator shared with them initially. When they began the project, the teachers felt confident in their own practice but were not confident that they could influence this problem. Through their observations, they began to see areas for improvement and also developed an appreciation of how their actions and the classroom experience influenced students' behavior. With these experiences, they began to reconceptualize their role as teachers and develop new action plans.

Like most teachers, initially, their focus was primarily on students' academic achievement and classroom management. Now, they realized how children's psychological experience directly influenced their engagement in the classroom and began to consider how they could address these needs. The most significant change came in their understanding of relatedness. Just a few weeks before, the teachers became aware that they did not address children's needs for belonging. Now they realized that relationships play an important part in learning, and they, as teachers, could help. Gail explained:

> I feel it is now my responsibility to expand her realm of friends and help her learn to play with other children. I think an increased sense of belonging will help her focus more on her work. I am going to find ways to increase opportunities for Dina to engage in activities with students that she doesn't know well.

As they shared ideas, their plans took form. They hoped to show the students they cared about them personally; they also intended to support positive peer interaction. Their strategies included the following:

- Use active listening and descriptive feedback to encourage the student to share problems and feelings and let the student know the teacher wants her or him to feel comfortable and cared for in the classroom.
- Spend more personal time with the student.
- Increase positive attention; decrease negative attention.
- Encourage new relationships to expand the circle of friends, within the classroom and the school.
- Monitor choice time so that the student is not excluded.
- Praise classmates who interact positively with the victims.
- Promote classroom conversations about empathy, caring, and feelings.
- Increase the use of literature involving empathy, caring, and feelings.

With respect to competence, since the teachers realized that their selected students were not getting their fair share of these experiences, they planned to do the following:

- Provide recognition for students' accomplishments in the classroom, spotlighting oral presentations, displaying written work and projects, and generally praising positive attitude and effort.
- Develop opportunities for students to show off their strengths.
- Always connect the student's name with a positive experience; downplay negatives and increase positives.

The teachers began to see how important choice was for their students and how few choice opportunities occurred in the daily routine. They also realized that autonomy was more important for some students than for others and that it was not only acceptable but also important to individualize. "After observing James," Carol commented, "I've realized he seems happiest and most engaged when he has a say in the activity he is doing. I am going to provide choices for him as much as I can. Hopefully, this will help him feel more comfortable in the classroom."

To support autonomy, the teachers planned to do the following:

- Increase center activities in the classroom.
- Allow kids more freedom in choosing where they work—on the rug, in a chair, reclining on the floor.
- Allow more freedom of choice for the student looking for more self-direction.
- Allow choice of assignments where possible.
- Allow choice of partners and groups, but safeguard against hurt feelings by setting rules precluding rejection.

Their ideas and practice were changing. Before they had focused on deficits in the children; now they were considering how they could change their own teaching practice to make a difference.

Experimentation: Action and Assessment

With the plan in place, the teachers begin to engage in intentional action. They had developed a new way of thinking about the problem and had identified strategies that reflected this new perspective. They were testing a new theory of action, and the cycle of reflective practice essentially began anew. As the teachers engaged in action, they continued to examine their experience. By gathering data about what they were doing and the effects of these practices, they assessed the validity of this new way of thinking, and the efficacy of their actions reinforced and enriched their new conceptualization.

So how did the plan work? The teachers presented their plans on May 3rd, and the experimentation phase continued for six weeks until the end of the school year. During that time, they met three times to report on their progress. During these discussions, the teachers described how their beliefs and practices had changed. They also explained how these changes affected the entire classroom environment as well as the experience of those students previously excluded by their classmates.

Changes in Teachers' Beliefs and Practice

Throughout the remainder of the project, teachers continued to note changes in their beliefs and practice. The greatest changes dealt with relatedness. Teachers began to pay attention to their students as children. They started listening to what was happening in their lives. When the students came into the classroom early, or during any quiet time, they would ask about what they did after school, what they had for dinner, or about their play dates (or activities) with friends. At first, the students were a bit wary of this new behavior and hesitant to respond, but soon teachers noted the students were smiling more and looking forward to these conversations. Knowing of James's upcoming birthday party and anticipating the reaction of his peers, Carol encouraged children to attend, noting that she never would have done this before. The extra effort and the extra time listening and talking to him led James to trust her and also changed her feelings toward him:

> When you get to know a child better, when you listen deeply to what he has to share, you start to understand his life. You can't help but feel for him. It took a while to get to know him because he was so closed off. When he opened up, it was wonderful. I have to attribute this change to my own change in belief about my role in the classroom and to my own change in actions.

Others offered similar examples of how, through conversation, they had come to empathize with their students and see the need to change their teaching practice. They also used the "I-message" to provide descriptive feedback to the victimized students and to their classmates. This strategy helped the children to speak about their feelings and find ways to resolve their own problems.

Knowing the children better and observing more carefully, the teachers were able to see when activities weren't working for the particular child and were able to develop an alternative tailored to the child's needs. Getting to this point was a difficult one. Carla explained:

> I feel my strength is that I've always been able to differentiate academically, and I've always tried to meet a child's academic needs. This process has made me realize that I have had a need to improve.

While the teachers initially espoused differentiation, their observations and experiences again helped them to understand that they had deep-seated feelings and beliefs that prevented them from treating children differently. As Carol explained, "I thought the students should all conform behaviorally— to act just the same as each other at all times, the way I wanted them to be." That understanding of their theory-in-use, combined with their growing realization that these children were indeed very different and had different needs, encouraged them to change their practice. "This process," as Carol explained, "has been an eye-opener."

With their new insight, they began to bend the rules. Janice, for example, realized that Michael had a strong need for self-direction and gave him more choice in activities than she gave the other students. As she did, she observed his satisfaction and also began to see improvement in his academic work. Carol developed a special project for James when his father took him out of the classroom for a week's vacation. When James returned, she also helped him develop his presentation and spotlighted him in class. In the past, she said she would have penalized him for his absence but explained, "I now think of the extra step I can take with a child who has a problem."

In their interactions with the children, they increased the positives and minimized the negatives. As their relationships with the children began to change, teachers noticed the other children began to treat these once-excluded children very differently. Carla explained:

> I don't know if my relationship with Farah changed because I changed or because she changed, but I do know that as our relationship changed, so did her relationships with the little girls in the class. I could now see she was a sweet little girl who needed to be brought out, and my guess is that the children in the class were now seeing her through my eyes.

Here, too, very different beliefs are apparent. While initially teachers attributed victimization to children's social deficits and felt helpless to address the problem, their understanding of the situation had now changed dramatically. They now realized they could make a difference. They understood emotionally and intellectually the importance of the student-teacher relationship; they knew they could nurture this relationship by attending to students' needs. By getting to know the children better, listening to their feelings, and taking a personal interest in their lives, the teachers understood the child better, and, as the children began to trust the teacher, they were more comfortable in the classroom. Teachers also discovered that they were models for other students' interactions with the previously victimized students. When the teachers demonstrated their caring and appreciation for these children, their peers did, too. They also appreciated the importance of teacher intervention to facilitate positive peer relationships and understood that classroom activities must facilitate supportive student interaction.

Here, too, is strong evidence of change in the theory-in-use. While espousals about elementary education typically emphasize the importance of child-centered and wholistic approaches, these teachers experienced the powerful force of a theory-in-use that urged them to resist personal relationships with these children. Through their observation and experience, however, they uncovered this theory and found it wanting. Through experimentation, they experienced the efficacy of strategies grounded in caring, and this helped to displace the original theory-in-use and embed more firmly the new way of thinking.

Aside from changing the nature of their own interaction with the children, teachers systematically structured classroom activities to encourage positive interaction and preclude exclusion. Most of the teachers had been using cooperative learning but didn't know how to deal with student exclusion. More attuned now to the effects of rejection, they became more committed to addressing the problem. Whether assigning students to groups or permitting choice, they set rules about appropriate behavior—no grimacing, no grumbling, and no one turned away. They articulated the new class rule: Every child is acceptable as a partner. They also reinforced positive behaviors, complimenting groups when they were inclusive and supportive.

With respect to competence, they witnessed how as students began to experience success, academically and socially, they developed the confidence to reach out to other students and develop friendships. As a result, teachers began to search for strengths and then figure out how to highlight these in the classroom. Sandra gave Ricky, a recent immigrant, an opportunity to teach his native language to small groups of students. When Ricky saw students "fighting over who could be in the first session, he was very excited." Ricky had a chance to demonstrate his skill; it also gave the students a chance to get to know each other better. Recognizing David's leadership skills, Leslie assigned him as group leader in science activities; "the children value his knowledge and make him feel very welcome, and David thrives." Gary had wanted to be a peer mediator but was not selected for the schoolwide program, so Kristin asked him to take on that role in her classroom. "When Gary feels competent," Kristin commented, "he's a different child." Similarly, the teachers saw how offering students choice in activities and relationships empowered them and had a powerful effect on their comfort in the classroom and their behavior.

Observing how choice affected Michael's interaction with others, Janice responded, "Although some kids only have choice on certain choice days, I set up choices for him every day. He thrives on making his own decisions. This works for him, so I incorporate it as much as I can."

Through this process of observation, reflection, and experimentation, the teachers developed a critical perspective on their own practice. As the comment from Gail illustrates, they came to recognize how their own negative interaction with these victimized students had provoked similar behaviors from their peers:

> I am so much more aware of how my actions affect the children. I have consciously changed my practice so that when I am feeling annoyed with Dina, I do not show it because I realize the children imitate my behaviors. This is a terrible thing to say, but because of all the tattling and bickering I would get annoyed with her. I didn't have a lot of patience. Now that I've stopped, Dina is feeling better about herself, and I see the children are less annoyed with her. I hesitate to say they may have been imitating me.

Continuing the discussion, Carla, too, expressed her opinion that the girls had mimicked her behavior in the past. Now, responding to the change in her own behavior, they were "much more sensitive and tolerant and accepting."

These changes in individual beliefs reflected a broader change in perspective regarding their role as teacher. At the last session, the teachers explained how they now believed that their jobs extended well beyond simply helping a student succeed academically. As one of the teachers noted, as sessions progressed, there were fewer negative comments about parents and more emphasis on what teachers themselves could do in the classroom. They seemed to shift from blaming and thinking of themselves as helpless to a belief that they, as teachers, have the power to create supportive communities in their classrooms and help students who are alienated socially.

The changed perspectives teachers articulated at the end of the project illustrate a change in the espoused theory as well as in the theory-in-use. The information they gathered during the observation led them to question their existing beliefs, assumptions, and practices. This set the groundwork for their experimentation, and, as they continued their efforts to address the psychological needs of their students and assess their own practice, the result of their efforts reinforced their new way of thinking. By the end of the project, their espousals were different and their actions were more closely aligned with their new conceptualization.

Changes in Students

What effects did these changes in practice have on students? Initially, teachers reported the students were reluctant to participate in class, seldom raised their hands, spoke in very quiet voices, and showed little skill in knowing how to join a group of children in a social setting.

After implementing their plans, the teachers reported a number of changes. They felt these students had become more comfortable socially, more outgoing, and better able to deal with social interaction. Where before, the children might react very defensively to exclusion, they were now more comfortable about seeking out other options:

> Farah is now branching out to other children. If the girls she seeks out aren't very receptive, she joins another group. The other girls seem happy to have her.
>
> Where Dina used to resort to name-calling when kids were mean to her, now the kids are not as mean and she has stopped the name-calling somewhat and is becoming friendly with the other girls.

Others saw their students telling jokes, "getting a personality." One teacher commented, "Life in school is better for him, and you can see it in his face."

The children also became less withdrawn and more engaged socially. James, for example, stopped reading at snack time and moved to the computer to join others and eventually started playing with other children. "Good news!" read a later journal entry. "James is playing Sorry with Leslie and Sean, one of our most popular boys." Reviewing her diary, Carla also noted changes in Farah and her classmates:

> I kept writing down things like, "Farah played nicely with the girls at lunchtime. They came in from recess holding hands and laughing." I eventually stopped because everything sounded wonderful. Things really changed for Farah. Even the conflicts with Charlie improved. . . . There is no question. I'm telling you their whole attitude—the way they [the other children] look at her is different—to see the change every day is amazing.

Teachers observed their students developing more confidence and becoming more engaged academically. As Gail began "focusing on the positives with Dina and increased opportunities for her to shine in front of her classmates, her self-esteem shot through the roof." Gail noted that Dina was "beginning to more readily answer questions, go first, and speak louder in class when responding in a group." Both Leslie and Sandra observed that David was more cooperative, smiled more, and participated more in class discussions. Ricky provided some direct feedback when he stopped his principal in the hall to tell her about his language project and concluded, "This is making me feel really good about myself. I really love school now." Other teachers offered similar observations, stating, "He joins in more now; he is part of what's happening in the room" and "He's on target. He's listening, paying attention, able to apply what I am asking."

There was no question that the children were happier. The teachers noticed it, the students described it in their words and actions, and even the parents were aware of changes taking place. At the end of the year, James's mom sent a note to his teacher, expressing gratitude for the terrific job she had done with James and the personal interest she had shown. David's parents, too, sent a note and gift and thanked Leslie in person for the "special interest, care and patience" she had shown to their son. Ricky's father, who had been very uncomfortable and uninvolved, thanked Sandra repeatedly for allowing Ricky to teach his classmates and commented that "his son felt happier coming to school this year, happier than ever before."

Discussion

Problems certainly were not eliminated, but they were alleviated. The teachers saw a positive response from their actions but realized that these children's problems required continual attention. Nonetheless, there were dramatic changes in the students' behavior and the nature of the interaction between these children and their peers.

What accounted for these changes? The involvement in the action research process and specifically the continuing and integral combination of observation, reflection, and experimentation facilitated new understanding. The most important change in their perception dealt with the children. Initially, when they thought about these victimized children, they focused strictly on their behavior. Attributing their behavior to personality, behavioral, or family defects, they were very critical of them. As they observed the children and talked with them more, they developed empathy. Instead of seeing their behavior, they began to experience their pain. With this new focus on the child as person, as one teacher commented, "I saw what was happening and everything began to shift." This reconceptualization motivated them to try new strategies. They began to care about these children, and, recognizing their need, they began to search for strategies. They were willing to try to apply the theoretical framework that had been presented to them because, as they observed, they began to see the children's needs. Their initial efforts to apply the theory, regardless of how minimal, worked, and this reinforced their new commitment. The subsequent changes in the students enhanced their efficacy as professionals—they saw the kinds of behavior and engagement that they hoped to see and realized that they were responsible for this change. They saw children who were now happy to come to class, engaged in the learning process, and developing academic and social skills.

When they processed their own experience at the end of the project, they identified aspects of the process that contributed to their learning. In the introductory chapters of this book, we emphasized the importance of collegiality, personal commitment, and organizational support. In addition to the importance of ongoing observation and reflection as they implemented their plans, the teachers also affirmed the importance of these factors. As Carla commented, "listening and sharing ideas with each other was the most important part. . . . Without this we wouldn't have made changes." Listening to everyone, as Leslie explained, "helped me see my own actions differently. I learned from everyone and from watching my plan make such a difference in my student's life." The continued support and feedback as well as the freedom to share their ideas and test them in a risk-free environment contributed to their sustained involvement as well as their personal growth and development.

In the initial chapters of this book and in the previous edition, we talked about the potentially painful nature of reflective practice. In this situation, however, there was little evidence of discomfort. Teachers revealed their dismay and distress as they developed an awareness of the inadequacy of their practice yet seemed comfortable sharing this information with their colleagues. Our guess is that the seriousness of the problem and the teachers' commitment to the solution as well as the strength of the feedback that they received from their students as they implemented their plans overshadowed whatever deficits they observed in their past practice. There was no opportunity for self-regret or recrimination since the predominant concern was addressing the newly observed needs of the children. These teachers were committed to children, and their new and rapid success in meeting their needs was sufficient reward. They were more concerned with where they were going than where they had been.

The introduction of the action research process also minimized the personal discomfort. In their initial observations, for example, the facilitator asked them to look for instances in their practice where they were successful. In doing this, they naturally became aware of the holes in their practice. They had focused on the goal, and, as Senge (1990) would explain, they experienced the tension between the goal and the current reality.

This was also a project in which the teachers retained personal control. They participated by choice and their progress was self-directed. No one told them what they would see or how to see it. They controlled their level of involvement and the analytic process. Their principal, as facilitator, set the process in motion, offered the theoretical framework to guide observation and discussion, provided organizational and psychological support, and arranged the meetings, but the teachers directed the process.

While the majority of the teachers agreed that they had actually changed their practices, the process was not successful for all. One of the teachers (interestingly, the only nontenured teacher in the group) participated but was never able to develop the same sense of empathy with her student as did others. At the conclusion of the project, she was still very critical of the child and continued to blame her for the problem. She was unable to develop a critical perspective on her own performance and was less successful in changing her practice. Why didn't she respond? Why didn't she come to see the situation as the other teachers did? One possible explanation is her status in the group. It is relatively well documented that experienced teachers, particularly those who are successful in their craft, are often the most responsive to professional development opportunities. It is possible that she did not experience the same level of comfort working with her principal as did the others or that her choice to participate was motivated by extrinsic concerns as well as by an intrinsic interest in the problem. An alternative explanation is simply that she wasn't ready for this type of change. Reflective practice, we believe, is a highly effective professional development strategy that is more likely to facilitate behavioral change than other strategies, but we do not claim that it works for everyone at all times or at the same rate. Learning is idiosyncratic, and reflective practice is no universal solution.

NOTE

1. The Fight Crime report also includes specific data and references regarding the long-range effects of bullying and victimization. It is available at no charge on the Fight Crime: Invest in Kids Web site: www.fightcrime.org.

Teachers and Kids as Reflective Practitioners of Their Learning

THE CONTEXT AND THE PROCESS

Testing and Student Failure

Testing rivets the attention and drives the behavior of educators. Testing is a single, narrow means of assessment and accountability. Yet with the implementation of No Child Left Behind, testing has become the main issue for teachers, administrators, parents, and children. No role escapes its powerful effects.

Joe, a fifth grader in a New Jersey public school, like countless other children, has had a bad day. He just completed an on-demand writing prompt taken from a prior version of the New Jersey Elementary School Proficiency Assessment.[1] His score placed him near the bottom—he failed. The on-demand prompt for the state test and Joe's essay response follow in Box 7.1.

Box 7.1

On-Demand Prompt for Fifth-Grade State Writing Examination

You have been stranded on a deserted wilderness island. Before your ship sinks, you are able to recover some items that might help you survive. What would you choose to recover? Why would you choose those items? What would you do with them?

(Continued)

(Continued)

Joe's Essay Response

If I were stranded on a deserted island I would need a knife, and axe, some sort of gluey stuff, & rope to repiar my ship. I would need a knife to cut rope and other stuff. An axe to wood. Also gluey stuff to glue wood. Then finally rope to tie stuff together like the sail. that's what I would need to repair my boat.

Two readers, each using a five-point holistic-scoring rubric, scored Joe's essay at a combined three out of ten possible points. He was assessed as having "Limited Command" of writing. The rubric identifies four main criteria: content and organization, usage, sentence construction, and mechanics. When the readers review the essays, they look primarily for a student's ability to create a well-structured and grammatically correct essay. In this task, organization receives more attention than content.

Like many other children, Joe doesn't do well on standardized (increasingly high-stakes) tests. When he performs poorly, Joe doesn't feel good about his score or himself, and his teacher doesn't feel rewarded or highly competent. Joe hasn't had many ideas of how to improve his performance on tests; his teachers haven't had much success helping him.

Test performance is a problem not only for Joe but also for teachers, schools, districts, and parents. While his success should be a concern under any circumstances, teachers and principals are under increasing pressure to improve test scores of kids just like Joe. To address this problem, districts, schools, principals, and teachers adopt different strategies—some successful, some not; some address underlying problems; others solve symptoms with quick fixes more political and symbolic than substantive in nature.

Some states have specific mandates. New York State, for example, mandated that students with unacceptable prior performances thought to predict low future test scores must be given Academic Intervention Services (AIS) to improve their performance on state tests. The state, however, provides little guidance about the content and structure of AIS and, like other remedial program efforts in the past, there is doubt as to the efficacy of these supplementary programs. Doctoral students in the leadership program at Hofstra University, for example, studied the AIS programs in their districts. The findings showed no significant relationship between participation in AIS programs and improvement in test scores. AIS programs provided minimal learning time, were often staffed by inexperienced or substitute teachers (low cost), and used the same teaching methods and often the same curricular materials as regular classroom instruction. Further, the criteria used to assign children to these programs were weak, predicting with only 30% to 40% accuracy actual test scores. Overall, the students concluded a little more of the same made no difference. Quick-fix, unfunded, compliance programs had political and symbolic import for districts; they had negligible effects on student learning as measured by test performance.

In Joe's case, there was a different approach with very different outcomes. In an effort to support children like Joe, his principal persuaded her superintendent and school board to experiment with an innovative professional development effort, the Let Me Learn Process® (LML). Unlike the traditional approaches that we described in Chapter 1, this development process offers intensive, personalized, and long-term support. Unlike other programs, this initiative is not a prepackaged solution but a developmental process aimed at helping both teachers and kids to develop a deeper understanding of themselves as learners and to use this new understanding to help them identify ways to improve their practice. In essence, this professional development process is a means to engage teachers and students in reflective practice. The focus is on the process of learning, the roots of the problem, rather than on the test score, a symptom. By enabling teachers and students to examine their beliefs and assumptions about learning and the link between these beliefs and their practice, the process seeks to create meaningful change through double-loop learning.

After only twelve weeks of student development, Joe and his classmates wrote on the same prompt a second time. Joe's second essay follows in Box 7.2.

Box 7.2

Yesterday, I got stranded on a deserted island. My ship destroyed, I must look for food and supplies for my ship. I thought about cutting down trees for wood. Also I could use vine to tie it together and fix my sail. Before I leave I should stock up on food. I'll start at sunrise.

Today is the day I'll try to leave. I'v got all my supplies the night before. I started my work I decided to use the mud and hay I found to patch the holes. By sundown I set sail. I got back home, to my land safely. When I was sailing back home I saw a mysterious ship with blue flames around it the ship, you could see right through. That ship I will visit it soon again, such a ghostly ship. That will be another story.

Joe's second essay is noticeably different. Comparing his two attempts, the number of words he used more than doubled. There are two paragraphs rather than one. He made fewer spelling and punctuation errors and wrote fewer sentence fragments in the second. His sentences varied more in form and length, and while not a criterion, he used more imagination in the second. His second essay was not stellar, yet it was sufficiently improved to move his performance from three to five points on the ten-point scale, an increase from "Limited Command" to the middle category, "Partial Command."

Joe was not the only one in his school to show improvement. Of the fifth graders, 55% improved their total scores by one point or more on the ten-point scale. Students who scored at the low end on the first writing prompt showed greater improvement than students who originally scored at the high end. In other words, students originally performing at the lowest levels showed the most gain—a desirable result. What happened to account for Joe and his classmates' improved writing performance?

Between Joe's first and second tests, Joe, his classmates, and his teacher along with five other colleagues and their students in Grades 3 through 5 were engaged in the Let Me Learn Process. The first phase of the professional development consisted of teachers working with their colleagues and a certified LML consultant on site in their school district to develop an understanding of the process and preparing to introduce it to students in their classrooms. While there is no standard format for delivering LML professional development,[2] in this school, the first phase totaled twenty-five hours. It began with 2.5 workdays in August followed by three hours a month from September to November. The facilitator began each session by asking the teachers what they got from the prior session and where they needed more help and then tailored the day's work on the spot to the teachers' self-diagnosed current development level. Implementation, the second phase, occurred from February through May. The consultant spent a total of fifty hours with the six teachers in individual classrooms working with them and their students, providing group coaching; timely, relevant, and one-on-one mentoring; and classroom modeling.

The Let Me Learn Process

Let Me Learn (Johnston, 1996, 1998, 2000) is an advanced learning system. It provides learners (child, teacher, parent, or administrator) with the means to understand and articulate who they are as learners and offers strategies to focus and guide their learning with intention. LML provides a vocabulary for communicating internalized and externalized learning actions (thoughts, feelings, actions) among learners. It enables learners to gain awareness of and to make explicit their tacit learning processes.

The conceptual framework for Let Me Learn is the Interactive Learning Model (ILM). This learning model depicts the brain as a triune system consisting of three mental processes: cognition (thinking), affectation (feeling), and conation (doing). Cognition includes mental acuity, memory, range of experiences, and ability to work with abstractions; conation refers to natural skill, pace, autonomy, use of personal tools, and degree of engaged energy; and affectation encompasses feelings, values, and sense of self (Johnston, 1996). This notion of the triune brain, or trilogy of the mind (Johnston, 1996), traces its origin to the ancient Greeks and is an important foundation for current research on the brain and learning (Keefe, 1992).

Philip (1936) observed variations in the way that adults and school children use these three processes as they approach learning tasks. Drawing on this work, Johnston (1996, 1998) empirically derived four patterned operations, each synchronous, or consisting of interactions of the three mental processes. These four patterned operations are Sequence and Organization, Specificity and Precision, Technical Performance and Reasoning, and Confluence and Risk Taking. Each patterned operation is distinct from the others, each interacts with the others, and each builds the wholeness of the learning process. Through the interaction of these patterns and the operation of mental processes, we make sense of the world and begin to learn (Johnston, 2003a). The ILM's depiction of the simultaneous interactions or synchronicity of the patterned operations (Sequence, Precision, Technical Reasoning, and Confluence) is found in Figure 7.1.

From the perspective of reflective practice, these mental processes and interactive patterned operations function very much like the assumptions comprising our theory-in-use. They are unknown to individuals directly. Yet they organize and drive each individual's particular, unique approaches to learning, and these actions affect the ability to achieve goals—in classrooms, workplaces, leisure pursuits, and family relationships. Like the theory-in-use, these mental processes are tacit, below the threshold of conscious awareness. Consequently, learners are unable to recognize or name them and need assistance to extrapolate and name these patterned operations.

LML provides a process and a vocabulary to enable learners to gain awareness of and to make explicit their tacit, unique, neurologically grounded bases for learning. Using the language of reflective practice, LML enables learners to understand and articulate the mental models or theories-in-use, which guide thoughts and actions about learning. In this case, however, the theory-in-use has neurobiological origins. With this

Figure 7.1   Synchronous Interaction of Three Mental Processes and Four Patterned
Operations

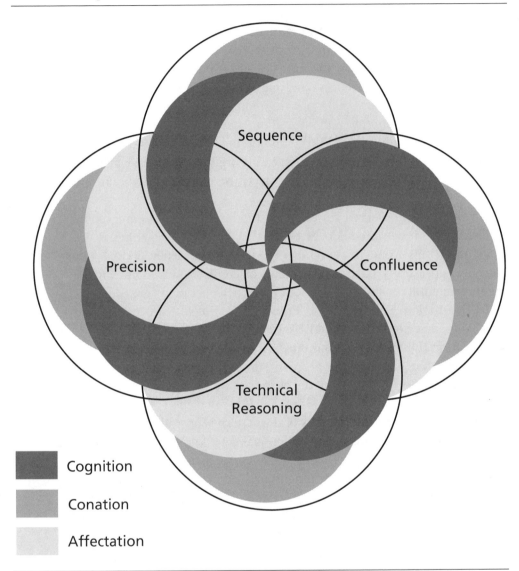

SOURCE: Used with permission. © 2000 LET ME LEARN, Inc. 2 Tiverstock Dr., Pittsgrove, NJ.

new understanding, learners can then identify and intentionally select
strategies that enable them to achieve their goals more effectively. As
teachers develop a deeper understanding of their own learning, they
become more sensitive and responsive to the learning needs of their
students (Bonich, Schlau, & Kottkamp, 2003). As students become more
aware of their own learning needs and processes, they are able to direct

their own learning and experience autonomy and efficacy. Using the language of LML, they approach learning with meta-awareness; they become intentional learners. Essentially, the LML process, by engaging the learner in reflective practice, enables the learner to experience double-loop learning about learning itself. In more outcome-oriented terms, LML enables teachers and students to improve their performance.

BECOMING REFLECTIVE LEARNERS THROUGH LET ME LEARN

Gathering Data About One's Self as a Learner

The professional development process begins with teachers taking the Learning Combination Inventory (LCI), an instrument developed by Johnston and Dainton (1997a). This inventory gathers self-reported data about how the individual learns, specifically about the extent to which the learner uses each of the four patterned operations.

Taking the LCI is akin to an interview probing a learner's personal experience. It is not a test; there are only valid-for-the-person responses, not correct ones. The interview consists of twenty-eight statements, including the following:

- I like to build and make things.
- I am a very organized person.
- I call out my ideas before being called on.
- I don't like having to do my work in just one way, especially when I have a better idea I would like to try.
- I ask more questions than most people because I enjoy knowing things.

The respondent answers these questions on a five-point continuum from *Never* to *Always*. Additionally, there are three open-response writing prompts: "What makes assignments frustrating for you?" "If you could choose, what would you do to show what you have learned?" "What hobby or sport do you do well? How would you teach someone else to do it?"[3]

The LCI yields four scores, each corresponding to one of the four patterned operations (Sequence, Precision, Technical Reasoning, Confluence) described previously. As we see in Figure 7.2, the numbers are marked on four continua ranging from 7 to 35, one continuum for each patterned operation. A certified LML facilitator then validates the LCI scores using internal indicators, including comparison of the closed questions with the three open responses (Johnston, 2000, pp. 39–57).[4]

Specifically, the validated scores on the LCI indicate the extent to which the person uses each of the processes: Sequence, Precision, Technical Reasoning, and Confluence. There are three ranges: Use First, Use as Needed, and Avoid. This information provides a framework for understanding the individual's learning behavior and experience in learning situations.

Debriefing the LCI: Understanding Patterned Operations and the Self as Learner

With their LCI scores in hand and working closely with each other and the facilitator, the teachers then begin to develop an understanding of this information. What do these scores mean and what are their implications for me as a learner and as a teacher?

To develop an understanding of this learning process, we illustrate using the LCI scores for Ms. J, Joe's teacher. Figure 7.2 shows the scoring grid with Ms. J's LCI scores. Scores from 7 to 16 are in the Avoid range; scores from 17 to 24 are in the Use as Needed range; and scores from 25 to 35 are in the Use First range. Higher numbers show stronger use of a pattern and lower numbers a weaker use. Even within a range, the strength of a pattern varies with its placement on the continuum.

As you can see from Figure 7.2, Ms. J has three patterned operations in the Use as Needed range, Sequence (20), Precision (24) and Technical Reasoning (20), and one pattern, Confluence (30), in the Use First range. This means that Ms. J tends to begin any task with Confluence and support it with her high-end Use as Needed pattern of Precision. The Sequence and Technical Reasoning processes are also available for her to use when they are needed, but she will not typically begin her learning with these.

At this point, concepts such as Confluence and Sequence still have little meaning for Ms. J or the other teachers, so the next step is to help them develop a personal understanding of these patterned operations. What are these patterned operations about? What do they mean?

While individuals have and use all four patterns, they use some patterns more readily than others. Persons with a Use First in Sequence, for example, approach tasks sequentially. Cognitively, as Figure 7.3 indicates, they organize information, mentally analyze data, and break tasks down into steps. If you were watching them begin a task, you would see them performing sequencing activities (conation): They make lists, organize, and plan. Characteristics of the situation also affect how they feel (affectation) when they are involved in the task. They thrive on consistency and dependability and need things to be tidy and organized. Conversely, if they feel rushed to complete tasks when the directions are not clear or keep changing midstream, they feel very frustrated.

Figure 7.2 The Learning Combination Inventory Scoring Grid

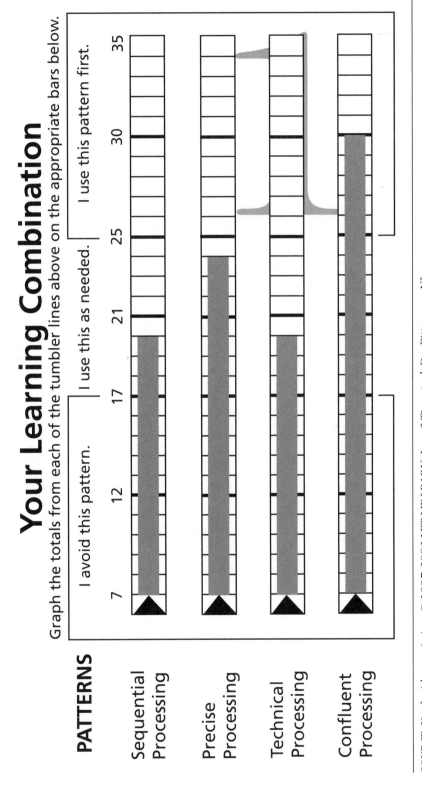

Your Learning Combination

Graph the totals from each of the tumbler lines above on the appropriate bars below.

SOURCE: Used with permission. © 1997–2003 LET ME LEARN, Inc., 2 Tiverstock Dr., Pittsgrove, NJ.

Figure 7.3   When I Have a Use First Pattern

I *Use First* Patterns	How I *think*	How I *do things*	How I *feel*	What I might *say*
Sequence	• I organize information. • I mentally analyze data. • I break tasks down into steps.	• I make lists. • I organize. • I plan first, then act.	• I thrive on consistency and dependability. • I need to be tidy and organized. • I'm frustrated when the game plan changes. • I feel frustrated when I'm rushed.	• Could I see an example? • I need to double-check my work. • Could we review those directions? • A place for everything and everything in its place. • What are my priorities?
Precision	• I research information. • I ask lots of questions. • I always want to know more.	• I challenge statements and ideas that I doubt. • I prove I am right. • I document my research and findings. • I write things down. • I write long e-mail messages and leave long voice mail messages.	• I thrive on knowledge. • I feel good when I am correct. • I'm frustrated when incorrect information is accepted as valid. • I'm frustrated when information is not shared with me.	• I need more information! • Let me write up the answer to that. • Wanna play trivia? • I'm currently reading three different books. • Did you get my e-mail on that? • Did you know that…
Technical Reasoning	• I seek concrete relevance—what does this mean in the real world? • I want as much information as I need—nothing extraneous.	• I get my hands on. • I tinker. • I solve the problem. • I do.	• I enjoy knowing how things work. • I feel good that I am self sufficient. • I'm frustrated when the task has no real world relevance. • I enjoy knowing things, but don't feel the need to share the knowledge.	• I can do it myself. • Let me show you how… • I don't want to read a book about it, I want to *do* it. • How will I ever use this in the real world? • How can I fix this? • I could use a little space…
Confluence	• I read between the lines. • I think outside the box. • I brainstorm. • I make obscure connections between things that are seemingly unrelated.	• I take risks. • I am not afraid to fail. • I talk about things—a lot. • I might start things and not finish them. • I will start a task first—then ask for directions.	• I enjoy energy. • I feel comfortable with failure. • I do not enjoy having my ideas criticized. • I'm frustrated by people who are not open to new ideas. • I enjoy a challenge. • I'm frustrated repeating a task over and over.	• What do you mean; "that's the way we've always done it"?! • The rules don't apply to me. • Let me tell you about…. • I have an idea…. • I have another idea….

SOURCE: Used with permission. © 1997-2003 LET ME LEARN, Inc. 2 Tiverstock Dr., Pittsgrove, NJ.

Each patterned operation is distinctive. People with Use First Precision ask lots of questions and are driven to know more. They challenge; they document their research and findings in great detail and strive to be right. When they are correct and recognized, they feel good; when they can't get enough information or don't get it right, they are frustrated.

Those with Use First in Technical Reasoning look for personal relevance in tasks and want only as much information as needed to accomplish the task. They like to work with their hands and solve problems. They take satisfaction from knowing how things work and being self-sufficient. They have no need to share what they know and are particularly frustrated when they must complete a task that, for them, has no real-world relevance. They like physical movement, many times want to work alone, and often feel very constrained and frustrated in the order-oriented context of schooling.

Individuals with Use First in Confluence like to approach tasks differently. They brainstorm and think outside the box of custom and make what others may see as strange connections. They take risks in learning and have little fear of failure. They also tend to start projects—without asking for directions—but don't always follow through to completion. They are frustrated by demands for conformity and feel misunderstood or unappreciated when their ideas are considered too off the wall, or strange.

Consult Figure 7.3 for more detail on the conative, cognitive, and affective processes functioning within each patterned orientation in the Use First range. It also lists frequently heard comments associated with each learning pattern.

Those who Avoid certain patterns also think, feel, and do in very predictable ways as shown in Figure 7.4. When confronted with a situation that requires of them a pattern that they avoid, they experience discomfort. At a cognitive level, they reject the task itself as meaningless or undoable; they have difficulty engaging in the actions that are necessary for success, and they are unhappy with the learning task, frequently experiencing a sense of incompetence and frustration. People who Avoid Sequence, for example, have difficulty understanding or following directions and see no sense in repetition. They have difficulty putting things in order, ignore anything looking like a list (table of contents, indexes), and feel scattered.

Those who Avoid Precision don't like extensive reading or writing; they resent assignments requiring information and recall. They like to deal in generalities and seldom have specific answers; they read by skimming and take few notes. When confronted with details, they feel overwhelmed.

Learners avoidant of Technical Reasoning hate to make things and prefer doing tasks requiring talking or writing. They rely on directions rather than figuring things out for themselves. Feelings of ineptitude, even fear, arise when they confront working with mechanical things or using tools. They rely on technical specialists to fix things or simply throw out what is broken and buy a new one.

People with Avoid Confluence have difficulty with open-ended unstructured tasks. They don't like improvising and imagining conditions that are not defined or given parameters. They pine for focus and definition. They don't want to think about taking social or intellectual risks. In unstructured or ambiguous situations, they feel unsettled and chaotic.

Figure 7.4 When I Avoid a Pattern

I Avoid Pattern	How I *think*	How I *do things*	How I *feel*	What I might *say*
Sequence	• These directions make no sense! • I did this before. Why repeat it? • Why can't I just jump in?	• Avoid direction; avoid practice. • Can't get the pieces in order. • Ignore table of contents, indexes, and syllabi. • Leave the task incomplete.	• Jumbled • Scattered • Out of synch • Untethered • Unfettered • Unanchored	• Do I have to do it again? • Why do I have to follow directions? • Does it matter what we do first? • Has anybody seen…?
Precision	• Do I have to read all of this? • How am I going to remember all of this? • Who cares about all this "stuff"?	• Don't have specific answers. • Avoid debate. • Skim instead of read. • Take few notes.	• Overwhelmed when confronted with details. • Fearful of looking stupid. • Angry at not having the one right answer!	• Don't expect me to know names and dates! • Stop asking me so many questions! • Does it matter? • I'm not stupid!
Technical Reasoning	• Why should I care how this works? • Somebody has to help me figure this out! • Why do I have to make something; why can't I just talk or write about it?	• Avoid using tools or instruments. • Talk about it instead of doing it. • Rely on the directions to lead me to the solution.	• Inept • Fearful of breaking the object, tool, or instrument. • Uncomfortable with tools; very comfortable with my words and thoughts.	• If it is broken, throw it away! • I'm an educated person; I should be able to do this! • I don't care *how* it runs; I just want it to run!
Confluence	• Where is this headed? • Where is the focus? • What do you mean, imagine?	• Don't take social risks. • Complete one task at a time. • Avoid improvising. • Seek parameters.	• Unsettled • Chaotic • No more change or surprises, please!	• Let's stay focused! • Where did that idea come from? • Now what? • This is out of control!

SOURCE: Used with permission. © 1997-2003 LET ME LEARN, Inc. 2 Tiverstock Dr., Pittsgrove, NJ.

During the debriefing sessions, for example, as she and the other teachers review the characteristics associated with Use First (Figure 7.3), Ms. J sees herself depicted. Scanning the thinking, feeling, and doing behaviors associated with Confluence, her strongest pattern, she recognizes herself. She thinks outside the box, seeks nontraditional ways of doing things, reads between the lines, loves to brainstorm, and sees connections others simply cannot. She takes risks with learning, is not defeated if something new does not work out, talks a lot about her work, jumps in immediately and balances a lot of things simultaneously. She affirms the feelings, too. Teachers who refuse to change drive her nuts. She is always seeking a challenge and feeling energetic. Colleagues who dismiss her many "wild" ideas before she can even explain them frustrate her. She actually says the things in the "What I might say" column. "Wow," she thinks, "This inventory really describes me well." Then she looks at the Precision row and also affirms many of the things there as well: asking and wanting to know; writing a lot and challenging things not correct; liking to have knowledge; and feeling frustrated when people withhold information. "Wow! More right on target descriptors." Then she looks at the Technical Reasoning and Sequence rows. She acknowledges that, while she can make lists and outlines, organize things, wield a screwdriver, and attack practical problems, these are not what she typically does. She also scans Figure 7.4 describing the behaviors characterizing those who avoid a particular pattern but does not find a great deal there she resonates with. She has no pattern in the Avoid range, so this also makes sense to her.

Having considered her LCI scores and the data in Figures 7.3 and 7.4, she thinks that they not only describe her as she sees herself but also match how her colleagues think of her. She has the reputation of being a bright, knowledgeable, energetic, innovative teacher, who is often suggesting ways to do things better and is the first to volunteer for new programs and curricula. She is known as a doer. People come to her for help with understanding the larger context. Her principal assigns kids to her who would drive many other teachers crazy. She does this because she knows that Ms. J quickly tries other learning approaches with kids if the original way of doing something does not result in success. Again, she thinks, "Wow, this LCI really describes me very well!"

Other colleagues in her professional development group have the same experience and find that their LCI scores correspond well with their own behaviors and feelings. They also discover that their descriptions vary considerably from each other, and Ms. J doesn't find anyone much like her. However, as a group, teachers tend to have Sequence and Precision as their highest patterned operations and Technical Reasoning as their lowest (Johnston, 1997).

Analyzing their own scores, they begin to develop an understanding of themselves as learners. As the workshop continues, they also engage in different activities that demonstrate in an experiential way their attraction to or avoidance of certain types of tasks. In one of the activities, for example, they each receive straws, pipe cleaners, and marshmallows and directions to represent with these materials where they learn best. While they do the task, they keep track of their thinking and feeling. With the task complete, they take turns describing what they made, how they felt, and what they thought.

A teacher with Use First Sequence and Avoid Technical Reasoning used pipe cleaners to construct a simple, two-dimensional rectangle, representing a desk. She learns best in a classroom where expectations are clear. She had very negative feelings about the activity, felt inept and inadequate having to make an object, and was extremely frustrated with the way that the task was presented. She wanted to know exactly what the facilitator wanted from her and found the directions too vague. The whole thing reminded her of the hands-on science kits the district had recently distributed. She's very uncomfortable with the thought of using them and unsure about how to proceed, so they're still untouched in the closet.

In contrast, a teacher with Use First Technical loved the project. She represented her favorite place to learn through a fully three-dimensional representation of herself in her woodshop, complete with tools. She felt great about doing the project because she learns best from hands-on activities. She commented on how unusual it is to do hands-on activities in professional development sessions and how it would be good to have more like this one. It reminded her, too, of those science kits, which she loves to do with her kids.

Ms. J depicted herself in a theatre. Recall that she has Use First Confluence. She learns a great deal engaging in amateur theatrical productions. Sometimes she acts, but more often she helps with the sets, coming up with different ideas based on a mix of research and her broad understanding of the meaning of the play, which she represents metaphorically in set design. She expresses joy that this professional development approach allows her to use different and unique approaches.

Led by the facilitator, these teachers discuss how different their places of learning are as well as their feelings about the activity and thoughts they had while doing it. Through these interactions they again affirm that their LCI scores made sense in what they did and how they felt and thought about it. The concepts of LML begin to take on personal meaning. They see themselves as learners, unique learners, not at all like everyone else.

Understanding Interactions Among Learners

The teachers also begin to see connections between their own learning patterns and their experience in the classroom. As they share observations, they notice that their colleagues with Use First in Sequence have orderly classrooms, hand in everything on time exactly the way it was asked for, and are more reluctant to try new things, preferring to stay with the tried and true. They discover that a third of them avoid Technical Reasoning, but few avoid other operations.

They also begin to see that their reactions toward children differ depending on their patterns. Pushing further, those avoidant of Technical Reasoning are the teachers who express relief that Ms. J is willing to take some of the "squirrelly" kids who wiggle a lot, don't sit in their chairs in normal ways, always have their hands busy, and always start doing before the directions are complete.

Over the course of the professional development sessions, these teachers engage in many more activities. One entails giving the LCI to a family member or close friend. Most choose a spouse. After completing one LCI, many ask for LCIs for additional family members. They discuss together what they are learning. They develop insights on interpersonal dynamics. One teacher with Use First Precision discovered that her husband avoids Precision and learns with Use First Technical. Her insistent questions bother him a lot; she also discovered that his high level of Technical Reasoning explains some of why he needs space and time to be alone. Another learned that because of her Use First Sequence she desires her home to be orderly and neat. This helps to explain her frustration with her son's messy room. He uses Precision and Confluence first but avoids Sequence.

Continuing over time, these teachers get a clearer understanding of how their own arrays of learning patterns provide deeper understanding of not only how they learn but also how they teach, what kinds of assignments they make, and how they give feedback and grade papers. They also grasp new understandings of how they interact with others, both in the school and elsewhere (Rusch, Haws, & Krastek, 2002). They begin to understand how emotions about their own learning, their work, and their close relationships are tied to their learning patterns (Bonich et al., 2003; Kottkamp, 2002). Some explain how understanding themselves better as learners and beginning to understand others in these ways reduces frustration and friction. After six months' work with LML, one third-grade inclusion teacher explained as follows:

> I have learned that when you know what a student's learning pattern is it helps you feel good about the student. What I mean is sometimes I feel guilty because there are students you just don't like because they get on your nerves. Once I understood that it's the way they are because that is how they learn, then I learned to relax and really not be put off by the student. Instead I've learned how to help that student put together a way that makes learning work for them. That may include working with someone similar to them in learning patterns or it may mean sitting down and talking through our differences. All I know is I like the feeling of being more patient and more accepting.

With new insight about the interaction between teacher and student learning patterns, they also begin to change their practice. A fifth-grade teacher, who had worked with LML for six months, for example, described her work with a difficult student:

> I want to talk about Matt. He's a very cognitive student, but he was very frustrated with writing. His writing scores were very poor, and he usually shut[s] down at a writing assignment. He loved to express himself through art, but even the quality of the art wasn't very good. He was comfortable talking in front of the group and sharing his ideas, even when they were way out there. Sometimes his ideas had nothing to do with what we were talking about, but he was always excited about his idea, so I thought his scores would be highly Confluent. When he took the LCI (S 19, P 15, T 34, and C 26), his Technical score surprised me, but it did help me understand him better. His written answers were also interesting: What frustrates me most? "I don't like writing a lot." "I would make myself a project," to show how he learned, and he would "give a diorama or 3-D project that had to do with what we learned," would be how he would teach others.
>
> He has been diagnosed LD and diagnosed ADD. He also received occupational therapy every week. I used to think Matt couldn't remember details and the lack of details was part of his "learning disability." Now I understand if the Precision is related to something that is a part of his real-world interest, he can stretch his Precision. For example, we were doing something in science. And I talked about atomic numbers and his hand went up. He said, "I know about atomic numbers. Like the atomic number for gold is 79." His response caught me by surprise. I wasn't sure he was right, but I looked it up and sure enough he was. I was surprised he knew this fact because most fifth graders don't know it. He had seen a program about it on television, and he thought that was interesting.
>
> Every marking period, the boys and girls have to give a book report to their small group. My kids work on it at home and then bring it in. They bring in props, but it is usually a minor part of the project. Matt spent three whole choice-time periods, which is a half an hour each, working on this project. It was driving me crazy (my scores were S 25, P 27, T 21, and C 19), but I thought, let him do it. I thought he was spending too much time building this creation, but it really helped him understand the story, so I let him do it. The written work was horrible, and we need to work on that, but I don't know that without this project, he would have been able to do as well as he did.

She then showed a video she made of his presentation.

"This is the story of the boy who fooled the dragon," Matt began, "and here's the set up I made of the story," which proved to be a complex many-charactered plot where the hero, a young boy, destroyed the evil king, and lived happily ever after. A key prop in the story was a castle that he built.

Matt's teacher talked about his approach to his work:

As difficult as it was, he wouldn't have been able to tell the story without this thing which he created. That piece of it was so important for him. For someone like him, 19 Sequence and Precise 15, it helped him recount detail as I have not heard him do before.

She was also clear about the implications for her own teaching:

On the one hand, I know I need to be more patient and let him build those things. I can't stay locked in my idea of what learning is. Watching Matt learn to use who he is as a learner has required me to rethink how to allow him to develop. Six months ago, I would have insisted that his book report be only in one way—my way.

Now she had a different way.

As teachers begin to understand themselves as learners and see how they interact with other teacher learners and child learners, they become more sensitive and responsive to the learning and personal needs of others (Bonich et al., 2003). Children have a similar experience. They, too, learn about LML in a group situation, and since this descriptive information is shared openly, the kids become aware of the patterned operations of all their colleagues. They use that information to organize groups for cooperative learning—groups are more effective when all of the pattern strengths are represented (Marcellino, 2001; Probasco, 1997). The information also affects the quality of their interpersonal relationships. One endearing snippet of a videotape made about Let Me Learn features two third graders and classmates Zach and Corey. Zach leads his learning with Precision, while Corey leads hers with Confluence. Zach looks at Corey and says, "I used to think you were crazy; now I understand you are just Confluent!" Corey looks at Zach with a smile and whispers, "Thank you." Knowledge of each another as learners has put them on a different interpersonal footing as well, a much healthier one.

By learning about themselves as learners and by getting to know their students in a different way, the teachers are beginning to change their ideas about themselves and their work. In the vocabulary of reflective practice, they have gathered and analyzed data and begun to develop a very different perspective on themselves and their own work. They have already begun to reconceptualize. The learning process is deeply personal and they have found the experience different, exciting, and motivating. In the classroom implementation phase of professional development, teachers introduce the LML process to their students and begin to develop a deeper understanding of their students as learners. They also continue to gain insight into their own work.

Implementing Let Me Learn With Kids

When it comes time for Ms. J and her colleagues to implement Let Me Learn with their students, much of the information they deliver and many of the activities they use are parallel to what the teachers have already done. They simply adjust activities to the level of younger learners. They administer the LCI, share the information with students, and help them to develop a personal understanding, just as they did. One of the experiential learning activities involves giving students a list of the kinds of statements found in the "What I might say" column of Figure 7.3. The instructions are for students to cut out the statements that best describe them and paste them on a piece of construction paper. Joe, whose learning LCI scores are Sequence-23, Precision-27, Technical Reasoning-34, Confluence-24, created a "Joe the Learner" poster (see Box 7.3).

Box 7.3

JOE the LEARNER

- I can do it myself!
- I want hands-on activities, which interest me instead of taking notes, doing book work, or writing about it.
- How can I *fix* this?
- I learn better if I can do what I am learning about.
- I need to run around outside and get things to make sense in my head!
- I could use a little space. . . .
- Let me build things!

Joe's poster is all about Technical Reasoning. His scores show why. Although his Sequence and Confluence are in the Use as Needed range and Precision is Use First, his 34 in Technical Reasoning, at the top of the range, simply overpowers the other patterns. His performance in the on-demand writing prompt grows increasingly understandable.

Like their teachers, the kids create art projects that reflect their learning patterns. Those with Use First Sequence tend to have very symmetrical artistic depictions. Those with Use First Precision often label various parts of pictures with words, such as door, window, chimney, and driveway when depicting a house. Kids with Use First Technical Reasoning often draw pictures with a great deal of mechanical/technical detail, such as cars or tractors or airplanes. Kids with Use First Confluence tend to make projects unlike those with other pattern arrays. They use more types of media and incorporate materials like ribbon, straw, or textured grass.

Like their teachers, children don't take long to see the connections between their LCI scores and their experience as learners. In a journal writing activity, students describe instances when they are using each of their patterned operations or combinations of them. The following examples come from fourth graders in rural Vermont:

Peter: I was in sequential when I made power notes in outline form while I read about earthquakes and when I listed my words for spelling. I am using my precision when I want to know stuff—like when I am learning facts about animals. I used my technical pattern when I drew cars and when I made an ice pack bandage with a rubber band, plastic bag and a frozen paper towel. I was in my confluence when I created a game during recess. It is called "Hide and Seek Freeze Tag."

Iris: I used my sequential pattern when I was problem solving and made a chart for my guess and check strategy for math. I also used it when I organized my wordbook in columns to be neat. Well, several have said [they're using Precision] when they look up facts, so I will add "I use precision when I am correct in spelling all the time." I built a cube out of paper using my technical process in math to show a number. I also built a dog-food feeder that is my height so I could feed my dog with less hassles. I am pretty high in confluence and have been writing songs. I used my confluence to solve a math problem my own way.

As with the adults, through information, experience, and discussion, students develop understanding of themselves as young learners and begin to see and affirm the relationship between LML concepts and the concrete, personal experience of doing, thinking, and feeling in ways that the concepts describe.

ANALYZING LEARNING TASKS

The purpose of reflective practice is to facilitate improvement in performance. The LCI provides teachers and students with information about their learning orientation. Like theories-in-use, the learner's approach to learning tasks, while influential, is not deterministic. As learners become aware, it is possible for them to select and use strategies with intention to change the way they approach learning tasks. The goal of reflective practice is to facilitate change. The specific goal of the LML process is to enable the learner to learn with intention.

To this point in the development process, learners have been developing a functional understanding of themselves as learners. They understand that their patterns influence how they approach tasks. Tasks differ, however. While some tasks require sequence, other tasks require confluence. As a simple example, if the task is to alphabetize a series of names, the primary patterned operations needed include the organization of Sequence and the detail and drive for correctness of Precision. These strategies will accomplish the task. In contrast, the desire of Confluence to do things differently is not congruent with this task and will not lead to success.

The successful learner uses task-appropriate strategies. Congruence between the patterned operations the learner brings to the task and those required by the given task determine the level of success. To respond appropriately, with intention, the learner must analyze tasks to determine what the requirements are. So, once the learner has a functional understanding of self, the next developmental step is learning to analyze tasks for patterned operation requirements.

Actually, the segue from learning about one's self as a learner to task analysis is already under way during the first stage of development. When teachers discussed the relationship between their LCI scores and their use of hands-on science kits, they were implicitly engaged in rudimentary task analysis. Kits and other experiential learning materials require the availability of Technical Reasoning (to at least the Use as Needed level) for the teachers to use them as intended and to feel positively about the experience. Teachers who Avoid Technical Reasoning and especially those who also Use Sequence First are not likely to use hands-on strategies successfully and tend to turn experiential and exploratory curricula into step-by-step didactic lessons. When the fourth graders discussed previously identified patterned operations associated with various school and nonschool tasks, they engaged in implicit task analysis.

In the task analysis phase of LML professional development, teachers address explicitly the primary question: What does that particular task require of me if I am to perform it well? Initially, the teachers deal with various learning tasks, including writing essays to particular prompts, working with science kits, and organizing and running a field day. As they begin to understand their own cognitive and affective reactions to different tasks, they begin to develop understanding of their students' reactions and begin to see the relationship between their students' learning patterns and their work as teachers.

Success in teaching, as in any other task, is determined by the congruence or dissonance between the teacher's approach and the student's needs. LML frames this issue by examining congruence between teacher and student learning patterns. To illustrate this principle in an experiential way, but before their students have completed the LCI, teachers draw on their own experience to respond to the following task:

> Select a specific student from your current class who best represents each of the following descriptors.
> - The one who drives me *nuts*
> - The ideal student
> - The Know-It-All
> - The organizer
> - The "Where did that idea come from?"
> - The one I can't seem to reach (Johnston, 2000, pp. 71-73)

As the teachers report their findings, patterns emerge. The "ideal student" is very much like the teacher. The "one who drives me nuts," the problematic child, is one who learns quite differently from the teacher. But the "ideal student" for one teacher may also be the "one who drives me nuts" for another and vice versa.

Later, when LCI scores are available for the kids, the teachers compare their scores with their students and find their original observations affirmed. The "ideal student" always has an LCI array very close to that of the teacher; the "one who drives me nuts" always has one very different from the teacher's. As the inquiry and discussion goes on, teachers begin to apply the lexicon of LML terms to the patterns they are describing and to what they have only experienced emotionally, often viscerally in the past:

- My "ideal student" has LCI scores much like mine. Aha! How I like to learn is how I like to teach! Kids who learn the way I learn and the way I teach do well in my class and are perceived by me as good students!

- The "one who drives me nuts" has an LCI score array very different from mine. Aha! Kids who learn differently from the way I do can drive me nuts! They are probably not learning well in my class because the way I teach is not how they learn!

- Everyone's "Know-It-All" has a Use First Precision score. Aha! Kids with high Precision know a lot of facts and like to make them known! This can get my goat, especially if my Precision score is not as high as the kid's.

- Everyone's "Organizer" has a Use First Sequence score. Aha! High Sequence is visible in organization and neatness! Whether I feel positive or less so about this depends on my Sequence score!

- Everyone's "Where did that come from" has a Use First Confluence score. Aha! Kids who often bring up things that seem offtrack from the logical progression of the lesson or discussion are kids with high Confluence! My positive or negative feeling about going offtrack is related to my Confluence score!

- The one doodling in the back of the room, the "one I can't seem to reach," is often a kid who has a Use First Technical Reasoning score. Aha! High Technical Reasoning is associated with not freely giving a lot of information to teachers, not writing much . . .

The longer term assignment is to pay particular attention to these six students, observe them carefully, and write descriptions of what they do and say. As teachers gather additional information, their understanding becomes clearer, and they develop a compelling rationale for changing their teaching practice.

In later sessions, with data from the observations at hand, the facilitator helps teachers to explore what they are finding. Then, the whole group begins to see the following: Aha! LML provides language, description, analysis, insight, and meaning to the feelings we have had about these kids from the beginning of the year. Aha! We teachers in here together have different LCI arrays; the particular kids we have difficulty or success with are not the same kids or kinds of kids in LML terms. The interaction of our patterned operation matrices and those of the kids is hugely related to the success or lack of success we experience with the kids and our emotional reactions to them. Thus, the complexity of task analysis related to the task of teaching particular kids is approached indirectly through gathering and analyzing data about experiences teachers are already having and often find problematic. The complexity comes together not in the form of another tough thing to do that takes up a lot of time or "another rock in my bag," but rather in the form of Aha, a problem understood! Of liberation from things not understood that drive good people crazy!

Students learn to do LML learning task analysis, too. One of the most useful LML tools is Cue Words Word Wall, developed by an elementary teacher who used LML with her classes since its inception. This tool, shown in Figure 7.5, simply lists the verbs, nouns, and adjectives commonly found in directions for or statements of learning tasks (e.g., writing prompts; homework assignments; end of chapter questions; project, term paper, and dissertation instructions) arranged in four clusters corresponding to the dominant patterned operation required to complete the task successfully. Teachers put up a chart that covers a large portion of the wall, hence the term *Word Wall*, as a reference for kids as they go about their daily schoolwork.

Recall that in preparing their essays for the writing prompt, students must respond to three questions: Before the ship sinks, *what would you choose to recover? Why would you choose those items? What would you do with them?* Using the Word Wall, students examine the first sentence and then use the chart's contents to identify the strategies that are called for. To answer the first question—what would you choose to recover, for example—students would need to make a *list*, a sequential process. The second question asks students for a rationale in choosing to save the list of items. Using the Word Wall, students determine that this part of the task requires them to *describe, explain, give reasons*, and *document*, all Precision verbs. The third question asks the students to *detail, describe, and identify specific* uses for items saved; it requires more Precision but may also draw on Technical Reasoning to *illustrate, demonstrate*, and *problem solve*, all related to practical problem solving. Predominant in all three questions is the need to plan, organize, and order (Sequence) and provide detail (Precision). Task analysis is complete, and it is clear to the students (and teachers) that the task as set out requires of the student a good amount of Sequence and Precision and a dab of Technical Reasoning. As we can see, Joe's LCI array of S-23, P-27, T-34, C-22 is not ideally suited for this task. While he has a Use First level of Precision, his extremely high Use First Technical Reasoning, which is not congruent with the task, completely overpowers his Precision if he remains in an unreflective state.

But the story is not complete yet. Joe now knows that his learning pattern array is not congruent with the on-demand prompt writing task. So what is he to do? This is the same question the teachers raised earlier when they engaged in task analysis: "OK, we see that the task and the

Figure 7.5 Cue Words Word Wall

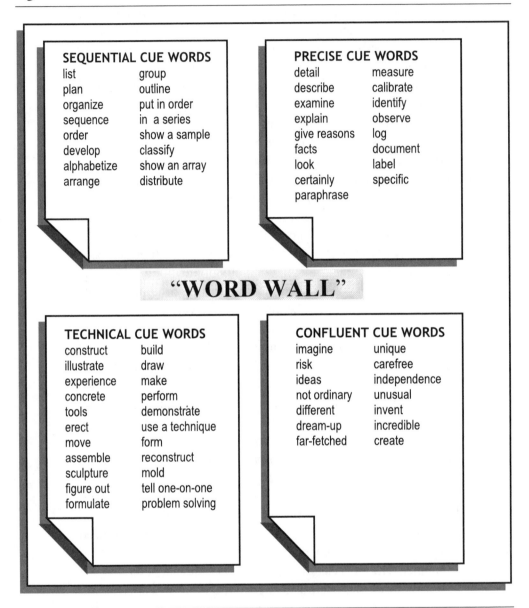

"WORD WALL"

SEQUENTIAL CUE WORDS

list	group
plan	outline
organize	put in order
sequence	in a series
order	show a sample
develop	classify
alphabetize	show an array
arrange	distribute

PRECISE CUE WORDS

detail	measure
describe	calibrate
examine	identify
explain	observe
give reasons	log
facts	document
look	label
certainly	specific
paraphrase	

TECHNICAL CUE WORDS

construct	build
illustrate	draw
experience	make
concrete	perform
tools	demonstrate
erect	use a technique
move	form
assemble	reconstruct
sculpture	mold
figure out	tell one-on-one
formulate	problem solving

CONFLUENT CUE WORDS

imagine	unique
risk	carefree
ideas	independence
not ordinary	unusual
different	invent
dream-up	incredible
far-fetched	create

SOURCE: Used with permission. © 1997-2003 LET ME LEARN, Inc. 2 Tiverstock Dr., Pittsgrove, NJ.

learner are incongruent in terms of patterned operations. So what do we do?" To answer these questions brings us to the highest and most sophisticated level of development: meta-analysis and intentional learning.

The whole process of learning task analysis or decoding is a powerful lifelong strategy for reflective learners, and the Word Wall is just as applicable to tasks assigned by a foreman in a factory or at a construction site, by a project manager in a software company, or by a platoon leader in the military. Task analysis is not just a test preparation strategy; at the same time, it can be very useful to both teacher and students preparing to perform a task such as the on-demand writing prompt that stumped Joe. Through involvement with LML, Joe, along with classmates and teachers, now has an understanding of his pattern matrix. They have learned to analyze tasks, and now the objective is to help them expand their repertoire of strategies so that they can be more effective on tasks that are difficult, given their specific patterns.

META-AWARENESS: BECOMING INTENTIONAL LEARNERS AND TEACHERS

Possessing knowledge of self as a learner, understanding the requirements embedded in learning tasks, and understanding how to analyze tasks has motivated teachers and students to use this new knowledge and understanding to improve their practice. They are ready to move to the final level of development. They are ready to experiment with new strategies.

For teachers this means engaging in intentional teaching. To teach intentionally means to teach with full awareness of children as learners and with a conscious effort to support them in using their unique, very personal learning-patterned operations matrices. Intentional teachers value the learner first and encourage kids to take responsibility for their own learning. Intentional teaching fosters trust and supports learners to move beyond their comfort zones in using learning processes and tools they would not have attempted to use prior to forming an LML learner-teacher partnership (Johnston, 2000).

Intentional learning is the learner response to intentional teaching; it is characterized by the desire to grow in understanding and responsible ownership of the learning experience, rather than pleasing the teacher and merely scavenging for answers. Intentional learners make the learning process work for them by recognizing how they use their own learning processes to explore, understand, and grow in their ability to learn effectively. They accomplish this by developing workable, personal learning strategies, negotiating with the learning environment (most important, the teacher), and developing respect for various learning modes (Johnston, 2000). Intentional learning is reflective learning. Joe, for example, needs to become an intentional learner to improve his performance significantly on the vast majority of learning tasks school sets before him. While Joe and his classmates now know that this specific writing prompt requires Sequence and Precision, what they learn more generally as they continue task analysis on a daily basis is that almost all school tasks require Sequence and Precision. Students low in Precision are particularly disadvantaged because tasks increasingly demand those precision-related strategies as they progress into secondary and postsecondary education (Pearle, 2002).

As a result, students with certain patterns are less likely to succeed. A study of high school freshman, for example, showed that students in the college-prep track had higher than average Sequence and Precision scores than those in the general track (see Table 7.1). The general track students, in contrast, had higher than average scores in Technical Reasoning and Confluence. Students with specific learning disorders had the highest scores in Technical Reasoning and the lowest in Precision with 81% using Technical Reasoning first and 50% avoiding Precision (Johnston, 2003b). Similarly, at the elementary level, among those classified for special education are a disproportionately high percentage of students with high scores in Technical Reasoning. The likelihood of classification increases as the Sequence and Precision scores move into the Avoid range. Other learning patterns also place students in jeopardy in the classroom. Students who have low scores in Sequence may succeed academically but are frequently the target of disciplinary action. The combination of Avoid Precision and Use Technical Reasoning First is particularly dangerous because the student avoids reading and writing (Grandin, 2002; Johnston, 2003b; Spadoni, 2002).

Table 7.1 Mean LCI Scores and Percentages for Those Who Use Technical Reasoning First and Avoid Precision Among Tracked Freshmen in One New Jersey High School

	Mean LCI Scores					Percentages of Students Who . . .	
Tracks	Sequence	Precision	Technical Reasoning	Confluence		Use First Technical Reasoning	Avoid Precision
• College Preparatory	28	22	20	20		32	14
• General Education	24	20	24	23		52	29
• Specific Learning Disability	24	18	29	22		81	50

SOURCE: Used with Permission. ©1997-2003 LET ME LEARN, Inc. 2 Tiverstock Dr. Pittsgrove, NJ.

Intentional teaching and learning become the goal for the final development stage in learning the LML process. But neither teachers nor children simply leap into this new level of learning accomplishment. Rather, there is additional understanding to gain and additional skills and tools to make one's own before the goal of internationality in teaching and learning is achievable. Understanding of and practice with the process of meta-processing and meta-awareness are what propel student and teacher learners into intentionality.

Meta-processing is the internal self-talk of learning that occurs whenever a learner is confronted with a learning task. It is a conversation among the mental processes of cognition, affectation, and conation. It uses cognition to recall all of the memorable learning experiences—good and bad. It uses conation to begin the task. It is also our gut or affective reaction, reminding us of prior feelings of failure, success, boredom, or excitement from involvement in learning. Using meta-processing strategies, learners are able to articulate what before they experienced but could not express. Through their experience in LML, they gain insight into these implicit beliefs, values, and assumptions about learning. They are expressing their theories-in-use.

The meta-processing strategies enable learners—children or adults—to gather information about their learning experience and to share information with others to gather valuable feedback:

- Mulling, for example, involves raising internal, self-talk questions in the middle of an assigned task, questions about feelings, prior experience, expectations, and needed resources.
- Connecting is a conscious effort to connect with the task requirements, to draw on experience and knowledge of self and others.
- Rehearsing is exactly that—the self-talk of trying out your response to get feedback and counsel before completion, but, at this step, it is done privately and the only audience (and critic) is the self.
- Expressing is the public performance, the authentic assessment, and, within the framework of LML, this is a public activity that welcomes feedback and encourages more reflection by the student on his or her own performance. Why did I use those words? What was I thinking when I answered the question this way?
- Revisiting, the final step, involves returning to the same or similar learning task to try it again, using the insight gained through this reflective process.

The culmination is Learning. By completing each of these phases, the student of whatever age has demonstrated the ability to grow, change, and develop and to do so with personal responsibility and intention (Johnston, 2000).

While these meta-processing strategies all support individual learning, they also change the nature of learning in several ways. First, they redefine learning as a collaborative effort rather than an individualistic and competitive process. Learners assume personal responsibility for their own work and develop skill in drawing on their own personal resources. They also learn to rely on others to support their learning. They learn to value critical feedback because they see its positive effects on their own work. The quality of conversation about work is not about brilliance or incompetence but on ways to enhance performance. Since learning is described as a developmental process involving multiple iterations—from creating a first draft and rehearsing to giving a final presentation and then revisiting the performance to conduct a self-assessment, identifying strengths and weaknesses—the emphasis is on effort and progress rather than ability (Kessler & Johnston, 2003). This task focus, while extremely important as a motivational strategy, is seldom found in learning environments (Maehr & Midgley, 1996). In each LML activity, learners are engaging in reflective practice, gathering information about their performance, assessing their performance relative to their intentions and their goals, and revising strategies to improve their practice in the next situation.

By raising these thought processes to conscious awareness, learners are able to translate this internal talk into external, explicit communication with other learners and teachers using LML vocabulary. Bringing the processes from inside the mind into the real time action of learning allows learners to communicate about where they are stalled, what they are pondering or wondering, what phase of learning they are in. One particularly touching illustration involves Susan, a special education student, diagnosed with disabilities in reading (dyslexia), writing (dysgraphia), and speaking (aphasia). LCI data showed her Technical Reasoning and Confluence patterns are high, while her Sequence and Precision patterns are very low. The students were involved in a project for an entire year, with the Word Wall clearly visible. All of a sudden, Susan jumped up, saying, "I *know!* We can write down this, this, and this!" And she said, "Oh my God, look at what I just did!" She then ran over to the Word Wall, went right to Sequence, and put her hand on the word *list.* "That's what I'm doing!" Seeing a student with such severe disabilities doing that, the teacher reported, was one of the most powerful experiences she ever had as a teacher (Silverberg, 2002, pp. 120-121). One can presume that the experience was equally powerful for the student.

Communication of the internal to the outside world makes it possible for learners to provide teachers and other learners with the information enabling them to engage in effective teaching, coaching, mentoring, and support (Johnston, 2000). For example, having a means to make internal talk public enables Ms. J to coach Joe more effectively about writing to on-demand prompts. Because their patterned matrices are quite different, they experience writing to a given prompt very differently, but externalizing their unique internal experiences using a common vocabulary enables them to communicate effectively about writing improvement strategies.

When learners are able to use meta-processing with intention, they arrive at the highest state of self-awareness, meta-awareness. Meta-awareness consists of the learner's knowledge of self as a learner. At this level, learners have knowledge and understanding of their learning processes, the interaction of those processes, their potential to achieve and to miscue on a given learning task (Johnston, 2003a). When students achieve this level, they can use their learning power with intention and deliberateness:

> They have become conscious of their transformation from being a passive student to an engaged learner. They know how to think through, rehearse, implement, and reflect upon their highly personalized learning strategies. They know how to get around the roadblocks, how not to become overwhelmed or underwhelmed by an assignment. They can literally work their way through the learning task. The learner who achieves this level of personalized proficiency as a learner is truly a model of educational accountability. (Johnston, 2000, p. 7)

In the classroom, Ms. J, as facilitator, will guide Joe and his classmates in using the seven phases of meta-processing, and they will become a normative part of the learning experience, a part of conversations about learning, assignments, testing, and other school tasks that take place between teacher and students and among peers, one-to-one or in small groups. As in numerous other classrooms, with practice, Joe and his classmates will likely reach the level of meta-awareness.

Teachers and professors using LML for themselves and with their students develop activities, lesson plans, and assignments to support learners in coming to know themselves as learners, to analyze tasks, and to develop meta-awareness. They also develop specific tools to facilitate those processes. An elementary teacher, for example, developed the Cue Words Word Wall. Another very powerful tool is the Power/Strategy Card.

The Power/Strategy Card is both an outcome of meta-processing and meta-awareness and a means for helping the learner maintain those processes of intentional learning during engagement in learning tasks. A Power/Strategy Card is metaphorically a meta-processing/meta-awareness crib sheet. It is a totally personal reminder of key strategies for a specific learner with a unique patterned matrix to improve performance on a particular kind of learning task.

The Power/Strategy Card contains three elements: the learner's LCI/patterned operations scores, the positive/negative attributes of each patterned operation in its specific range for accomplishing the specific task, and specific strategies to increase overall performance for each patterned operation. Once students achieve a sufficient level of meta-processing and meta-awareness to produce this information, they may develop different cards for different generic or specific learning tasks.

Joe, as we now know, uses Technical Reasoning and Precision first, but Technical Reasoning dominates. His Confluence and Sequence scores are lower: He uses them as needed, but unless he has a conscious awareness of task requirements and realizes that these skills are needed, he may not. When Joe has developed his skills in meta-processing and has achieved a minimal level of meta-awareness, he will understand his own learning needs, be able to analyze task requirements, and develop an appropriate strategy, in essence, counseling himself to change his own learning practice. At this level of development, Joe would have sufficient information and insight to be able to develop his own Power/Strategy Cards.

In Figure 7.6, we illustrate this tool with a Power/Strategy Card that a student with a patterned matrix like Joe's might create to help him improve his performance on the type of essay included in the state testing program. It responds to the task's particular embedded requirements and Joe's unique array of patterned operations. Note that Joe's Power/Strategy Card basically has strategies to tether (tone down) his Technical Reasoning and to extend (ratchet up) his Sequence and Precision. Other learners with different patterned operations matrices would have cards containing different general and specific strategies.

With experience, students as early as third grade are able to achieve surprising levels of meta-awareness and intentionality. Alex, a fifth-grade special education student in Joe's school, provides a startling example of a child who has progressed quite far in his development toward meta-awareness and intentionality. According to Alex's teacher, when he was participating in a hearing to determine his placement for the following year, he offered the following recommendation:

Figure 7.6 Joe's Personal Power/Strategy Card for On-Demand Writing Prompts

My Personal Strategy Card	Sequence	Precision	Technical Reasoning	Confluence
Joe's Scores ⟹	23 Use as Needed	27 Use First	34 Use First!	22 Use as Needed
Ways in which I would *"naturally"* use each of these patterns	I would not normally organize, make lists, plan, break an assignment into steps.	I can be fairly good at gathering information and asking questions, but don't like to write much.	This is **MY** pattern! I always get my hands on things, jump in and **DO** things that make sense to me. I only tell people information when I want to. I like to work alone. I don,t do things I don,t like.	I don't normally read between lines or see big pictures or do things very differently from others or brainstorm a lot.
	What is required of this patter?	*What is required of this pattern?*	*What is required of this pattern?*	*What is required of this pattern?*
What does the task or assignment require of each of these patterns?	Make a plan, organize my essay, list what I would take, follow directions carefully, and double-check my work.	Describe with details, explain my reasons, present facts, be specific, and write many more words than I like to.	Nothing at all!!	Maybe be a little inventive, but not too much.
	My personal strategy for using this pattern	*My personal strategy for using this pattern*	*My personal strategy for using this pattern*	*My personal strategy for using this pattern*
What I will say to myself. How will I use my patterns to accomplish the task?	**Extend a Lot!** Make a plan for the essay! Include an opening and closing. Make an outline of important points! Read the instructions carefully and note the points! Double-check my work when I think I am done!!	**Extend** Use more details and more words. Answer the questions directly. Pay attention to details of spelling, capitalization, punctuation, tenses, verb-subject agreement. Use logic in developing the essay. Communicate main ideas clearly.	**Tether!!** Write more words and details than normal. Give it all my energy even if I don't think it's important. Find a problem in it and enjoy solving it. Find more information than I think I need. Start with the sequence and precision issues. Don't start writing until I plan!!	**Tether!!** Use creative, imaginative ideas only if asked for. Brainstorm about details.

SOURCE: Used with permission. © 1997-2003 LET ME LEARN, Inc. 2 Tiverstock Dr., Pittsgrove, NJ.

You've got to put me with a teacher next year who knows Let Me Learn. See, I need a teacher who understands me because I'm not very organized, and I need to forge that [Sequence]. So if I am with a teacher who is sequential and understands that I'm not, then I can learn how to use my strategies better. (Johnston, 2003b, slides 45, 46)

His teacher reported, "I almost fell off my chair. He just opened up and said this, and then I said to myself, 'Wow! The kids get it. They really get it!'"

Out of the mouth of an "elementary," "problem" learner come amazing things! In the child's few words are many indicators of meta-awareness. He understands himself as a learner. He knows his patterned learning matrix and its meaning for school tasks, and he demonstrates competence in his use of LML vocabulary and concepts, accurately describing his learning and that of teachers and prescribing appropriately for himself. At a more general level, he also shows intentionality. He has an active rather than passive stance and is willing to negotiate with the learning environment to overcome obstacles. He is taking responsibility and accountability for his own learning and has a clear intention to learn well.

Any child brought to a special education hearing has had learning difficulty and undoubtedly has felt a great deal of frustration with school and learning tasks. Yet here Alex speaks as a very responsible kid working to meet personal needs and the goals school sets out for him; his attitude and intentions are sterling. LML and its use by at least one teacher have liberated him from much that before must have bound and taunted him. He is now an empowered and accountable learner. If he does experience the kinds of teachers he prescribes for himself in future, he is very likely to beat the odds of classified or otherwise labeled kids by developing a healthy self-concept and achieving as a learner.

There are data indicating that when teachers and students begin to engage in the Let Me Learn Process referrals to child study teams for the purpose of classification decline markedly. In a follow-up survey of twenty-three New Jersey and Ohio teachers who had worked with LML for a year, teachers reported that referrals of students were down more than 50% between the pre-LML year (1997) and 1998, the year of implementation (Johnston, 2003, personal communication). In 2001, an early childhood center in New Jersey also reduced the number of referrals by 40% (Grandin, 2002). Data like these, which contrast markedly with nationwide trends, have important implications.

LET ME LEARN AS REFLECTIVE PRACTICE

We contend that engaging in the Let Me Learn Process, including use of its concepts, vocabulary, activities, and tools, is a deep and broad exercise of reflective practice for both teachers and child learners. Through LML, teachers and students develop a conscious understanding of their own learning behavior. They become aware of the neurologically based patterns that influence their beliefs, assumptions, feelings, and actions when they confront learning tasks. They develop an experiential understanding of the triune mind, its processes and patterned operations, and, with this knowledge, they begin to reconceptualize learning itself. Teachers become aware of their own learning behavior and understand how their patterned operation matrices influence their action. Teachers also develop a new understanding of their students. Seeing commonalities and differences among them, they are able to empathize. They begin to respond to their students in different ways and diversify their teaching strategies.

Students who experience LML also develop a very conscious understanding of their own learning behavior. They have real information about their work as learners and begin to interact differently with teachers, with peers, and with the learning situation. They become empowered and personally accountable learners. They understand what's happening; they see their strengths and their weaknesses. More important, they now have information that empowers them. They have a language to communicate about their own learning, and they have developed a repertoire of strategies to help them to be more successful on a variety of tasks. They know how to help themselves learn. They are no longer dependent on the teacher. They are no longer powerless in a system that they can't understand. With this new paradigm, they change their behavior. While they may still not like tests, they know what they need to do to be successful on them.

As a result of their involvement in LML, teachers and students change individually, but the level of change extends beyond that to change the very nature of the relationship between teachers and students in the learning process. A constructivist professional development model, like that described in Chapter 1, the LML Process has enabled teachers and students to break the hierarchical boundaries that typically divide them and to create in the classroom what Silverberg (2002) described as relational spaces, where teachers and students work as partners in learning.

The LML Process has been introduced in twelve states and several other countries: United Kingdom (England and Northern Ireland), Italy, Australia, Israel, and Malta, where it is a required part of the teacher certification process.[5] The largest venue is public elementary schools. The process is also used in early childhood centers, secondary schools, technical schools, community and four-year colleges and universities, businesses, and corporations. In some schools, parents and families have also been introduced to LML, a strategy that has created parent, teacher, and child partnerships, able to work together productively to support student learning. At Hofstra University, we regularly introduce LML in advanced leadership programs and find it valuable not only as a means to change leaders' perspectives on learning but also as a strategy to support graduate learning.

Regardless of the locale or the level, responses are similar to those described here. The participants—adults and children—find the process relevant, helpful, and for some a literally life-changing experience that leads them to approach their work in very different ways. It leads to change in perception and to change in practice. In Chapter 1, we speak critically of prepackaged solutions, which may be very well developed and useful but fail to engage teachers in a deep analysis of their own thinking and their own practice. The LML Process clearly illustrates an alternate approach. Unlike programs that provide single-loop solutions, LML enables teachers and students to explore and change their own thinking and feeling as a means to developing individually constructed strategies to improve performance. LML engages teachers—and students—in a double-loop process of change.

LML has a unique, rich, and scientifically developed conceptual framework that is relevant to all learners in all settings. We believe that it is additionally powerful because it is introduced in a way that facilitates reflective practice, and we present it here as an important illustration of how professional development can be designed to achieve meaningful change.

Throughout the chapter, we made only passing references explaining LML as reflective practice. We now move to framing many of the experiences, activities, and experiences within the experiential learning cycle of reflective practice.

Teachers are initially engaged in the learning process as they focus on a key problem: that certain kids in their classes aren't learning and, like Joe, are failing the test. As the teachers begin discussion, they personalize the problem: They are not being successful with certain children.

Learning to use the LML Process involves the learner in rich and multiple loops of observation and analysis, the second stage of the experiential learning cycle. The LML process begins almost immediately with data gathering. Through the use of the LCI, teachers gather information about themselves, as learners. In collaborative and supportive settings, they share this information, and, through activities and discussion, they learn about their colleagues. As they share experiences, they also learn more about themselves as spouses, parents, friends, teachers, and colleagues.

As they analyze this information, they develop an understanding of their beliefs and assumptions about learning. While the patterned operations and the mental processes of cognition, conation, and affectation synchronously nested in each of them have neurobiologic roots, they are similar to the theory-in-use in several ways:

- They are largely tacit and reside below the level of conscious awareness.
- They drive the learner's learning behavior.
- They may produce desired or undesired outcomes.
- Unless they are explicitly known and controlled by the individual, they guide behavior in ways that may be dysfunctional.

While the patterned operations are fixed, the learner who reaches and is able to maintain the reflective state of intentional learning and the teacher who achieves the state of intentional teaching are able consciously to override the unreflective state of their neurologically anchored patterned operations by consciously/reflectively tethering those that are too strong for the given learning task and extending or forging those that the task calls for in a higher range.

The LCI plays a particularly valuable role in the LML process because it facilitates the identification of these important underlying theories-in-use about learning. It is a powerful tool to tap and measure the strength of the patterns directly. In other areas of inquiry, while there are different indirect ways to identify theories-in-use, there are no such valuable single tools available for finding and naming theories-in-use directly.

Teachers also gather information about students through observation and through the LCI. Students gather information about their learning theories and about their own behavior as learners through systematic data (the LCI), direct observation (experiential activities), and reflective assessment (journaling, meta-processing). Observational opportunities are broad and deep, and they take place continuously throughout the process, supplementing and enriching the ongoing analysis.

The analysis, as we have mentioned, focuses on teachers and children as learners, understanding the connections among the LML concepts, behaviors as learners, and the outcomes of these actions. Using tools like the Word Wall, students and teachers also gather information about the requirements of various learning tasks and again assess their own learning behavior. This knowledge is an important prelude to developing more successful action strategies. Both students and teachers grow in understanding of how to align strategies with the requirements needed for successful accomplishment of various tasks. In short, everything and anything related to learning that is observed becomes a potential opportunity for analysis, and every analysis generates the potential for additional observation and data collection.

Reaching the stage of reconceptualization signals that double-loop learning is in process, that the learner is reconstructing assumptions. It signals minded activity rather than simple behavior adjustment to a problematic situation. Teacher and child learners who reach the stage of reconceptualization are empowered and literally take off in new directions. It is in this stage that they begin active use of meta-awareness, that they become intentional learners and intentional teachers. In their internal talk they start to articulate different assumptions: "If I use intentional teaching and learning, I can make it work!" They also begin to act on the belief that the learner is in charge of his or her own learning. Teachers become more open to learner requests; children begin to initiate suggestions. It means that teacher and child learners liberate themselves from some of the traditions of schooling that actually inhibit rather than support learning. The child learner voice of Alex in his hearing is the counterpart of the teacher perspective. Like the teachers, Alex, too, is saying, "I understand myself as a learner. I can make this work for me, especially if I have a teacher who understands me and is willing to work it out with me"—amazing empowerment from a kid who has many reasons to be less optimistic.

The final stage of the experiential learning cycle of reflective practice is experimentation. With new understanding, teachers and students begin to experiment with new teaching and new learning strategies. Teachers begin to structure cooperative learning groups based on the LCI scores of their child learners. Teachers honestly begin to perceive and experience themselves more as learners. (Initially, every teacher proclaims being a learner or lifelong learner, but after engagement in LML will sometimes say that was not really true.) They say it explicitly to their students and demonstrate it. Teachers begin to embed LML concepts into lesson planning and experiment with multiple ways to fulfill assignments. They are open to kids' ideas about what works for them (and they discover it is not just more work for them).

Kids analyze tasks before beginning their work, try out Power/Strategy Cards, and develop their skill in meta-processing. They share their experience, facilitating their own learning as well as that of their peers and teachers. Experimentation with LML often leads to success; when it works with one kind of learning task, they are eager to apply these strategies to other tasks. Success encourages additional observation and analysis, reconceptualization and experimentation. Through practice, many of these children become skilled as learners. Where the experiments do not work out, the process has taught teachers and kids alike to work in collaborative communities and to consult others for help. In some classrooms, and increasingly in schools, the idea of a learning organization has become an exciting reality.

We believe that the idea of children becoming reflective practitioners of their own learning is one with amazing and as yet untapped potential. The potential is not only for the near view of success in school or the exceedingly myopic issue of high-stakes test performance. It is the much more exciting and hopeful vision of kids as intrinsically motivated, truly empowered, joyful, and effective learners. It is also a vision for teachers to derive deep satisfaction from teaching and to realize the goal that initially drew them to the profession, the desire to nurture children, helping them to discover for themselves the keys to unlock their capacity and will to learn.

NOTES

1. All references to Joe's case in this chapter were taken from an experiment in a single school district to determine whether participation in the Let Me Learn Process would be associated with increases in writing scores. A prompt drawn from the NJESPA was used as a pre- and posttest. Essays were scored using the regular state rubric by teachers from another district.

2. LML professional development is tailored to meet the unique needs of schools and districts. Ideally, the sessions are scheduled during the school year. This enables teachers to collect and analyze information about students and their own interactions with them prior to and during implementation. Highly compressed development, as in a five-day summer workshop with little follow-up, results in a much diminished sense of efficacy among teachers and lower implementation.

3. The LCI comes in three reading/experience levels. It has been assessed as both valid and reliable at all three levels when administered and validated by a certified facilitator or teacher (Johnston & Dainton, 1997b).

4. Deeper validation occurs over time as the individual compares his or her LCI scores with many forms of behavioral data from present and past personal experience (work products, artwork, emotional responses to learning tasks, group behavior, photos from childhood, activities, etc.).

5. Let Me Learn, Inc., is a not-for-profit organization, organized exclusively for educational purposes under Section 501(c)(3) of the Internal Revenue Code. For information about LML, the LCI, LML materials, or research and development opportunities, contact Let Me Learn, Inc., at info@letmelearn.org.

Reflective Practice for Empowerment

In the first four chapters of this book, we developed several key points. We emphasized the importance of ideas as sources of action and discussed how those ideas are often an imperfect interpretation of reality. We described reflective practice as a cycle of experiential learning that helps us to reframe experience and to develop new action theories and strategies. We talked about the catalytic role of valid information and the importance of open, descriptive, and nonjudgmental communication. We also explained how the traditional concept of appropriate organizational behavior (Model I thinking) with its emphasis on unilateral control deters reflective practice. Most important, we claimed that reflective practice is a potent and effective professional development strategy for enhancing individual learning, creating change, and shaping learning organizations.

The three cases presented here, we believe, illustrate each of these points and lend credibility to these arguments far beyond our abstract language. At the same time, when we look at these cases, we see neither a pat formula nor one best approach. To the contrary, as the narratives demonstrate, reflective practice takes different forms. In Chapter 5, we saw educators experiencing reflective practice as they completed a required assignment. The teachers were participants in a class but engaged in reflective practice largely through a dialogue between themselves and the instructor or facilitator. In Chapter 6, we saw teachers coming together on a volunteer basis to engage in action research with their principal and one another on an issue they defined as serious and worthy of their attention. In their reflective practice, they worked closely with one another in a collaborative and supportive situation. The facilitator, the school principal, played a supportive but nonintrusive role. Her primary tasks were to explain the process, arrange meetings so that teachers would have the opportunity to share their findings, and support their inquiry by listening and reflective questioning. At the end, she also facilitated by asking the participants to articulate their learning. In Chapter 7, we described teachers and students engaging in reflective practice as a result of a data-based intervention. The educators did not intend to engage in reflective practice. Nonetheless, confronted with new information, they, too, became reflective practitioners, learning about themselves as learners and teachers, and, by sharing information openly, they engaged their students in reflective practice, enabling them to develop new understanding and strategies in approaching their own learning.

The facilitator role while nonobtrusive was important in establishing the groundwork for reflective practice. In the Problematic Student Project, Kottkamp set the stage for reflective practice by designing an intervention that would facilitate observation and reflective analysis and by introducing ideas and information from the formal knowledge base that provided a deeper understanding of what the prospective administrators were doing and why. Siris (2001) raised consciousness about the problem of bullying among teachers and then introduced a new conceptual framework that helped teachers to reassess the situations in their classrooms. Christine Johnston (1996, 1998, 2000) developed a conceptual framework (LML) and an analytic tool (LCI) that literally reframes teachers' understanding of learning and designed a professional development process that effectively leads to change because it engages teachers and their students in reflective practice. In that professional development process, the facilitator is an outside consultant but relies on experiential rather than didactic learning methods. While showing the importance of the facilitator and additional resources, it also shows how ideas and information from the formal knowledge base become the means rather than the end. They are tools to assist educators as they develop knowledge and chart their own professional development path.

Not all of those involved in reflective practice completed all of the stages of the experiential learning cycle. Since the intent of reflective practice is improved professional performance, ideally the goal is to complete all four stages. Nonetheless, each stage of the process contributes to personal learning. The cases also demonstrate how all stages of the process are essential to double-loop learning or second-order change. Change is the combined effect of identifying a problem, gathering comprehensive information about the problem, analyzing the data in relationship to our own goals and values, and then actually experimenting with the new ideas and strategies emerging from this analysis. At the same time, it should be apparent that reflective practice is not necessarily a linear process. The process can begin at different points, and learners may revisit earlier stages. One constant, however, is the intense power of valid data to stimulate reflective practice and learning. Confronted with data, practitioners often move rapidly into analysis, reconceptualization, and action planning. Data are indeed powerful!

These cases about reflective practice also document the importance of experiential and contextually based learning. Learning does not occur in a predictable time frame. In fact, each case documents great learning in relatively little time, but the time frame was flexible enough to meet the needs of the group, and the learning took place in the context of the work environment. As one of the action research participants mentioned, "It's different than a one-shot staff development lesson" (Siris, 2001, p. 132). For her, the hands-on dimension of the learning—the opportunity to learn from everyone, planning, and then watching her plan make such a difference in her student's life—was critical.

The relationship between ideas and action is also well developed. It is quite evident how teachers' perceptions influence their behavior and how their growing awareness of their assumptions and their practice creates change. What is also interesting is to see the way that Model I assumptions influence teacher behavior in the classroom. Concern with control and the use of control strategies is predominant. Students were so problematic because their behavior challenged teachers' ability to maintain control. The work of Argyris (1982, 1990) and others documented the effect of this meta-theory on leadership behavior in organizations. Fishbein (2000) showed how this control theory is integrated into the socialization pattern that prospective educational administrators experience during their internships, and these cases show us how this theory-in-use emerges in the classroom with very serious consequences.

At the same time, these cases affirm that reflective practice is an effective intervention. Confronted with valid information about their work, educators overcome these lifelong lessons and change their practice. In very short time periods, professionals develop profoundly different perspectives of themselves and their own work. More important, they use these new understandings to change the nature of their work in ways that have almost immediate positive effects on students' learning.

We know that organizational expectations, norms, and conditions affect the continuity of behaviors. Student teachers, for example, frequently lose sight of the progressive student-oriented strategies embedded in teacher education programs when they confront the reality of schools that value and demand doctrinaire approaches to instruction. Similarly, we observe prospective administrators shedding their ideals as they, too, move into traditional bureaucratic, hierarchically dominated systems.

Nonetheless, we believe that the depth of the learning and the strength of the responses may sustain learning. Educators who develop a deeper understanding of themselves, change their ways of thinking and doing, and experience the positive effects of these changes are more likely to persist in continuous learning.

In Chapter 6, we also provided evidence of how reflective practice can begin to reshape organizational norms. For these teachers, it was the first opportunity in their professional careers to work so intensely with a group of their colleagues and principal on a professional development issue. All of them found it enjoyable and rewarding and credited their learning to the support and stimulation they received. "Listening and sharing ideas with each other was the most important part. . . . Without this we wouldn't have made changes. . . . Without it, I definitely would not have known how to get there" (Siris, 2001, pp. 131, 132). Whether the strength of their experience will prompt them to continue to seek out opportunities for collaboration or whether the school structure will change to include more opportunities for collaborative reflection and action are issues for further research. In Chapter 7, we saw community developing in the classroom, as teachers and students developed a very different working relationship, becoming partners in learning. Working together as reflective practitioners, working with their students, brought teachers and students together in what Silverberg (2002) described as a relational space.

The ability to understand themselves and their students, the tools and vocabulary allowing them to communicate effectively with their students, created a possibility of connection. Integration of new knowledge, assumptions, and beliefs about their students, themselves, and their professional practice removed the separation between them and brought them into the same relational space. This relational space is the place where the teacher and students can work together toward an increasingly connected relationship that grows in its ability to meet the learning (thinking, feeling, and doing) needs of both the teacher and the student (Silverberg, 2002, p. 143).

These cases are not inclusive. In Chapter 2, we gave examples of how reflective practice can be integrated into school practice. In our work with prospective administrators, for example, we regularly see the way that communicating objective data transforms the supervisory process into reflective practice. In case after case, we see how teachers, whether new or experienced, invariably initiate self-analysis after having the opportunity to review only the descriptive information gathered during the class observation. Although this practice, widely recommended by professional organizations and researchers, literally revolutionizes the supervision process and facilitates a collaborative relationship between supervisor and teacher, common practice requiring the supervisor to assess and recommend before consultation with the teacher remains the norm. We also know from research and experience that many school leaders—principals and superintendents—integrate reflective practice into their everyday work. They use data to assess school performance, they share information openly with all members of the school community, and they engage their staff and constituents in problem analysis and problem solving. We would like to see more cases documenting these practices and their effects.

With respect to the effectiveness of reflective practice as a professional development strategy, our language is an understatement in comparison with lived experience. Highlighting differences in the process also serves to highlight similarities. One of the most important constants is that reflective practice leads to real professional development, where deep personal learning actually takes place. In a recent conversation, one of our graduate students talked about how amazed he was to be learning and contrasted his current experience with six years of undergraduate and graduate education. Before this, he said, he hadn't really known what learning felt like. Siris (2001) and her teachers became convinced that the mode of professional development they experienced was the only way to do it. One teacher related the following summary:

> [It was] a powerful force in making me realiz[e] things that were missing in my classroom. Meeting on a weekly basis, listening to what everyone else was doing with their plan, becoming conscious of my behavior towards children, and reflecting on what children were doing on an affective level were all wonderful and gave me insight into myself as a learner. (p. 133)

People who experience the power of reflective practice describe it as an astounding and often life-changing experience, unlike anything in their past: "one of the most significant learning experiences and change agents in my nineteen years as an educator" (Berkey et al., 1990, p. 220). In one sense, this is a gratifying response. On the other hand, considering that most educators bring nearly twenty years of formal education to the classroom in addition to countless hours of professional development, the absence of learning experiences like these is distressing.

Educators who engage in reflective practice give similar reports about how the process has affected them. The changes they describe are both personal and organizational. They talk about their changing view of the world and about seeing things in new and different ways. They talk about changes in their attitudes, beliefs, and assumptions and about new meaning. They talk about new understanding of themselves, as learners and teachers; they talk about understanding their students in very different ways. Those who worked in a group talk about change in the nature of their relationships with professional colleagues and how they came to see themselves as part of supportive teams with shared goals and values rather than as isolated individuals struggling in an uncaring environment. Finally, they talk about changes in their practice, how even well into their careers they are changing the way they do things, often with surprising and dramatic results.

Given the consistencies in these reports, it would be difficult to deny that the reflective process stimulates new thinking that leads to changes in professional practice. But why? What in the process enables people to reconsider long-held beliefs and to break patterns of behavior reinforced by habit and culture? Although this question could result in a very complex answer, there are clearly three aspects of the process that are particularly supportive of professional growth and development. Throughout the book, we commented repeatedly that data are the keystone to the process. Good information is essential for meaningful change to occur. In the process of reflective practice, professionals gather information about the problematic situation; they also gather information about themselves.

In a somewhat atypical fashion, reflective practice both thrives on and helps to develop an environment of open communication and collaboration. It works best when reflective practitioners work together as a group to gather and assess information. Sharing information increases the resources available to all. The descriptive and nonjudgmental nature of the information further enhances communication and nurtures collaboration. Finally, reflective practice works because it is an empowering process. It respects the autonomy of professionals and enhances their sense of efficacy.

INFORMATION

Information is the power of reflective practice. Engaging in the process, reflective practitioners gather information about problem situations. They also gather information about themselves and their practice.

The necessity to visit and revisit what are often everyday situations leads professionals to develop a new and different understanding. As they systematically gather information about situations and events, exploring emotions, actions, and outcomes, they reframe situations and see the taken-for-granted in a new and different light: The problematic student no longer seems problematic. They begin to see different dimensions of the problem; through observation and analysis, its complexity emerges. This outcome in itself is a valuable one. An accurate and comprehensive understanding of the problem is the most critical element of problem solving. Failure to identify the real problem leads to symptomatic solutions. As the problem becomes clear, the solutions—meaningful solutions—become evident (Senge, 1990; Senge et al., 2000).

In the observation and analysis stage, the reflective practitioners also develop a deeper understanding of themselves. As they examine the problematic situation, they focus on their own practice in a very comprehensive way. As they do this, they develop a new perspective of their action, and they are invariably drawn to assess their work in the light of their values and beliefs. Observing problematic students leads teachers to identify previously unidentified strengths in these children. These insights, in turn, lead them to revisit and reflect on some of their deeply held beliefs about teaching and learning that had been ignored in the pressure of professional life. In many instances, they begin to see that they are part of the problem.

The teachers scrutinize their assumptions, the interpretations they make about everyday events, critique them in the light of data, and eventually uncover those deeply held beliefs grounded in culture and reinforced through experience. This is a truly unique aspect of reflective practice. It engages people in the learning process as individuals. It requires them to be involved wholly, not simply as professionals but also as thinking, feeling, caring, and responsible human beings. It emphasizes and honors the personal in what is becoming an increasingly impersonal organizational world. As they come to understand themselves more deeply, they are then able to understand others better. As teachers learn about themselves as learners, they are better able to empathize with their students; they are more patient, less frustrated. And, of course, the reverse is also true. As they come to understand others better, they develop a deeper understanding and acceptance of themselves.

Whether directly or indirectly, reflective practice encourages an examination of personal beliefs and values. As we mentioned earlier, what seems a simple task—to describe personally held professional beliefs and values—proves to be surprisingly difficult. When the vision is clear, however, a number of things happen. The discrepancies—the contradictions between what we say and what we do—become more obvious. As professionals articulate goals and assess the current situation, action strategies become readily apparent, and teachers report the amazing utility of this seemingly simple value articulation process in dealing with a wide range of professional and personal problems.

The contrast between the preferred situation and the reality not only defines the problem more clearly but also becomes an incentive to take action (Senge, 1990; Senge et al., 2000). "Why were we willing to make commitments and why were we willing to take risks?" queried teachers involved in a reflective practice project. "Because we cared about closing that gap between the reality that we saw in the classroom and the idea that we could envision" (Berkey et al., 1990, p. 216).

A great deal has been written about the importance of vision for leadership. Beginning with the effective schools research and the importance of expectations in shaping a culture of achievement, educational and organizational researchers have highlighted the importance of clearly defined values, beliefs, and goals (Leithwood et al., 1994; Peters & Waterman, 1982; Senge, 1990; Senge et al., 1999). The articulation of values, beliefs, and goals—the development of vision—is central to reflective practice. At every stage, the individual examines his or her personal beliefs within the organizational context. What is it that I want to accomplish? What are my beliefs about good schools, and what facilitates learning? Where do I stand as an educator, and what are the implications for how I should act? As Wafa experienced, developing a more conscious sense of her basic values and goals renewed her own sense of responsibility to revitalize her practice.

Through articulating a platform, the individual begins to see the self in a different perspective. Where before the system may have been the dominant figure, now the individual emerges from the background as focal. The emphasis is no longer organizational constraints but individual options. DeCharms's (1968, 1976, 1984) concept of origin/pawn is useful here in explaining how the origin functions within the context of organizational constraints. For the pawn, all individual actions are shaped by beliefs about what the system will or won't allow. In contrast, the origin working among constraints no less real shifts the focus to determine what she or he intends to do given the existing obstacles. The organization hasn't changed, but the individual has refocused the lens to construct a different reality. Like Matt, Susan, and Alex, Ms. J, and the other teachers, origins shift the focus from "I can't" to "I can." Reflective practice enables us to experience ourselves as origins within educational settings.

COMMUNICATION AND COLLABORATION

Reflective practice thrives in an environment of open communication and collaboration. There is more information; people speak freely to one another about their ideas, concerns, successes, and failures; and their conversations build on valid data rather than inference, speculation, and innuendo. Because there is so much conversation, so much interaction, and because most of it focuses on professional work issues, the reflective practice environment—whether a small group of teachers or administrators, a class, or an entire school—becomes a learning environment. Reflective practitioners focus on their own work in an effort to develop a deeper understanding and a higher level of competence. As they share ideas and information, they develop new and better strategies. They learn—from and with one another. As a result, their sense of efficacy and effectiveness increases. All of these interrelated aspects of enhanced work-related communication are clearly in evidence in this book. They are also reported in other narratives and studies about reflective practice environments (Berkey et al., 1990; Cambron-McCabe, 2003; Kottkamp & Silverberg, 2003; Silverberg, 2002, 2003).

The flow of information in the process of reflective practice is very different from what professionals typically encounter. In many schools, teachers have limited access to information. On an organizational level, few educational organizations engage in systematic and regular assessment. While some data may be a matter of public record, access to information is often restricted. On an individual level, although performance feedback is a critical element in professional growth, it is a rare situation in which individuals actually have access to meaningful feedback about their own work (Osterman, 1994). Feedback is offered infrequently and, when provided, is often unrelated to the needs or interests of the practitioners, whether teachers, administrators, or students. In most organizations, formal evaluations provide one of the few opportunities for professionals to obtain information about their performance, yet we know the process seldom yields information helpful to the recipient. Information about the performance is usually gathered and interpreted by a supervisor. Similarly, the supervisor frequently develops the assessment and accompanying recommendations, privately and unilaterally, often without substantive input from the recipient.

Within the reflective practice model, there is more and different information, the information is generated in a different way, and the interpretation of information is usually self-directed with the support of others. The reflective process generates a great deal of information about performance, and that information is shared openly. There is also an emphasis on valid descriptive data rather than judgment or prescription. The observational data are shared, not simply the interpretation of that information. In addition, the practitioner—teacher, administrator, or student—often plays a key role in gathering the information, analyzing it, and making decisions about subsequent action. Because the facilitator and other members of the group avoid the role of evaluator and prescriber, the locus of control remains with the practitioner. In reflective practice, the facilitator is not a judgmental superior but a collaborator, stimulating professional growth in a way consistent with the needs of the individual. Teachers, students, and administrators work together and the traditional superior-subordinate relationship becomes one of collegiality and collaboration.

Our ability to engage in reflective practice and to share performance information openly with one another is colored by our beliefs that professionals need and want more information and are able to discuss problems in an open way with colleagues. While it is not too difficult to accept the idea of providing positive feedback about successful effort, it is much more difficult to believe that professionals want to know where and when their performance is less than perfect. Yet the experience of reflective practitioners, as well as a substantial body of research, supports the position that individuals need, want, value, and use information about their performance, even when the information highlights problems. Although Schon (1983) talked about how reflective practice requires the practitioner to "give up the rewards of unquestioned authority, the freedom to practice without challenge to competence, the comfort of relative invulnerability, and the gratifications of deference" (p. 299), the experience of reflective practitioners suggests these rewards are more likely to be a burden compared to the satisfactions derived from honest and open communication. In her work with a group of therapists, for example, Mattingly (1991) reported that "Nearly everyone mentioned their relief at being able to speak of their practice as a place where things often did not run smoothly and where they and their patients often did not seem to agree about what should happen in therapy" (p. 254). In each of the cases reported here, there was surprise when practitioners discovered the inconsistencies and shortcomings in their practice, but there was no angst. To the contrary, being able to see the problem as well as their own role in the problem seemed to enhance their sense of efficacy. Where once they could generate no meaningful responses, they now could see not only room for improvement but also ways to improve. Experiencing the positive results from those strategies was even more empowering.

This open flow of communication about professional issues has a number of positive effects. According to Senge (1990), providing people with information about performance enables them to develop a better picture of the current reality. The contrast between what is and what we would like, the contrast between the reality and the vision, Senge maintained, is the source of the creative tension essential to personal and organizational growth. Through the reflective process, individuals become more aware of these discrepancies; they also become more aware of their own role in the problem. They assume personal responsibility. As people have more information about their practice, they are better able to identify ways they can improve their own performance and are more likely to take action.

Through reflective practice, individuals learn about their own performance. Because of the emphasis on exploration, analysis, and collaboration, individuals also have access to more information about alternative strategies. The process of reflective practice expands the pool of resources available to any individual. By bringing more people into the process, it also provides multiple perspectives. At the conclusion of the action research project described in Chapter 6, the teachers were emphatic about the importance of collaboration. "Listening and sharing ideas with each other was the most important part. Without this, we wouldn't have made changes." "Listening to everyone's ideas helped me see my own actions differently." They gained information from others; they gained information by more carefully observing their own practice. The most important feedback, however, came as they began to experiment. "I learned from everyone—and from watching my plan make such a difference in my student's life." "I was getting ideas from other teachers and actually implementing them. Often, I'll start something new and stop it. This, I continued because we had so much feedback." The expertise of colleagues and personal experience enriches learning in important ways, but we have also seen how other information and knowledge drawn from research can be introduced successfully, meaningfully, and effectively into the learning process.

School personnel—teachers and administrators—work in very isolated ways within their districts and buildings. Teachers are bound by their classrooms or departments and have few opportunities for collegial discussion, let alone focused discussions about their work. Administrators, too, principals and superintendents alike, lead lonely existences, meeting infrequently for professional conversation with their colleagues. Reflective practice expands the dialogue and provides a structure in which colleagues can share information and ideas.

This flow of open and descriptive communication creates a climate of caring and collaboration and helps to create partnerships that transcend hierarchical boundaries (Barnett, 1990; Fishbein, 2000). Likert (1961), for example, was one of the early theorists who emphasized the importance of interaction and influence among members and leaders in organizations: When individuals are involved with others, they are more fully implicated as a person, more committed, more involved. When people talk and work with others, they are more likely to like them (Baumeister & Leary, 1995; Homans, 1950). The more they like and care about each other, the harder they will work to ensure team success (DeRosa-Karby, 2002; DeRosa-Karby & Osterman, 2002; Fullan, 2001; Sagor, 1991).

EMPOWERMENT

Those who participate in reflective practice often describe a feeling of empowerment and, in their practice, become more comfortable empowering others. In each of the cases, teachers talked about being able to do things that they hadn't realized they could do. They began to see connections where they had seen none before. They began to realize that they could make a difference. With this growing sense of efficacy, they began to make changes. Silverberg (2002) also noted increases in self-efficacy among teachers who had worked with the Let Me Learn Process. As teachers developed understanding of themselves and students, they no longer perceived the students as problematic, and they were able to identify strategies that worked.

Individuals have basic motivational needs to experience competence, autonomy, and relatedness (Connell & Wellborn, 1991). As students, teachers, or administrators, individuals need to experience themselves as capable of producing desired outcomes and avoiding negative outcomes; they need to feel competent. They also need to experience autonomy, which grows out of the experience of connectedness between one's actions, personal goals, and values as well as control over one's activities. Finally, people need to feel securely connected to others in their environment and need to experience themselves as worthy and capable of love and respect. People—adults and children—need to feel that others care about them.[1]

The process of reflective practice responds to each of these motivational needs. It provides the information needed for people to effect positive changes in performance; it respects the right of individuals to exercise self-direction and, even more, enhances their ability to exercise control over their own learning and their own actions. It respects choice. Finally, it engages people in a collaborative process of professional development that responds to their needs for relatedness. As professionals come to understand themselves better, they have a better understanding and appreciation for others—colleagues and students. Because the rich learning environment of reflective practice generates such valuable information, professionals not only identify productive strategies but also have the opportunity to experiment. The experience of success with problems that once seemed daunting enhances the sense of efficacy, another critical motivational factor directly related to performance. No example conveys this more powerfully than the ecstatic response from Susan, the student with multiple handicaps: "Oh my God, look at what I just did!"

As we saw in these cases, as educators themselves feel more empowered, they are also more comfortable in empowering others. We saw teachers recognizing children's need for self-direction and developing a sense of comfort in accommodating those needs. As they experienced their own autonomy, they were more comfortable in recognizing and addressing their students' needs for autonomy.

In sum, reflective practice is an empowering and motivational process because it responds to basic human needs for competence, autonomy, and relatedness. The central reflective processes of communication and collaboration are empowering. They enable individuals to be more effective, to assume greater responsibility for their own performance and learning, and to work more closely and more productively with others in the workplace. When individuals are more effective, they enable organizations to be more effective.

REFLECTIVE PRACTICE IN AN AGE OF REFORM: A CAVEAT

In Chapter 1, we posed the hypothesis that reflective practice was a viable means to school reform. This statement, however, should not be viewed as simplistic or overly idealistic. Obviously, organizational change, and school reform in particular, are extremely complex phenomena. Nonetheless, the chances for success increase to the extent that there are multiple perspectives and a variety of strategies (Bolman & Deal, 1991; Fullan, 1999, 2001; Hargreaves & Fullan, 1998; Lambert et al., 2002). Reflective practice is a human resource strategy. Sorely missing from discussions of school reform, this theoretical perspective maintains that organizations and people depend on one another and that processes satisfying human needs also serve organizational purpose. Reflective practice is a process that empowers and motivates individuals and groups through an ongoing process of professional development. In this process, as people begin to envision new possibilities and to work together in different ways to achieve newly defined goals, the possibility of change on a broader level becomes more real.

Reflective practice creates a sense of optimism about organizational change, a sense that meaningful change is possible. Unlike national and state efforts to achieve school reform through federal funding, revised certification standards, and standardized testing, however, reflective practice is a grassroots approach. Schools will become better places when teachers in classrooms and principals in schools and superintendents in districts begin to talk more about the vision and the reality and when they begin to work together to create knowledge and to devise better and more appropriate ways to meet the needs of the children they serve. "Better schooling will result in the future—as it has in the past and does now—chiefly from

the steady, reflective efforts of the practitioners who work in schools"
(Tyack & Cuban, 1995, p. 135).

Thus, reflective practice is empowering at both the individual and
organizational levels; it is a powerful, multilevel source for individual and
systemic change. But we are using empowerment in a particular way.
Empowerment is a buzzword, and, in general conversation, especially
among persons who think in traditional hierarchical terms, it is often
assumed to be something given to subordinates, something controlled by
superiors and parceled out in specific amounts. This is not our understanding of empowerment. As already illustrated by statements from educators, it is not something given but something emanating from the self. It
is not an entity distributed through a chain of command but a willingness
and drive to act professionally and responsibly, grounded in a sense of
self-esteem, competence, and autonomy. Reflective practice is a major
vehicle for empowerment as we conceptualize it, but it is antithetical to
the concept of empowerment as a controlled and distributable resource.
At the same time, organizations can be structured in ways that encourage
individuals to become origins rather than pawns.

The caveat concerning reflective practice and school reform is that
precisely controlled and externally prescribed reform outcomes simply
cannot be achieved through this process. We cannot mandate highly specific reform outcomes of the kinds that state legislatures and departments
of education have propounded in recent times. We cannot specify reflection as the means for introducing or changing a particular program, a
particular curriculum, or a particular disciplinary procedure. We cannot
reach an externally produced, preordained end through genuine reflective
practice processes. Because reflective practice leads individuals to improve
their own performance, the process ultimately enriches the organization's
ability to achieve goals, but it is also quite likely that through reflection
many alternative and effective paths to the same goal will emerge.

This is not to say that reflective practice leads in no predictable direction. In fact, reflective practice invariably moves individuals and organizations toward Model II and away from Model I assumptions and behaviors
in a broad way. It helps to create professional learning communities and
minimizes the need to rely on top-down control strategies. In a sense,
reflective practice not only directs but also deflects. As it moves us toward
the development of thoughtful and collaborative learning communities,
it moves us away from those aspects of organizational behavior that
generate defensiveness, isolation, powerlessness, and alienation. It moves
us away from unilateral imposition of power, strict externally controlled
accountability mechanisms, competition that pits colleagues against
one another—all organizational realities characterizing so many of the

reform attempts during the past several decades. Instead, it moves us toward the development of professional communities, bonded in the intent to improve the quality of education for all children but particularly for those who have been least successful.

Reflective practice is a potentially powerful avenue for school improvement and systemic change. We say potentially because it has not been tried yet in any serious way. To try it seriously means calling off business as usual and trusting professional educators and parents in ways not even considered under many contemporary reform proposals and our pervasive and persistent reliance on traditional ways of doing things. To try it seriously means accepting on a broad front the kinds of beliefs and attitudes we recommended for facilitators. To try it seriously means those in power in schools, districts, state departments of education, governors' offices, and legislatures will need to trust those in the field to improve education and give them adequate time to develop, implement, assess, and revise action alternatives. To try it seriously means that academics in professional preparation programs need to relinquish control over the learning process by becoming less didactic and more focused on the link between the classroom and the world of practice. Ironically, we cannot mandate reflection—no more than we can mandate collaborative decision making. What we can do is to provide the space, time, and support for those who already have the volition to try it. Certainly this nation could afford and profit from some genuine experiments in reflection as means of change and improvement.

We seek colleagues who will join us in this quiet approach to change, who will move to the frontier that awaits us in almost every school and university in this nation, and who are willing to take risks to grow and improve their own professional practice while working with others to improve themselves. If we have learned anything in our personal journeys with reflective practice, we have learned that it is only through changing ourselves that we have any hope of changing others. That simple and overlooked truth is at the very center of becoming reflective practitioners. We seek colleagues who are prepared to risk changing. And perhaps we would also encourage those who share these understandings of professional development and change to be less quiet.

NOTE

1. The following are some sources for additional discussion of the importance of caring in schools: see Altenbaugh, Engel, and Martin (1995); Beck (1994); Murphy et al. (2001); Noddings (1992); and Osterman (2000, 2002).

References

Altenbaugh, R. J., Engel, D. E., & Martin, D. T. (1995). *Caring for kids: A critical study of urban school leavers.* Bristol, PA: Falmer Press.

Amrein, A. L., & Berliner, D. C. (2002). High-stakes testing, uncertainty, and student learning. *Educational Policy Analysis Archives, 10*(18). Retrieved February 10, 2003, from http://epass.asu.edu/epass/v10n18/

Argyris, C. (1982). *Reasoning, learning, and action: Individual and organizational.* San Francisco: Jossey-Bass.

Argyris, C. (1990). *Overcoming organizational defenses: Facilitating organizational learning.* Boston: Allyn & Bacon.

Argyris, C. (1991). Teaching smart people how to learn. *Harvard Business Review, 69*(3), 99-109.

Argyris, C. (1993). *Knowledge for action: A guide to overcoming barriers to organizational change.* San Francisco: Jossey-Bass.

Argyris, C., Putnam, R., & Smith, D. M. (1985). *Action science: Concepts, methods, and skills for research and intervention.* San Francisco: Jossey-Bass.

Argyris, C., & Schon, D. A. (1974). *Theory in practice: Increasing professional effectiveness.* San Francisco: Jossey-Bass.

Argyris, C., & Schon, D. A. (1978). *Organizational learning.* Reading, MA: Addison-Wesley.

Baaden, B. (2002). *High stakes: An examination of feedback during the use of alternative assessment in the classroom.* Unpublished doctoral dissertation, Hofstra University, Hempstead, NY.

Babad, E., Bernieri, F., & Rosenthal, R. (1991). Students as judges of teachers' verbal and nonverbal behavior. *American Educational Research Journal, 28*(1), 211-234.

Barnett, B. G. (1990). Peer-assisted leadership: Expanding principals' knowledge through reflective practice. *Journal of Educational Administration, 28*(3), 67-76.

Barnett, B. G., & Brill, A. D. (1989, October). *Building reflection into administrative training programs.* Paper presented at the Annual Convention of University Council for Educational Administration, Cincinnati, OH.

Baumeister, R. F., & Leary, M. R. (1995). The need to belong: Desire for interpersonal attachments as a fundamental human motivation. *Psychological Bulletin, 117*(3), 497-529.

Beatty, B. R. (2000). The emotions of educational leadership: Breaking the silence. *International Journal of Leadership in Education, 3*(4), 331-357.

Beck, L. G. (1994). *Reclaiming educational administration as a caring profession.* New York: Teachers College Press.

Beebe, S. A., & Masterson, J. T. (1994). *Communicating in small groups: Principles and practices* (4th ed.). New York: HarperCollins.

Belenky, M. F., Clinchy, B. M., Goldberger, N. R., & Tarule, J. M. (1986). *Women's ways of knowing: The development of self, voice, and mind.* New York: Basic Books.

Berkey, R., Campbell, D., Curtis, T., Kirschner, B. W., Minnick, F., & Zietlow, K. (1990). Collaborating for reflective practice: Voices of teachers, administrators, and researchers. *Education and Urban Society, 22*(2), 204-232.

Berlak, A., & Berlak, H. (1981). *Dilemmas of schooling.* New York: Methuen.

Berliner, D. C., & Biddle, B. J. (1995). *The manufactured crisis: Myths, fraud, and the attack on America's public schools.* Reading, MA: Addison-Wesley.

Blase, J., & Kirby, P. C. (1992). *Bringing out the best in teachers.* Thousand Oaks, CA: Corwin.

Blase, J., & Kirby, P. C. (2000). *Bringing out the best in teachers* (2nd ed.). Thousand Oaks, CA: Corwin.

Bolman, L. G., & Deal, T. E. (1991). *Reframing organizations: Artistry, choice, and leadership.* San Francisco: Jossey-Bass.

Bolton, R. (1979). *People skills: How to assert yourself, listen to others, and resolve conflicts.* New York: Simon & Schuster.

Bonich, M., Schlau, J., & Kottkamp, R. (2003, April). *Integrating the Interactive Learning Model with reflective practice for adult learners: Cases of empowered learning and change in self and others.* Paper presented at the Annual Meeting of the American Educational Research Association, Chicago.

Borko, H., Michalec, P., Timmon, M., & Siddle, J. (1997). Student teaching portfolios: A tool for promoting reflective practice. *Journal of Teacher Education, 48*(5), 345-357.

Borman, G. D., Hewes, G. M., Overman, L. T., & Brown, S. (2003). Comprehensive school reform and achievement: A meta-analysis. *Review of Educational Research, 73*(2), 125-230.

Bredeson, P. V. (1999, April). *Paradox and possibility: An examination of teacher professional development.* Paper presented at the Annual Meeting of the American Educational Research Association, Montreal, Canada.

Bredeson, P. V. (2003). *Designs for learning.* Thousand Oaks, CA: Corwin.

Bridges, E. M. (1986). *The incompetent teacher.* Philadelphia: Falmer Press.

Bridges, E. M. (1992). *Problem-based learning for administrators.* Eugene, OR: ERIC Clearinghouse on Educational Management.

Brookfield, S. (1992). Uncovering assumptions: The key to reflective practice. *Adult Learning, 3*(4), 13-18.

Brookfield, S. D. (1995). *Becoming a critically reflective teacher.* San Francisco: Jossey-Bass.

Brookfield, S. D., & Preskill, S. (1999). *Discussion as a way of teaching: Tools and techniques for democratic classrooms.* San Francisco: Jossey-Bass.

Brown, J. S., Collins, A., & Duguid, P. (1989a). Debating the situation: A rejoinder to Palincsar and Wineburg. *Educational Researcher, 19*(4), 10-12.

Brown, J. S., Collins, A., & Duguid, P. (1989b). Situated cognition and the culture of learning. *Educational Researcher, 18*(1), 32-42.

Burns, T., & Stalker, G. M. (1961). *The management of innovation.* London: Tavistock.

Cambron-McCabe, N. (2003). Rethinking leadership preparation: Focus on faculty learning communities. *Leadership and Policy in Schools, 2*(4), 285-298.

Carson, T. R. (1995). Reflective practice and a reconceptualization of teacher education. In M. F. Wideen & P. P. Grimmett (Eds.), *Changing times in teacher education: Restructuring or reconceptualization* (pp. 151-162). Washington, DC: Falmer Press.

Clandinin, D. J., & Connelly, F. M. (1991). Narrative and story in practice and research. In D. A. Schon (Ed.), *The reflective turn* (pp. 258-281). New York: Teachers College Press.

Clarke, A. (1995). Professional development in practicum settings: Reflective practice under scrutiny. *Teaching and Teacher Education, 11*(3), 243-261.

Cohn, M. M., & Kottkamp, R. B. (1993). *Teachers: The missing voice in education.* Albany: State University of New York Press.

Connell, J. P., Halpern-Felsher, B. L., Clifford, E., Crichlow, W., & Usinger, P. (1995). Hanging in there: Behavioral, psychological, and contextual factors affecting whether African American adolescents stay in high school. *Journal of Adolescent Research, 10*(1), 41-63.

Connell, J. P., & Wellborn, J. G. (1991). Competence, autonomy, and relatedness: A motivational analysis of self-system processes. In M. R. Gunnar & L. A. Sroufe (Eds.), *Self processes and development* (Vol. 23). Hillsdale, NJ: Lawrence Erlbaum.

Corcoran, T. B. (1995, June). Helping teachers teach well: Transforming professional development. *CPRE Policy Briefs.* Retrieved April 25, 2003, from http://www.ed.gov/pubs/CPRE/t61/index.html

Coutinho, M. J., Oswald, D. P., & Best, A. M. (2002). The influence of sociodemographics and gender on the disproportionate identification of minority students as having learning disabilities. *Remedial and Special Education, 23*(1), 49-60.

Cuban, L. (1984). *How teachers taught: Constancy and change in American classrooms 1890–1980.* New York: Longman.

Cuban, L. (1988). *The managerial imperative and the practice of leadership in schools.* Albany: State University of New York Press.

deCharms, R. (1968). *Personal causation: The internal affective determinants of behavior.* New York: Academic Press.

deCharms, R. (1976). *Enhancing motivation.* New York: Irvington.

deCharms, R. (1984). Motivation enhancement in educational settings. In R. Ames & C. Ames (Eds.), *Research on motivation in education* (Vol. 1, pp. 275-308). New York: Academic Press.

Deci, E. L. (1980). *The psychology of self-determination.* Lexington, MA: D. C. Heath.

Deci, E. L., & Ryan, R. M. (1985). *Intrinsic motivation and self-determination in human behavior.* New York: Plenum.

Deci, E. L., Vallerand, R. J., Pelletier, L. G., & Ryan, R. M. (1991). Motivation and education: The self-determination perspective. *Educational Psychologist, 26*(3-4), 325-346.

DeRosa-Karby, N. (2002). *Teachers' organizational commitment and the factors and the processes that may contribute to it.* Unpublished doctoral dissertation, Hofstra University, Hempstead, NY.

DeRosa-Karby, N., & Osterman, K. F. (2002, November). *Leadership, organizational commitment, and student learning.* Paper presented at the Annual Convention of University Council for Educational Administration, Pittsburgh, PA.

Dewey, J. (1938a). *Experience and education.* New York: Macmillan.

Dewey, J. (1938b). *Logic: The theory of inquiry.* New York: Holt.

Doyle, M., & Straus, D. (1982). *How to make meetings work.* New York: Jove Books.

Elmore, R. F. (1992). Why restructuring alone won't improve teaching. *Educational Leadership, 49*(7), 44-48.

Elmore, R. F. (1995). Structural reform and educational practice. *Educational Researcher, 24*(3), 355-374.

Elmore, R. F., Peterson, P. L., & McCarthey, S. J. (1996). *Restructuring in the classroom: Teaching, learning, and school organization.* San Francisco: Jossey-Bass.

Ershler, A. R. (2001). The narrative as an *experience text:* Writing themselves back in. In A. Lieberman & L. Miller (Eds.), *Teachers caught in the action: Professional development that matters* (pp. 159-173). New York: Teachers College Press.

Falk, B. (2001). Professional learning through assessment. In A. Lieberman & L. Miller (Eds.), *Teachers caught in the action: Professional development that matters* (pp. 118-140). New York: Teachers College Press.

Fight Crime: Invest in Kids. (2003). *Bullying prevention is crime prevention.* Washington, DC: Author.

Firestone, W. A., & Corbett, H. D. (1988). Planned organizational change. In N. J. Boyan (Ed.), *Handbook of research on educational administration* (pp. 321-340). New York: Longman.

Fishbein, S. J. (2000). *Crossing over: The roles and rules of the teacher-administrator relationship.* Unpublished doctoral dissertation, Hofstra University, Hempstead, NY.

Fishbein, S. J., & Osterman, K. F. (2000, November). *Crossing over: The roles and rules of the teacher-administrator relationship.* Paper presented at the Annual Convention of the University Council for Educational Administration, Albuquerque, NM.

Fullan, M. (1997). *What's worth fighting for in the principalship.* New York: Teachers College Press.

Fullan, M. (1999). *Change forces: The sequel.* Philadelphia: Falmer Press.

Fullan, M. (2001). *Leading in a culture of change.* San Francisco: Jossey-Bass.

Fullan, M., & Hargreaves, A. (1996). *What's worth fighting for in your school.* New York: Teachers College Press.

Fullan, M. G. (1991). *The new meaning of educational change.* New York: Teachers College Press.

Furman, G. (Ed.). (2002). *School as community: From promise to practice.* Albany: State University of New York Press.

Glanz, J., & Sullivan, S. (2000). *Supervision in practice: 3 steps to improving teaching and learning.* Thousand Oaks, CA: Corwin.

Glasser, W. (1997, April). A new look at school failure and school success. *Phi Delta Kappan, 78,* 597-602.

Goleman, D. (1998). *Working with emotional intelligence.* New York: Bantam Books.

Goleman, D. (2000, March-April). Leadership that gets results. *Harvard Business Review,* 78-90.

Goodlad, J. (1984). *A place called school: Prospects for the future.* New York: McGraw-Hill.

Gordon, T. (1980). *Leader effectiveness training.* New York: Bantam Books.

Grandin, R. (2002). *Report of progress, State of New Jersey Goals 2000 grant.* Washington Township, NJ: Washington Township Public Schools.

Greenfield, T. (1991). Re-forming and re-valuing educational administration: Whence and when cometh the phoenix? *Educational Management and Administration, 19*(4), 200-217.

Greenfield, T. B. (1986). The decline and fall of science in educational administration. *Interchange, 17*(2), 57-80.

Griffiths, M., & Tann, S. (1992). Using reflective practice to link personal and public theories. *Journal of Education for Teaching, 18*(1), 69-84.

Hargreaves, A. (2001). The emotional geographies of teachers' relations with colleagues. *International Journal of Educational Research, 35*(5), 503-527.

Hargreaves, A. (2002). *Teaching in the knowledge society.* Retrieved September 14, 2003, from http://www.cybertext.net.au/tct2002/keynote/hargreaves.htm

Hargreaves, A., Beatty, B., Lasky, S., Schmidt, M., & James-Wilson, S. (in press). *The emotions of teaching.* San Francisco: Jossey-Bass.

Hargreaves, A., Earl, L., & Ryan, J. (1996). *Schooling for change: Reinventing education for early adolescents.* Washington, DC: Falmer Press.

Hargreaves, A., & Fullan, M. (1998). *What's worth fighting for out there.* New York: Teachers College Press.

Hart, A. W. (1990). Effective administration through reflective practice. *Education and Urban Society, 22*(2), 153-169.

Holborn, P. (1988). Becoming a reflective practitioner. In P. Holborn, M. Wideen, & I. Andrews (Eds.), *Becoming a teacher* (pp. 196-209). Toronto, Canada: Kagan and Woo.

Homans, G. C. (1950). *The human group.* New York: Harcourt, Brace, and World.

Ingersoll, R. M. (2003). *Who controls teachers' work? Power and accountability in America's schools.* Cambridge, MA: Harvard University Press.

Jentz, B. (1982). *The hiring, start-up, and supervision of administrators.* New York: McGraw-Hill.

Jentz, B. C., & Wofford, J. W. (1979). *Leadership and learning.* New York: McGraw-Hill.

Johnson, D. W., & Johnson, F. P. (1991). *Joining together* (4th ed.). Englewood Cliffs, NJ: Prentice Hall.

Johnson, D. W., & Johnson, R. (1989). *Cooperation and competition: Theory and research.* Edina, MN: Interaction Book Company.

Johnson, S. M. (1990). *Teachers at work: Achieving success in our schools:* New York: Basic Books.

Johnston, C. A. (1996). *Unlocking the will to learn.* Thousand Oaks, CA: Corwin.

Johnston, C. A. (1997). *LCI patterns by majors.* Unpublished institutional research report, Rowan University, Glassboro, NJ.

Johnston, C. A. (1998). *Let me learn.* Thousand Oaks, CA: Corwin.

Johnston, C. A. (2000). *A personal guide to implementing the LML Process K–12.* Pittsgrove, NJ: Let Me Learn.

Johnston, C. A. (2003a, July). *The constructs and the knowledge base of the Let Me Learn Process.* Presentation at the Sixth Annual Let Me Learn Summer Institute, Philadelphia.

Johnston, C. A. (2003b, July). *Drop dead data.* Keynote address delivered at the Sixth Annual Let Me Learn Summer Institute, Philadelphia.

Johnston, C. A., & Dainton, G. (1997a). *The learning connections inventory.* Pittsgrove, NJ: Let Me Learn.

Johnston, C. A., & Dainton, G. (1997b). *The learning combination inventory users manual.* Pittsgrove, NJ: Let Me Learn.

Keefe, J. (1992). Thinking about the thinking movement. In J. Keefe & H. Wahlberg (Eds.), *Teaching for thinking.* Reston, VA: National Association for Secondary School Principals.

Kelsey, J. G. T. (1993). Learning from teaching: Problems, problem-formulation and the enhancement of problem-solving capability. In P. Hallinger, K. A. Leithwood, & J. Murphy (Eds.), *A cognitive perspective on educational administration* (pp. 231-252). New York: Teachers College Press.

Kessler, P. R., & Johnston, C. A. (2003, September). *The effects of innovative teaching on student growth in knowledge of economics and the intentional use of their learning processes.* Paper presented at the Development in Economics and Business Education Conference, Edinburgh, Scotland.

Knapp, M. S., Copland, M. A., Ford, B., Markholt, A., McLaughlin, M. W., Milliken, M., et al. (2003). *Leading for learning sourcebook: Concepts and examples.* Seattle, WA: Center for the Study of Teaching and Policy, University of Washington.

Kofman, F., & Senge, P. M. (1994). Communities of commitment: The heart of learning organizations. In S. Chawla & J. Renesch (Eds.), *Learning organizations: Developing cultures for tomorrow's workplace* (pp. 15-43). Portland, OR: Productivity Press.

Kohn, A. (1999). *Punished by rewards: The trouble with gold stars, incentives plans, A's, praise, and other bribes.* New York: Houghton Mifflin.

Kolb, D. A. (1984). *Experiential learning: Experience as the source of learning and development.* Englewood Cliffs, NJ: Prentice Hall.

Kolb, D. A. (1985). *The learning style inventory: Technical manual.* Boston: McBer.

Kottkamp, R. B. (1982). The administrative platform in administrative preparation. *Planning and Changing, 13*(2), 82-92.

Kottkamp, R. B. (1990). Means for facilitating reflection. *Education and Urban Society, 22*(2), 182-203.

Kottkamp, R. B. (2002, July). *Problematic person project: Integrating reflective practice and Let Me Learn.* Poster session presentation at the Fifth Annual Let Me Learn Summer Institute, Philadelphia.

Kottkamp, R. B., & Silverberg, R. P. (1999a, April). *Exploring the mental models of administrative aspirants: Assumptions about students, teaching and learning.* Paper presented at the Annual Meeting of the American Educational Research Association, Montreal.

Kottkamp, R. B., & Silverberg, R. P. (1999b). Learning formal theory through constructivism and reflective practice: Professor and student perspectives. *Educational Administration and Leadership: Teaching and Program Development, 11,* 47-59.

Kottkamp, R. B., & Silverberg, R. P. (1999c, March). *Reconceptualizing students at risk: Teacher assumptions about "the problematic student."* Paper presented at the Research Network: Children and Youth at Risk and Urban Education, European Education Research Association, Valletta, Malta.

Kottkamp, R. B., & Silverberg, R. P. (2003). Leadership preparation reform in first person: Making assumptions public. *Leadership and Policy in Schools, 2*(4), 299-326.

LaBoskey, V. K. (1994). *Development of reflective practice: A study of preservice teachers.* New York: Teachers College Press.

Lambert, L., Walker, D., Zimmerman, D. P., Cooper, J. E., Lambert, M. D., Gardner, M. E., et al. (2002). *The constructivist leader* (2nd ed.). New York: Teachers College Press.

Leithwood, K. (1993, October). *Contributions of transformational leadership to school restructuring.* Paper presented at the Annual Convention of the University Council for Educational Administration, Houston, TX.

Leithwood, K. (1995). Cognitive perspectives on school leadership. *Journal of School Leadership, 5*(2), 115-135.

Leithwood, K., Aitken, R., & Jantzi, D. (2001). *Making schools smarter: A system for monitoring school and district progress* (2nd ed.). Thousand Oaks, CA: Corwin.

Leithwood, K., Begley, P. T., & Cousins, J. B. (1994). *Developing expert leadership for future schools.* London: Falmer Press.

Leithwood, K., & Jantzi, D. (1990, April). *Transformational leadership: How principals can help reform school cultures.* Paper presented at the Annual Meeting of the American Educational Research Association, Boston.

Leithwood, K., Jantzi, D., & Fernandez, A. (1994). Transformational leadership and teachers' commitment to change. In J. Murphy & K. S. Louis (Eds.), *Reshaping the principalship: Insights from transformational reform efforts* (pp. 77-98). Thousand Oaks, CA: Corwin.

Leithwood, K., & Steinbach, R. (1995). *Expert problem solving: Evidence from school and district leaders.* Albany: State University of New York Press.

Lieberman, A. (1988). *Building a professional culture in schools.* New York: Teachers College Press.

Likert, R. (1961). *New patterns of management.* New York: McGraw-Hill.

Little, J. W. (2001). Professional development in pursuit of school reform. In A. Lieberman & L. Miller (Eds.), *Teachers caught in the action: Professional development that matters* (pp. 23-44). New York: Teachers College Press.

Lortie, D. (1975). *Schoolteacher: A sociological study.* Chicago: University of Chicago Press.

Louis, K. S., Kruse, S. D., & Associates. (1995). *Professionalism and community: Perspectives on reforming urban schools.* Thousand Oaks, CA: Corwin.

Maehr, M. L., & Midgley, C. (1996). *Transforming school cultures.* Boulder, CO: Westview.

Manzoni, J. F., & Barsoux, J. L. (1998). The set-up-to-fail syndrome. *Harvard Business Review, 76*(7), 101-113.

Marcellino, P. A. (2001). *Learning to become a team: A case study of action research in a graduate business management course.* Unpublished doctoral dissertation, Hofstra University, Hempstead, NY.

Marks, H. M., & Printy, S. M. (2003). Principal leadership and school performance: An integration of transformational and instructional leadership. *Educational Administration Quarterly, 39*(3), 370-397.

Marshall, C., & Mitchell, B. A. (1991). The assumptive worlds of fledgling administrators. *Education and Urban Society, 23*(4), 396-415.

Mattingly, C. (1991). Narrative reflections on practical actions: Two learning experiments in reflective storytelling. In D. A. Schon (Ed.), *The reflective turn* (pp. 235-257). New York: Teachers College Press.

McGregor, D. (1960). *The human side of enterprise.* New York: McGraw-Hill.

McLaughlin, M. W., & Pfeifer, R. S. (1988). *Teacher evaluation: Improvement, accountability, and effective learning.* New York: Teachers College Press.

McLaughlin, M. W., & Talbert, J. E. (2001). *Professional communities and the work of high school teaching.* Chicago: University of Chicago Press.

McLaughlin, M. W. (with Zarrow, J.). (2001). Teachers engaged in evidence-based reform: Trajectories of teacher's inquiry, analysis, and action. In A. Lieberman & L. Miller (Eds.), *Teachers caught in the action: Professional development that matters* (pp. 79-101). New York: Teachers College Press.

McNeil, L. M. (1986). *Contradictions of control: School structure and school knowledge.* New York: Routledge.

McNeil, L. M. (2000). *Contradictions of school reform: Educational costs of standardized testing.* New York: Routledge.

Miller, J. L. (1990). *Creating spaces and finding voices: Teachers collaborating for empowerment.* Albany: State University of New York Press.

Mintzberg, H. (1983). *Structure in fives: Designing effective organizations.* Englewood Cliffs, NJ: Prentice Hall.

Montalbano, J. (2001). *Utilizing action research to enhance self-efficacy beliefs of elementary school students.* Unpublished doctoral dissertation, Hofstra University, Hempstead, NY.

Murphy, J., Beck, L. G., Crawford, M., Hodges, A., & McGaughy, C. L. (2001). *The productive high school: Creating personalized academic communities.* Thousand Oaks, CA: Corwin.

Murphy, J., & Datnow, A. (2003a). Leadership lessons from comprehensive school reform designs. In J. Murphy & A. Datnow (Eds.), *Leadership lessons from comprehensive school reforms* (pp. 263-278). Thousand Oaks, CA: Corwin.

Murphy, J., & Datnow, A. (Eds.). (2003b). *Leadership lessons from comprehensive school reforms.* Thousand Oaks, CA: Corwin.

Murphy, J., & Louis, K. S. (Eds.). (1994). *Reshaping the principalship: Insights from transformational reform efforts.* Thousand Oaks, CA: Corwin.

Myers, I. B., & McCaulley, M. H. (1985). *Manual: A guide to the development and use of the Myers-Briggs Type Indicator.* Palo Alto, CA: Consulting Psychologist Press.

National Board for Professional Teaching Standards. (2001). *NBPTS Middle childhood generalist standards* (2nd ed.). Arlington, VA: Author.

National Policy Board for Educational Administration. (2002). *Standards for advanced programs in educational leadership.* Arlington, VA: Author.

National School Safety Center. (Producer). (1992). *The broken toy* [Videotape]. Zanesville, OH: Summerhill Productions.

Natriello, G., & Dornbusch, S. M. (1984). *Teacher evaluative standards and student effort.* New York: Longman.

Newmann, F. M. (Ed.). (1992). *Student engagement and achievement in American secondary schools.* New York: Teachers College Press.

Noddings, N. (1992). *The challenge to care in schools: An alternative approach to education.* New York: Teachers College Press.

Ogawa, R. T., & Bossert, S. T. (1995). Leadership as an organizational quality. *Educational Administration Quarterly, 31*(2), 224-243.

Osterman, K. F. (1990). Reflective practice: A new agenda for education. *Education and Urban Society, 22*(2), 133-152.

Osterman, K. F. (1991). Case records: A means to enhance the knowledge base in educational administration. In F. C. Wendel (Ed.), *Enhancing the knowledge base in educational administration* (pp. 35-47). University Park, PA: University Council for Educational Administration.

Osterman, K. F. (1994). Feedback in school settings . . . No news is bad news. *The Journal of Management Systems, 6*(4), 28-44.

Osterman, K. F. (1999). Using constructivism and reflective practice to bridge the theory/practice gap. *Educational Leadership and Administration: Teaching and Program Development, 11*, 9-20.

Osterman, K. F. (2000). Students' need for belonging in the school community. *Review of Educational Research, 70*(3), 323-367.

Osterman, K. F. (2002). Schools as communities for students. In G. Furman (Ed.), *School as community: From promise to practice* (pp. 167-195). Albany: State University of New York Press.

Osterman, K. F., & Kottkamp, R. B. (1993). *Reflective practice for educators: Improving schooling through professional development.* Newbury Park, CA: Corwin.

Osterman, K., & Pace, D. (1999). Preservice teacher beliefs about student disengagement. *Teaching Education Journal, 10*, 2.

Pearle, K. M. (2002). *Metacognition as vehicle for organizational change: How "thinking about thinking" and intentional learning break the mold of "heroic" teaching in higher education.* Unpublished doctoral dissertation, Rowan University, Glassboro, NJ.

Peters, T. J., & Waterman, R. H. (1982). *In search of excellence.* New York: Harper & Row.

Philip, H. (1936). An *experimental study of the frustration of will, acts and conation.* Cambridge, UK: Cambridge University Press.

Pounder, D., Ogawa, R. T., & Adams, E. A. (1995). Leadership as an organization-wide phenomenon: Its impact on school performance. *Educational Administration Quarterly, 31*(4), 564-588.

Prestine, N. A., & LeGrand, B. F. (1991). Cognitive learning theory and the preparation of educational administrators: Implications for practice and policy. *Educational Administration Quarterly, 27*(1), 61-89.

Probasco, D. (1997). The *construction of effective cooperative learning groups for successful high school biology instruction.* Unpublished masters thesis, Rowan University, Glassboro, NJ.

Reagan, T., Case, K., Case, C. W., & Freiberg, J. A. (1993). Reflecting on "reflective practice": Implications for teacher evaluation. *Journal of Personnel Evaluation in Education, 6*, 263-277.

Rosenholtz, S. J. (1989). *Teacher's workplace: The social organization of schools.* New York: Longman.

Rusch, E., Haws, E., & Krastek, R. (2002, November). *A key to unity in diverse learning communities: Learning about learning within a cohort.* Roundtable presentation at the Annual Convention of the University Council for Educational Administration, Pittsburgh, PA.

Ryan, R. M. (1995). Psychological needs and the facilitation of integrative processes. *Journal of Personality, 63*(3), 397-427.

Ryan, R. M., & Powelson, C. L. (1991). Autonomy and relatedness as fundamental to motivation and education. *Journal of Experimental Education, 60*(1), 49-66.

Sagor, R. D. (1991). *Operationalizing transformational leadership: The behavior of principals in fostering teacher centered school development.* Paper presented at the Annual Convention of the University Council for Educational Administration, Baltimore.

Sarason, S. B. (1971). *The culture of the school and the problem of change.* Boston: Allyn & Bacon.

Sarason, S. B. (1990). *The predictable failure of educational reform: Can we change course before it's too late?* San Francisco: Jossey-Bass.

Schon, D. A. (1983). *The reflective practitioner: How professionals think in action.* New York: Basic Books.

Schon, D. A. (1987). *Educating the reflective practitioner.* San Francisco: Jossey-Bass.

Senge, P., Cambron-McCabe, N., Lucas, T., Smith, B., Dutton, J., & Kleiner, A. (2000). *Schools that learn: A fifth discipline fieldbook for educators, parents, and everyone who cares about education.* New York: Doubleday-Currency.

Senge, P., Kleiner, A., Roberts, C., Ross, R., Roth, G., & Smith, B. (1999). *The dance of change: The challenges of sustaining momentum in learning organizations.* New York: Doubleday-Currency.

Senge, P., Kleiner, A., Roberts, C., Ross, R. B., & Smith, B. (1994). *The fifth discipline fieldbook: Strategies and tools for building a learning organization.* New York: Doubleday-Currency.

Senge, P. M. (1990). *The fifth discipline.* New York: Doubleday-Currency.

Sergiovanni, T. J. (1991). Constructing and changing theories of practice: The key to preparing school administrators. *Urban Review, 23*(1), 39-49.

Sergiovanni, T. J. (1992). Reflections on administrative theory and practice in schools. *Educational Administration Quarterly, 28*(3), 304-313.

Silins, H. C., Mulford, W. R., & Zarins, S. (2002). Organizational learning and school change. *Educational Administration Quarterly, 38*(5), 613-642.

Silva, D. Y. (1998, November). *Structured observation: A collaborative supervision tool for promoting teacher reflection.* Paper presented at the Annual Meeting of the New England Educational Research Organization, Portland, ME.

Silver, P. F. (1986). Case records: A reflective practice approach to administrator development. *Theory into Practice, 25*(3), 161-167.

Silverberg, R. P. (2002). *From marginalization to relational space: A descriptive phenomenological study of teachers who changed their assumptions and beliefs about problematic students.* Unpublished doctoral dissertation, Hofstra University, Hempstead, NY.

Silverberg, R. P. (2003). Leading in the relational space. *Journal of School Leadership, 13*(6), 688-706.

Siris, K. (2001). *Using action research to alleviate bullying and victimization in the classroom.* Unpublished doctoral dissertation, Hofstra University, Hempstead, NY.

Spadoni, L. (2002, June). *More than a cute face.* Presentation at the Annual Conference of the National Association of Education for Younger Children, Albuquerque, NM.

Stein, S. J., & Book, H. E. (2000). *The EQ edge: Emotional intelligence and your success.* Toronto, Canada: Multi-Health Systems.

Stone, D., Patton, B., & Heen, S. (1999). *Difficult conversations: How to discuss what matters most.* New York: Viking Penguin.

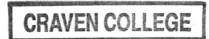

Straus, D. (2002). *How to make collaboration work: Powerful ways to build consensus, solve problems, and make decisions.* San Francisco: Berrett-Koehler.

Sullivan, S., & Glanz, J. (2000). *Supervision that improves teaching: Strategies and techniques.* Thousand Oaks, CA: Corwin.

Taylor, D. (1998). *Beginning to read and the spin doctors of science: The political campaign to change America's mind about how children learn to read.* Urbana, IL: National Council of Teachers of English.

Thompson, S. (2001). The authentic standards movement and its evil twin. *Phi Delta Kappan, 82*(5), 358-362.

Tyack, D., & Cuban, L. (1995). *Tinkering toward utopia: A century of public school reform.* Cambridge, MA: Harvard University Press.

Walls, L. (2000). *Bullying and sexual harassment in schools.* Retrieved September 14, 2003, from http://www.cfchildren.org/article_walls1.shtml

Weber, M. (1947). *The theory of social and economic organization* (Henderson, A. M., & Parsons, T., Trans.). New York: Free Press.

Wehlage, G. G., Rutter, R. A., Smith, G. A., Lesko, N., & Fernandez, R. R. (1989). *Reducing the risk: Schools as communities of support.* Philadelphia: Falmer.

Wise, A. E. (1988). Two conflicting trends in school reform: Legislated learning revisited. *Phi Delta Kappan, 69*(5), 328-333.

Index

CORWIN PRESS

The Corwin Press logo—a raven striding across an open book—represents the union of courage and learning. Corwin Press is committed to improving education for all learners by publishing books and other professional development resources for those serving the field of K–12 education. By providing practical, hands-on materials, Corwin Press continues to carry out the promise of its motto: **"Helping Educators Do Their Work Better."**